The Craftsmen of Dionysus

AN APPROACH TO ACTING

••••••••••••

NEW AND REVISED

with a new chapter on Auditioning

••••••••••••

FOOTNOTE TO THE TITLE

The Craftsmen of Dionysus was the first known actors' guild.
It originated in Athens in the fourth century B.C.

The name was derived from the annual festivals held in honor of Dionysus,
the god of fertility, to ensure the rebirth of the land.
These festivals combined religious ceremonies and drama;
the most important of them was called The Great Dionysia.

The guild established branches in many cities of the Greek-speaking world.
It regulated wages and working conditions and managed the organizations
and bookings of troupes to the provinces and at festivals.
The religious nature of the drama elevated the actors to priestly eminence;
they were highly respected and enjoyed privileges not accorded other citizens.
This book is addressed to the ever-present and future craftsmen of Dionysus.

THE APPLAUSE ACTING SERIES

The Craftsmen of Dionysus

AN APPROACH TO ACTING

NEW AND REVISED

with a new chapter on Auditioning

JEROME ROCKWOOD

APPLAUSE
BOOKS
211 WEST 71 STREET • NEW YORK NY • 10023

THE CRAFTSMEN OF DIONYSUS
AN APPROACH TO ACTING
New and Revised

Library of Congress Cataloging-in-Publication Data

Rockwood, Jerome.
    The craftsmen of Dionysus : an approach to acting / Jerome
Rockwood.
        p.   cm. — (The Applause acting series)
    "New and revised, with a new chapter on auditioning."
    Includes bibliographical references and index.
    ISBN 1-55783-155-6 (pbk.) : $16.95
    1. Acting. I. Title. II. Series.
PN2061.R55 1992
792' .028—dc20   92-25206
                                                            CIP

Applause Theatre Books
211 West 71st Street
New York, NY 10023
Phone: 212-595-4735 Fax: 212-721-2856

SECOND APPLAUSE PRINTING: 1997

For Norma
First and Always

Acknowledgements

I wish to extend my sincere gratitude to Professor Elmer E. Baker, Jr., and to Professor Louise Gurren, who so kindly arranged for that most vital element in the writing of a book—the time in which to write it. And for the drawings in the section entitled "Movement in Period Plays," my deep appreciation to Mr. Ervin Nussbaum.

Prologue

In creative affairs, one plus one equals three; it is bad form for the artist to come out even, to have his product equal the sum of his materials. It is paradoxical, but the very thing we look for in art is the very thing we cannot define—that elusive essence, that extra dimension that makes us feel there is more present than meets the eye.

When we translate poetry from one language to another, we can translate everything but that which makes it poetry; something is lost which can only be felt. Just the opposite obtains when we translate a character from the script to the stage. When an actor brings the gift of life to the words on the page, he does far more than the playwright is able to do. He extends those printed words and ideas into another dimension imbued with his living presence. He creates a new, compounded reality which is greater than our own everyday reality, for to the invention of the playwright he adds the sum of his being.

To put it otherwise: within the seed is the entire plant. But the seed is not yet the plant. It is the potential plant. It must be placed in the right soil, watered, exposed to the right amount of light. Nurtured.

So it is with talent. Talent is not the performance. It is the potential for the performance. Talent, too, must be nurtured. Shaped into a conscious technique, bolstered with discipline.

A funny word, talent. We toss it around freely to mean anything from flair to insight to almost any special ability. Now talent varies both in kind and degree. It might be an ability to mimic other people's characteristics, or an ear for dialects, or a naturally comic response to situations—or dozens of other aptitudes useful for the actor. But how many of us are endowed with everything?

It is important for the actor to learn his strengths and weaknesses. To rely only on his strengths, as some personality actors do, is to severely limit his range and sharply reduce the kinds of parts he can play. If he wants to grow and develop as a versatile actor he must work on the weaker areas to bring them up to performance pitch.

What was that you said? You have terrific instincts? You're a "natural"? So is a monkey. A monkey is amusing to watch, but he lacks a few essential elements that would make him an artist. And those are a point of view and the conscious command of a technique with which to present it. I'm sure you know the old adage about Inspiration being 90% Perspiration. So let's get to work. This book is an attempt to assign to the actor his very responsible task and to equip him with the skills to meet it.

Contents

Introduction

In creative affairs, one plus one equals three; it is bad form for the artist to come out even, to have his product equal the sum of his materials. It is paradoxical, but the very thing we look for in art is the very thing we cannot define—that elusive essence, that extra dimension that makes us feel there is more present than meets the eye.

When we translate poetry from one language to another, we can translate everything but that which makes it poetry; something is lost which can only be felt. Just the opposite obtains when we translate a character from the script to the stage. When an actor brings the gift of life to the words on the page, he does far more than the playwright is able to do. He extends those printed words and ideas into another dimension imbued with his living presence. He creates a new, compounded reality which is greater than our own everyday reality, for to the invention of the playwright he adds the sum of his being.

This book is an attempt to assign to the actor his very responsible task and to equip him with the skills to meet it.

one

A point of view

*O*nce upon a very long time ago, Robert Edmond Jones has mused, a caveman was out in search of sustenance for his family. Suddenly, he was accosted by a savage stegosaurus, who offered to eat him. A fearful fight ensued, but the caveman finally felled the stegosaurus with a frightful wallop. Shaken but triumphant, the hunter returned home and gathered his family and friends around the fire to relate the incident. But instead of just telling it, he acted it out. He played both parts; now he was himself, now the stegosaurus. He groaned and growled, he ducked and dodged, he staggered and struck. It was terribly exciting; and at the death blow, the spectators yowled and banged sticks and stones to show their appreciation. The drama was born.

Soon, however, the caveman's audience began to reflect on what it had seen. Some of the spectators thought the stegosaurus hadn't been represented well at all. At least, they had never seen a stegosaurus quite like that. Others held that the stegosaurus was properly fearsome, but they doubted that the hero was as brave as he pretended. So it began. So it continues.

The Paradox of the Actor

Wherever plays are performed, the paradox of the actor tantalizes audiences. Can he who moves us to such intense feeling remain unmoved himself? If the actor does not feel the emotions of his character, why are we touched by his pretense? Opinions are as varied as the people who proffer them; to wit:

This excitement of compassion, this adjuration of all gods and men, of citizens and allies, was not unaccompanied by my tears and extreme commiseration on my part; and if, from all the expressions which I then used, real concern of my own had been absent, my speech would not only have failed to excite commiseration, but would have even deserved ridicule.

Cicero, 106 – 43 B.C.[1]

At the very moment when he touches your heart he is listening to his own voice; his talent depends not, as you think, upon feeling, but upon rendering so exactly the outward signs of feeling, that you fall into the trap.

Denis Diderot, 1713–1784[2]

. . . Unless he can enter into the feelings of his heroes, however violent they may be, however cruel and vindictive they may seem, he will never be anything but a bad actor. . . . How can he convince another of his emotion, of the sincerity of his passions, if he is unable to convince himself to the point of actually becoming the character that he is to impersonate?

Sarah Bernhardt, 1844-1923[3]

. . . The actor must have a double personality. He has his first self, which is the player, and his second self, which is the instrument. . . . Whether your second self weeps or laughs, whether you become frenzied to madness or suffer the pains of death, it must always be under the watchful eye of your ever-impassive first self. . . . The famous maxim, if you wish to make me cry, you must cry yourself, is therefore not applicable to the actor.

Benoit Constant Coquelin, 1841-1909[4]

I must become capable of identifying myself with one or another personage to such an extent as to lead the audience into the illusion that the real personage, and not a copy, is before them. . . . [criticising Bernhardt] I could not help noticing . . . a seeking after effects that were discordant with the position and character of the personage.

Tommaso Salvini, 1829 – 1915[5]

1. Cicero, *Cicero on Oratory and Orators*, trans. J. S. Watson (New York: Harper and Brothers, 1860), p. 137.

2. Denis Diderot, *The Paradox of Acting*, trans. W. H. Pollack (London: Chatto and Windus, 1883), p. 16.

3. Sarah Bernhardt, *The Art of the Theatre* (London: Geoffrey Bles, 1924), pp. 103–104.

4. Benoit Constant Coquelin, "Acting and Actors," *Harper's New Monthly Magazine* (May 1887), p. 906.

5. Tommaso Salvini, *Leaves from the Autobiography of Tommaso Salvini* (New York: The Century Company, 1893), pp. 71, 189.

Different Approaches: Presentational and Representational Acting

There are, of course, as many methods of creating a role as there are actors. Each actor finds, through study and experience, the things which work best for him, and eventually he emerges with an approach peculiarly his own. Although this would seem to indicate a staggering variety of techniques, they are all traceable to two basic, but fundamentally different, approaches to the problem.

In one method, sometimes called *presentational acting,* the actor "presents" the character to the audience by imitating the speech, movement, mannerisms, and emotional manifestations he thinks the role requires. Often he really "feels" the emotion during rehearsals, but for performance he carefully imitates the tones and gestures which he has developed and established during those rehearsals. Adherents of this method believe that only in this way can the actor reproduce exactly the effects he seeks; for if he were really to feel all the emotions called for during a performance, he would lose the absolute control necessary to imitate faithfully the actions of the character. Moreover, he would be worn out before the end of the performance.

The presentational method calls for scrupulous attention to voice and movement, since these are the two major tools with which such actors express themselves. The actor rehearses his lines, carefully planning each vocal nuance and inflection. His movements are similarly planned; sometimes facial expressions are practiced in a mirror. In this way, the actor finds that particular expression which most fully conveys his intention and then repeats it exactly at each performance.

In the second method, sometimes called *representational acting,* the actor attempts to represent his role by actually thinking the thoughts and experiencing the emotions of the character he is portraying. While recognizing the importance of voice and movement, the representational actor places far greater emphasis on the evocation of the internal — the psychological and emotional — determinants of the character. He believes that every moment on stage must be alive with the inner life or spirit of the character, where as the presentational actor relies more on a series of carefully calculated signs or external manifestations to convey the concept of his character.

The distinctions between the presentational and representational methods are sometimes oversimplified with labels which create misunderstanding. It is not simply a matter of "imitating nature" versus "distorting nature," or "life" versus "art." Both methods are based on observations of nature; both strive to present the truth of the human spirit on the stage. It is in the *procedures* for attaining this goal that the difference lies. The presentational method imitates what it sees in nature; the representational approach attempts actually to recreate the natural condition. Nor can we say that one method is more "realistic" than the other; for if the imitation is perfect, how will we distinguish it from the real thing?

A common misapprehension is that the representational method is better suited for modern, realistic plays, whereas the presentational method is superior for period plays. This is indeed a fallacy, for actors of both schools successfully apply their techniques to either type of play. The presentational actors argue that they can copy modern life as readily as they can imitate a Restoration gentleman, and the representational actors hold that King Lear is no less full of live thoughts and passions than a character in a Tennessee Williams play.

Accusations are hurled back and forth by both camps. The presentational actor is accused of being "external," "shallow," and "empty inside"; the representational actor is charged with boring his audience with an excess of realistic trivia. These are, of course, bad actors. When we put fine actors of both schools side by side, it isn't always easy to tell which actor is practicing which method. Moreover, there are probably very few purists in either camp. The able actor borrows this, alters that, rejects the other until, as we have noted previously, he comes up with his own unique system — a blend of anything and everything that works for him. For this reason it is wise for the actor to study and work with as many different kinds of teachers and directors as possible.

Here, however, we must add a word of caution: the actor must not try to learn several techniques at once, lest he become confused and unable to apply any one of them effectively. Imagine, for example, a student who knows nothing about painting. He goes to an art school and is immediately shown three different ways of mixing paints and six different techniques for applying paint with assorted brushes, and is introduced to a number of contrasting views on symmetry and asymmetry. He will never really have the time and opportunity to master any of the techniques or fully comprehend the concepts.

Taking Sides

This book offers an approach to the representational method of acting. As we have already emphasized, all actors have always had the same aim: to make the audience believe them. Only their methods and training differ. Let us now examine how and why the particular method of training advocated in this book came about.

Actors have a special problem which is not shared by other

artists. The painter or sculptor decides what he wants to do and then tries to do it. There is no one to intervene. The actor, however, is one of a team of several artists who must collaborate on the production; he cannot work in isolation. As a result, his performance is affected by many factors.

For example, the actor has had to contend with the changing physical playhouse. It makes a significant difference whether he performs in an outdoor theatre before 20,000 spectators, as did the ancient Greeks, or in an intimate indoor theatre before an audience of 100; whether he walks on a stage floor that slants or one that is level; whether weak candlelight forces him to stay down front and center so that he can best be seen, or the more adequate illumination of gas burners permits him greater freedom of movement; whether he recites his lines in front of painted scenery or has three-dimensional doors and windows to handle.

The actor's greatest adjustment, however, has been to the materials provided him by the playwright—new styles of plays and new types of characters. In the collaborative art of the theatre, the playwright has usually been the first to experiment with new forms; the actor's task has been to find ways to interpret and convey the new characters which have been written for him.

The trend in drama from the earliest times to the present has been from external reality to internal, or psychological, reality. The drama as a story has given way to the drama as an expression of experience. Plot is still surely an element in modern drama, but most modern playwrights do not support Aristotle's contention that it is the most important factor in drama. Dialogue and characterization often overshadow plot. For a very long time, characters in plays were stereotypes used as pawns by the author to tell his story. Gradually he has become more interested in the things that make people tick, their inner drives and needs and fears. He is no longer as interested in the plot as in the characters involved; he wants their motivations to be clear; he wants us to understand them as people with all the complexities of human beings rather than see them as stereotypes whose behavior conforms to a standard, predictable pattern.

The modern drama is generally considered to have begun with Ibsen and Strindberg, whose plays are superb demonstrations of character revelation and insight. These playwrights brought to a pinnacle a movement which had started earlier. The seeds of realism were being planted in Europe during the early part of the nineteenth century. Political and social conditions were oppressive. The Industrial Revolution had created misery for large masses of people who had poured into the cities to work in factories and were forced to live in terrible conditions. In the middle of the century, Darwin's *Origin of Species* caused an uproar and redirected men's thinking. Heredity and environment replaced Fate as the factors conditioning man's character and behavior. The whole idea of evolution fitted in neatly with man's unhappy condition; for if evolution could work physically, why not socially as well? There was now nothing cosmic or mysterious in the factors which affected a man. He could be studied objectively, just like any other natural thing. Science could do that; science was the new god. Science would find out the truth, because the truth was limited to knowledge gained through the five senses.

The Impact of the New Realism

Since one of the basic concepts of the new realism was that environment shaped man's behavior, it was only natural that the first and most striking changes in the new drama were in stage settings. It was now considered of primary importance to create the illusion of a real environment on stage, one *within* which—and partially *because* of which—the actor would behave. Theretofore, the set had been a mere background, not an integral, organic part of the play. To be sure, scenery in the romantic theatre had become highly illusional, but the illusion had been simply spectacle—towns on fire, ships sinking, volcanoes erupting. Now the illusion was needed to create a believable environment which would exert its influence upon the people within it.

One of the chief advances in realistic settings was the box set, which had been experimented with as early as 1840. Briefly, the box set is one in which large flats (framed canvas screens painted to resemble walls, with functional doors and windows) are arranged to form the walls of a room which completely encloses the action. It is as though an entire room were constructed on the stage and then the fourth wall removed to permit the audience to look in and eavesdrop. Also, the stage floor for the box set is level, unlike the former stages, which sloped so that the actors upstage were higher and could be seen more easily.

By 1830, gaslight had replaced candles almost exclusively, and the resulting greater control of lighting permitted the creation of still more realistic effects. By 1880, electricity had begun to replace gas—a further advance toward an illusional theatre. And finally, with the innovation of extinguishing the lights in the auditorium during performances, the actor bade the audience good-by, moved behind the proscenium, and was swallowed up by his environment.

The dramatist, meanwhile, had looked around astounded at the wealth of new situations and new characters right outside his door. There was more drama, he decided, in one ordinary man and his problems than in ten legendary kings; and he lost no time in confronting the actor with the challenge of bringing that ordinary man and his problems to life on the stage.

One of the first important attempts to do this was made by André Antoine, a French actor-producer-manager who had founded a little theatre in Paris called the Théâtre-Libre. On March 30, 1887, he opened his theatre with four one-act plays, one of which was *Jacques Damour* by Émile Zola. Amazing things happened on that stage that night. The actors spoke only to each other and never so much as acknowledged the presence of the audience; sometimes an actor even turned his back to the audience! There were no asides or soliloquies; the entire action was contained within the set. The actors spoke in ordinary conversational tones and used simple gestures and movements such as ordinary folk do in real life. Wisely, Antoine had used amateur actors, for he knew professionals could not rid themselves of their flamboyancy and their tendency to declaim rather than merely converse. The furniture on the stage was real—it had actually come from Antoine's home—and the playing environment was filled with the many little accessories one might have found in any real apartment. The audience, bewildered and outraged, rioted. But Realism was here to stay.

Realism and Naturalism

It is important for the actor to understand fully the difference between realism and naturalism, for one of the accusations most frequently leveled at the representational actor is that he brings to the stage a segment of real life with all its dull detail, neglecting to select and heighten his material to achieve an artistic performance. Again, this is bad acting. It is not the aim of the good representational actor.

Naturalism was an extreme offshoot of the realistic movement. Its champion was Émile Zola (1840–1902), who advocated a pure, scientific approach to drama. The writer, Zola proclaimed, must observe and record with complete detachment, never allowing his own ideas or impressions to intrude. Any attempt to select or arrange his material would serve only to distort the truth. One of Zola's followers said the theatre should present a "slice of life," and indeed it appeared that the aim of the naturalists was to make the theatre as untheatrical as possible. In America, naturalism reached its apogee with the productions of David Belasco, whose transplantations of real life onto the stage were nothing short of spectacular. For *The Governor's Lady* (1912), he reproduced on stage a corner of a Childs restaurant down to the very silverware and the steaming hot cakes. But Belasco was doing nothing that the original builders of the Childs restaurant had not done. By bringing the restaurant into the theatre, he had simply eliminated the theatre. This type of transplanting hardly requires a theatrical artist.

Duplication Versus Art

An exact duplication of real life is not the purpose of the theatre—nor of any art. In order to present his special insights, the artist selects, heightens, and distorts. Thus a "naturalistic art" is, in fact, a contradiction. The closer we come to reproducing actual reality on stage, the less real it is, and the more confining. On the stage, a real restaurant can "say" no more than what it actually is: a single, specific restaurant. But an artistically ordered restaurant, a theatrical restaurant, can make a statement about all restaurants; it can present the very essence of "restaurantness"; it can reflect the writer's attitude toward restaurants; it can encourage the audience to reflect on their own feelings about restaurants. It is when the audience participates with its imagination that the life on the stage becomes most real. Thus the very unreality of the theatre is that which holds us fascinated and induces our belief. It is precisely because we cannot explain it that we believe so deeply. When the ghost is explained, he is no longer real.

The artist must, of course, base his observations on nature, on what he knows to be real; but what we consider realism in the theatre is actually a highly ordered piece of work in which the artist has done considerable tampering with nature. All the trivial remarks which fill real-life conversation are carefully pruned, and only the significant, telling dialogue is left. Characters "accidentally" happen on the scene at just the right moment to advance the events. Modern clothes, as well as period costumes, are chosen so that the colors and styles convey exactly the right impression. The actor whispers tender nothings in the girl's ear, but can be overheard by everyone in the top balcony.

We accept the production as "real" because we believe what it has to say, because there are insights into people and events which we feel are true, and because there is a sprinkling of real-life elements—bits of dialogue, props, furniture—with which we can associate. But this theatrical reality is quite different from the reality of everyday life. If it were not, if art and life were one and the same, why bother with art? If the beggar on the stage is absolutely no different from the beggar on the street, then we have learned nothing about beggars, and we have gained nothing from the performance.

While actors were excited about this new realism, they were at first floundering for a technique with which to express it. The romantic ranting and bravura posturing were no longer suitable, nor was the precise and stilted elocution demanded by alexandrine verse. Unfortunately, the actor's training had lagged far behind other advances in the theatre. Under the star system, or the actor-manager system in which the star managed his own company, there was no reason for the great talents to pass their methods on to others. (Besides, they were too busy acting to stop to teach others.) Supporting characters were considered unimportant; ordinarily, the traveling star didn't even bother to rehearse with the company he was visiting. Actors in these companies memorized a large stock of roles and learned to give the best stage positions to the star, while they remained as inconspicuous as possible. Unless an actor was ready to retire from the theatre, he did not dream of upstaging the star.

However, with the rise of permanent theatres came the idea of ensemble acting—a whole company working together, rehearsing and performing; and the need for training, in order to ensure high standards of acting from every member of the company, became apparent.

Delsarte: Acting by Formula

Earlier, a few attempts had been made to organize the instruction of the actor; but as they were not based on essential truths about art or human beings, these methods and their champions had had no lasting influence. One such acting technique had been advanced in 1839 by François Delsarte, a French theoretician who attempted to reduce acting to scientific principles. Gesture, he declared, was the agent of the soul; and the actor could imitate any emotion by learning the proper gesture, for identical feelings expressed themselves in identical patterns and movements.

According to Delsarte's theory, the expanded torso indicated excitement and vehemence; contracted, it expressed pain; relaxed, it expressed indolence. Leaning directly toward an object showed objective attraction; leaning obliquely toward an object, subjective attraction. The shoulders marked the degree of intensity of a passion; the elbows showed the degree of consciousness of self. The actor's hand could assail, affirm, deny, accept, reject, or support—according to the angle of the wrist and the position of the fingers. The feet had nine expressions; three with the weight upon the forward leg (animation, suspense, vehemence); three with the weight equally distributed (respect, insolence, decision); and three with the weight upon the back leg (repose, defiance, prostration). The actor must speak well, of course; and to that end, there were three important points of reverberation in the mouth: the physical, in the pharynx; the moral in the palatal arch; and the mental, behind the upper teeth.

This rigid, externally imposed formula for acting was a far cry from the technique needed to serve the new realism which was beginning to emerge. While the acting thus engendered might be consistent with the formality and pretentiousness of courtly presentation, Europe's eyes were now focused on "the common man." The new hero was not a nobleman, but our neighbor; and the actor's goal became to render himself indistinguishable from the man on the street. In consequence, he became more and more involved with imitating the minutiae of everyday life, and his acting became smaller and less imaginative. He offered the chaff with the wheat, cluttering his performance with insignificant trifles in order to present a completely true-to-life picture. It was as though he had lost his grip on his art; it seemed no longer necessary to be creative, to carefully select just the right elements for his character, to employ imagination and inventiveness, to exercise taste. To portray a groceryman, the actor simply imitated the inflections and movements of his grocer.

The novelty and excitement of realism, the eagerness to experiment, had caused the actor to overshoot the mark. When this happens to a movement, it remains for an individual with extraordinary understanding and sensitivity to temper the force, to harness the undisciplined energies and channel them into a creative and artistic form.

Stanislavski

In 1898, Constantin Stanislavski, together with Vladimir Nemirovich-Danchenko, founded the Moscow Art Theatre. He had studied the renowned actors of his time and of the past and had tried to find common elements in their acting. Great actors, he noted, had a certain "creative state" of mind by which they were able to react truthfully to the imaginary situations in a play. The events on stage seemed to be really happening, and the spectator was filled with a deep sense of belief in the character and his behavior. These actors possessed both the so-called *external* techniques—mastery of voice and body—and an *internal* technique which consisted of a thorough understanding of the psychology of the character and an ability to evoke emotions that rang true because they were conjured from the depths of the actor's own experiences.

Stanislavski concluded that actors could learn to command their bodies and their minds to a point where they could induce this "creative state," where their entire physical and spiritual being was organically working to bring "the life of the human spirit" onto the stage. He also realized the importance of integrating each and every character with the play, rather than allowing the play to serve as a vehicle for the special talents of a star. From these concepts, he developed a system of training actors which was really the first structured approach to the study of acting.

The Stanislavski system has been thought of as a "style" of acting, and one which is primarily suitable for "naturalistic" plays. This is not so at all; it is not a style but an approach to the actor's task, a technique of analyzing a role and of working on one's *inner and outer* resources so as to have complete control of one's craft and to be able to offer a fully realized and thoroughly illuminated character. It is an approach which may be applied to any kind of play, from Greek classics to modern farce. Stanislavski had a hearty dislike for the "ignorant maniacs" of the theatre whose megalomania interfered with their art. And he believed that the theatre was, above all, a place where people came to be *entertained.*

Stanislavski in America

The productions of the Moscow Art Theatre became world famous. News came to America about this startling company; and its first visit to New York, in 1923, created a sensation. Weeks before the first performance, every seat in the theatre had been sold out. After the company had performed here, its coup was complete. No one here had ever seen such magnificent ensemble acting. American actors were in a fever to learn this new technique.

Eventually, the concepts of inner truth and organic acting were to produce some truly fine performances in this country, but at first Stanislavski's ideas were imperfectly understood. Although his autobiography (*My Life in Art*) appeared in 1924, his first book on acting (*An Actor Prepares*) was not published in English until 1936. Prior to its appearance, there were occasional magazine articles, lectures, and class instruction by a few of his pupils and members of the Moscow Art Theatre who had remained in this country; but American actors found themselves grasping at straws and were not yet able to piece all the concepts together into a unified approach to their art.

The Group Theatre

In 1931, the Group Theatre was organized in New York City. Headed by Harold Clurman, Lee Strasberg, and Cheryl Crawford, it was a permanent company aimed at ensemble acting; and during its ten-year life it produced some excellent and exciting drama. The Group introduced the work of Clifford Odets and Sidney Kingsley, and produced plays by Maxwell Anderson, Paul Green, Robert Ardrey, William Saroyan, Irwin Shaw, and John Howard Lawson. It nurtured directors such as Elia Kazan, Lee Strasberg, Harold Clurman, and Robert Lewis. Some members of the acting ensemble were Stella and Luther Adler, Morris Carnovsky, Franchot Tone, John Garfield, Lee J. Cobb, Sanford Meisner, J. Edward Bromberg, Philip Loeb, Russell Collins, and Sylvia Sidney. The directors of the Group gave classes and rehearsed plays according to what were then understood to be Stanislavski's tenets, and which came to be known in America as "The Method." It is only natural for techniques to be modified as they are practiced by different people, and so today we find former members of the Group engaged in teaching acting methods which are based principally on Stanislavski's system but which differ in various respects. Clurman's *The Fervent Years*[6] is an excellent account of the Group's history and its struggles with The Method.

The Actors Studio

In 1947, the Actors Studio was founded in New York by Elia Kazan, Cheryl Crawford, and Robert Lewis. Its purpose was to provide actors with a workshop in which to develop their technique, based upon The Method. Admission was by audition; no fee was charged. In 1951, a difference of opinion caused Lewis to leave the Studio, and Lee Strasberg was invited to replace him. Prominent members of the Actors Studio have included Marlon Brando, Paul Newman, Marilyn Monroe, Geraldine Page, Eli Wallach, Julie Harris, Kim Stanley, Maureen Stapleton, Pat Hingle, Karl Malden, and Ben Gazzara.

The Actors Studio and its techniques have been the most hotly debated issues in the theatre in recent times. Some of the discord stems from Strasberg's alterations of Stanislavski's ideas, particularly in the matter of emotion memory, [7] which Strasberg encourages but which Stanislavski later relegated to a far less important position than it had occupied in his original thinking. An especially unfortunate situation has been created in which The Method and the Actors Studio have been stigmatized as a result of examples of horrible acting by some who call themselves "method actors" but who have misunderstood The Method and misapplied its techniques. These actors became entranced with the introspection and self-absorption prompted by the search for the "inner truth"—so much so that they

6. New York: Alfred A. Knopf, 1945.
7. For a discussion of emotion memory, see page 61.

disregarded the externals. In fact, these misguided actors viewed the externals as evil. They deliberately did *not* train their voices and bodies for fear that they would appear "theatrical," which they equated with "phony." If, for example, they used their naturally ungainly walk and a voice which could barely be heard in the tenth row, they thought they were being all the more "real."

Many audiences responded well to these "realistic" perform-ances, with the result that the actor with a natural eccentricity was often cast *because* of it. Directors and producers looked for actors who were "different"; and actors, accordingly, nurtured their personal peculiarities, thus strengthening the very system which actors have always despised—the type-casting system in which an actor always plays a similar kind of role. Happily, the pendulum now seems to be swinging away from this sort of "non-acting," and audiences are deriving pleasure from a theatre which is honestly theatrical.

THE EXEMPLARY ACTOR

An actor looks at a script. It is made up of a lot of words— speeches that people say to one another. An occasional stage direc-tion. No more. These words are the beginning and the end of the actor's work. Between his first reading of the words and his utterance of those words in performance lies the actor's task: the psychological and physical preparation needed to *say* those words so that they are more than mere mouthings.

The words are the beginning because they are the only clue to what the play is about. We must study the words to know who we are and what our relationships are to the other characters. But there comes a time when the order is reversed, and everything we have learned and deduced from the playwright's words now serves as preparation for the saying of those words. The words become the end, the culmination of the actor's experience on stage. First comes the impulse, the response or stirring within us which leads to the need to utter the words. We erupt into speech only when we cannot accomplish our aims through actions. If the vegetables taste flat to me, I reach for the salt. Only if the salt is not within my reach do I have to speak. If Joan of Orléans could step up to the supply sergeant and ask for a horse and a soldier's uniform, there would be no need for her to pour a verbal barrage into the dauphin's ear in an attempt to convince him that God has chosen her to lead the French to vic-tory.

Words do not pop out of our mouths as independent little spir-its, neatly manufactured by fluttering vocal cords and the articulatory mechanism. No, those are nonsense sounds. Real words, words that live because they have been born of need, have been through a gestation period. They have been through the emotional mill. They may slip out between our lips soft and weak, having been stripped of their backbones by the fear within us. They may come out the worse for wear, having been beaten by angry thoughts. Sometimes they dance out, all sparkling, because they have been caressed by happy feelings.

So we see that although the playwright supplies the words in their final pattern, the actor must go back to their beginnings and create within himself the motivations which will give birth to his *need* to say those words.

To elaborate, let us suppose that this is an ordinary Friday evening, and I decide to cancel a social engagement with some friends and go to a movie instead. This decision may have been prompted by a vague "feeling" or by a quite conscious and specific reason. Whether my decision is conscious or not, it has resulted from a complex of likes and dislikes, understandings and misunderstandings, or prejudices. When the occasion for decision is of greater moment, a much more intricate set of influence-factors is activated: all my wants and fears and needs—in short, the vast reservoir of experiences, learnings, and daydreams which blend to make me the unique individual that I am—are brought to bear upon that decision. Again, some are more conscious than others. When the actor on stage makes a decision or takes action in the person of his character, that decision or action must be backed by as vast a reservoir.

The audience, on leaving the theatre, should be deeply concerned with the people, problems, and ideas which have been presented. If the playgoer marvels at the actor's virtuosity, his splendid voice and bombast, his elegant carriage, but is not moved by the situations in which the actor is supposedly involved, that actor has failed.

Do not misunderstand; external technique is a must. The actor's voice and body are his instrument, a sensitive instrument which must respond to the most subtle nuances of thought and feeling. The instrument must be under complete control to produce the finest shadings as well as the boldest strokes.

The actor should be able to speak the verse of Shakespeare and the dialect of Tennessee Williams with equal facility. He should be comfortable and move with ease in a doublet, a cape, or a trench coat. He should be able to fence, to bow to a seventeenth-century lady, or to prance like a leprechaun. Yet all these external trappings can become just so much flummery if the actor does not reveal to us the inner spirit of the character as well. Consider two actors: the first, poised and graceful, has copied the gestures of the Restoration gentleman — turned-out leg, handkerchief delicately waved in front of the face — and he performs these externals very nicely. The second actor, equally poised and graceful, knows *why* he waves the handkerchief: It is loaded with perfume, and he waves it to dissipate the foul breath of his companion. Toothpaste was still a long way off.

The understanding which lies beneath the action of the second actor imbues the whole moment with life and meaning; whereas the action of the first, no matter how prettily executed, remains only an empty gesture. Jean-Louis Barrault says it this way: "A gesture is not sufficient; it needs to be clothed in thought." And what is the greatest compliment paid to a painter or sculptor? Is it not that he has captured the "inner essence" of his model?

Our exemplary actor creates his performance anew each night. The drives or motivations behind his actions are there every single time; his passions are freshly engendered each time he appears on stage. He presents a living, organic being, as fully alive as the man on the street — no, more so; for in the few hours allotted him on stage, he must pack in a wealth of living material; he must carefully select and balance; he must heighten certain elements and exclude others. He should be exhausted at the end of a performance, because the demands made upon an actor facing the crises and intensified situations in a good drama, the inner tensions and energies (if fully realized), are tiring indeed. Stanislavski once said that the role of Othello is so demanding that no actor could do it justice more than twice a week.

We have now come full circle and are back to the "how-much-to-feel" argument. No, the actor we have just described is not really *living* his role; he is *imagining* the situation and behaving as he would *if* it were real. Without this consciousness, the actor would be psychotic. Yet his feelings are nonetheless real. He perceives the *cause* of these feelings to be different. Because the actor realizes that he is only imagining the situation, he can abandon himself to the deepest grief or terror with the knowledge that after the performance everything will be just fine again.

To say that the actor *becomes* the character is to suggest some sort of transformation which defies all natural laws. A person cannot become another person. He cannot exchange his heart and his mind and his limbs for those of another. He is always in possession of his own faculties, physical and mental, and he uses them to show us how he would behave *if* he were the Prince of Denmark. Hamlet does not exist; only Olivier exists, using his own voice, his own memories and passions, and the best English make-up. Perhaps tomorrow night he will play Falstaff; he may deepen his voice, move differently, wear a big stuffed belly, and bring to bear a different set of memories and emotions — but always *Olivier's* memories and emotions. These matters will be discussed further in the section on characterization.

The Need for Conscious Control

In a song satirizing the Stanislavski system, Danny Kaye asks, "Who is the greatest actor in the world? And how did I get that way?" Indeed, how does one become an artist rather than just a competent craftsman? The answer is: *by work*—by putting in the same arduous, tedious hours of practice as the dancer, singer, pianist, painter.

If you couldn't play the piano, would you dream of approaching a symphony conductor and requesting an audition as concert pianist? Ridiculous, isn't it? Yet this kind of presumption is an everyday occurrence in the theatre.

It's a funny thing about actors. A great many of them do not see the need for study and practice. Only in acting does it happen that someone from another field wakes up one day and decides to be an actor. He has some photographs taken of himself and passes them around to the casting agents. No one can tell he is not a real actor, for his instrument is incarnate—he has a body and a voice. Perhaps his voice is peculiar. So much the better; that makes him a "character." When he applies for a role, the most that will be demanded of him is that he will be asked to read some lines from a play. Well, he can read. He can even put some "expression" into his reading. And if he appears to be the right physical "type," he is hired. What the director cannot possibly know is that this "actor" lacks the knowledge and experience to make his character mature into a vital and organic person during the four-week rehearsal period.

Our "instant actor" is either going to play this part from night to night as the mood strikes him, or else he will repeat his lines each night like a human tape-recorder. His performance will be erratic, ranging from good to terrible. He lacks control, a conscious technique which would make him absolute master of his creative and physical energies so that his every performance would be on the highest possible level. Inspiration is fickle; she does not always visit us when we need her. In her absence, the actor without a solid technique is lost.

Acting: Art or Craft?

There is an old, fruitless argument about whether acting is an art or a craft. Are the two so distinguishable? The fine craftsman, by dint of imagination and talent, will make of his work an art; the fine artist is one who can channel and control his creative imagination by his mastery of technique. The greater his knowledge and grasp of his craft, the more surely will the artist be able to put into effect his conceptions — or rather, the conceptions of a playwright — and to do this in such a way that the audience will be unaware of his *modus operandi*. A large part of the actor's art is the concealment of his craft.

It takes a lot of hard work to master a craft, and acting is one of the most difficult arts/crafts, depending as it does upon the undependable human instrument. The delicate and subtle balance of the myriad psychological and physical elements that produce a good performance can be easily upset by many unpredictable factors, such as bad news, a sleepless night, or indigestion. That is why there are certain foundation techniques that must become second nature so that the actor can devote his full concentration to more important things. If the mind is cluttered with a dozen concepts of technique which the actor is trying to synthesize, there is no room or energy left for the creative imagination. It is only through strict discipline of the basic techniques that the imagination can be freed to soar. Therefore, in order to ensure proper mastery of these fundamentals, they must be taken in some sort of order, carefully dissected and practiced, and time allowed for them to "set."

Within the first few months of many acting courses, the student performs in scenes ranging from the Greek classics through Tennessee Williams. Usually, he does not master one technique before he rushes or is rushed into another. It is an old failing: we have no patience for tedious practice. We only want to see results. Moreover, there is often little or no time for the teacher to discern and work on individual differences. Especially in the teaching of acting, different personalities must be drawn out by different means. We all have certain peculiarities and problems which interfere with our full and free expression on the stage. What moves one person emotionally has no effect on another. Tell one actor to be "aggressive," and he becomes a brute; tell another, and he is politely firm.

Each student must experiment with all the various exercises and discover which work best for him. In acting, we are not dealing with mathematical equations, but with human personalities. By trying, choosing, and discarding, each student builds his own method of creating a role. There is no single method which applies to everyone. Stanislavski himself would become very annoyed when anyone spoke of "his" system. It was not a question of "his" system or anyone else's system, he maintained; there was only one system, that of creative, organic nature; and all good actors used it whether or not they had ever heard of Stanislavski.

THE COURSE OF STUDY

This book, then, will deal with the specific sequential techniques needed by the actor for work on a role. Although discussions of speech and movement have been included, concentrated work on the voice and the body should be done in separate classes under teachers of those disciplines. Each demands a great deal of time and practice and cannot be properly covered in the usual acting course. Classes in developing the speaking voice, singing, diction, and dancing are the very least an aspiring actor should be expected to attend. The course of study proposed herein will treat the following areas.

Jargon and Geography of the Stage

The student is introduced to the environment in which he will be working — the stage — and is offered a basic vocabulary of terms used in the theatre to designate stage areas and types of movements. Certain rules, or conventions, of stage movement are discussed. Some are upheld, others are challenged.

The Actor's Instrument

This section is devoted to work on the instrument, which is to say the actor's self. He learns that relaxation and freedom from muscular tension are cardinal necessities, for tension interferes with thought and feeling no less than with physical movement. He learns to involve himself completely when on stage so that he can really *do* and *experience* an action rather than merely go through the outward motions. The greater his involvement in his activities, the more strongly will there be awakened in him emotions which he will then direct into meaningful and theatrically expressive actions.

The objective of a scene is pointed out as the goal toward which the actor must devote all his energies. He works on deepening the justification and the personal significance behind his actions in a scene. This strengthens his belief in those actions and makes the scene richer and more meaningful to him.

The "scenes" here mentioned are all of the actor's own invention. Improvisations are created, at first by the actor alone and then by two actors working together. When not tied to the words and story line of a script, the actor is free to respond spontaneously to an evolving situation. He has an opportunity to explore fully his personal reaction to a given event; for unless he can behave truthfully on the stage *as himself*, he will have no basis for the creation of a character for which, after all, he will have to borrow from his own store of emotions and experiences.

Exercises are done in "sense memory," the responding to imaginary stimuli involving the five senses. These deepen the actor's sense of truth and help him to individualize his responses. The controversial issue of "emotion memory," a technique involving the substitution of personal memories which evoke emotions analogous to those which the character in the play is supposed to be experiencing, is discussed but not advocated.

The concept of "preparation" is introduced—what the actor is to do during those few moments off stage immediately before an entrance. This is one of the most often neglected areas of the actor's training, yet those few seconds are crucial. They must be used properly to warm up, to "get the engine going."

Considerable emphasis is placed on developing the imagination, for the actor whose expression is in terms of the ordinary or the cliché will find that the audience is always one scene ahead of him. The imaginative actor will not use hackneyed symbols but will find unique and convincing ways to convey his ideas.

The Colors: Elements of Characterization

In this phase of our work, the student learns to choose specific colors, or character elements, for his role, and to steer away from trite or stereotyped representations. He learns to physicalize, or externalize, the psychological elements of his character so that he is not just "feeling" for himself but projecting his character for the audience. There are exercises with costumes, props, pictures, animals, and period literature designed to stir the imagination and to infuse a feeling for a particular character element or a given era. Music is used in the same manner. Students also develop portrayals of caricatures to demonstrate the fullest possible use of the physicalization of internal elements.

The Actor's Material: Analysis of the Script

In this section the work previously done on action, objective, and justification is applied to the written scene. Now the student develops the discipline of following the author's instructions and seeking for character clues within the play. He finds his character's place in relation to the theme of the play and to the other characters. The actor learns that by carefully studying the *other* characters, the stage directions, and all the many implications inherent in a play, he can extract a tremendous amount of material from the script for use in his characterization. As a model, Chekhov's one-act play *The Anniversary* is analyzed in detail; and the full text of Pirandello's *Sicilian Limes* is included in the Appendix for a class assignment in script analysis.

The Actor's Speech

Speech is one of the actor's most formidable tools. A flexible speech pattern, under strong control, can serve the actor in countless ways. Speech is a character element, a reflector of emotional states, a vehicle for rendering the rhythms of poetry. This section deals with those aspects of speech which are of particular importance to the actor: projection, standard stage speech, dialects and accents, the use of the voice as a character element, and the speaking of prose and poetry.

Special Problems in Style and Movement

Student actors are intrigued with the idea of playing with "style," but they often approach the problem of style as though it were merely an embellishment, a set of mannerisms to be superimposed on the performance. The student learns in this section that style is not a separate element, but part of the fabric of the play. By finding the truth of his character as the playwright conceived it, the actor will achieve the proper style.

Closely allied to the problem of style is the matter of finding the right movement for the character, especially in period plays. The actor discovers that his movement in a particular play will depend on the style of the play, the physical costume, the psychology of the costume, the manners and customs of the period, and the character being portrayed. Specific movements, such as bows and curtsies, as well as discussions of costumes and customs, are offered for the Medieval and Tudor, the Elizabethan, the Restoration, and the Victorian and Edwardian periods.

The Product: A Synthesis of the Techniques

The logical culmination of our work is the consolidation of all the foregoing techniques in the presentation of written scenes and one-act plays. Suggestions are offered for the choosing of practice scenes, and sources of scenes and plays are indicated. The dynamic use of rehearsal time is then considered. A scene is not simply repeated mechanically, over and over, until the players know it cold. Each time a scene is run, there must be a specific problem under consideration: now the actions, now the environment, now the relationship of the characters to each other, now the props to be handled, and so on. Finally, the student learns the vital technique of keeping the part fresh from night to night during performances.

The Audition

A new chapter has been added to this edition. Getting the role and creating the role are not the same thing. It's the difference between artistry and marketing. It is important for the actor to be aware of the special techniques needed for the adition—needed, that is, to get the job.

two

Jargon and geography of the stage

Every trade or profession has its jargon, a special set of terms used by its members to denote tools or materials used, or the processes which differentiate their work from that of everyone else. Jargon is fun; it makes us feel part of the "in group"; it gives us a sense of belonging. Jargon is especially necessary in the theatre, because every production finds an entirely new group of people working together. Without some common language, actors and directors would have a difficult time communicating with each other. We have to learn some basic terms.

It is to be expected, too, that a set of ground rules be understood by all the different actors and directors who may find themselves teamed up for a production; otherwise, each rehearsal period might have to begin with a lesson on the fundamental techniques of moving about the stage. The problem, however, is that not everyone agrees on which rules are rules and which are old-fashioned theories which ought to be discarded, which "fundamentals" can be disregarded with impunity and which ought to be strictly observed. Before we pitch camp and challenge some of these "rules," let's start with some definitions which occasion no argument.

Stage Geography

A playwright, in writing directions for movement or for the placement of furniture, needs to be able to refer to a particular section of the stage and feel sure that actors and directors will readily understand him. Similarly, the director needs to be able to give directions to his actors without climbing on stage and demonstrating every movement himself.

Right stage is that side of the stage which is on the actor's right as he faces the audience; *left stage* is on his left. *Downstage* is that part of the stage nearest the audience; *upstage* is away from the audience, toward the rear wall of the stage. The direction to *move down* means to come downstage, nearer the audience; to *move up* means to move upstage, away from the audience. If there is a desk on stage, to come *below* the desk means to come between it and the audience; to move *above* it means to go upstage of it.

For preparing promptbooks or for giving more specific directions, some directors divide the stage into as many as fifteen areas, as shown in Figure 1. For example, if the actor moves up from the exact *center* of the stage, he will be in the *up center* position; the area immediately to his left will then be *up left center;* further to his left will be *up left;* and so on. To come further *in* or *on stage* means to come closer to the center. *Off stage* refers to any part of the stage which is not visible to the audience because of interposing draperies or scenery.

UR	URC	UC	ULC	UL
R	RC	C	LC	L
DR	DRC	DC	DLC	DL

Figure 1.   THE PLAYING AREAS OF THE STAGE

The *apron* is that part of the stage which juts out toward the audience, in front of the main curtain. *Proscenium* refers to the wall which separates the auditorium from the stage; the audience sees the play through the *proscenium opening* or *arch.* The whole area which lies behind and beyond the stage proper is designated as backstage. The wings are the off-stage areas to the left and right of the stage. There are many, many more terms which the student will hear in the theatre, but those mentioned here are the ones most commonly used by directors and actors. Other terms relate to technical equipment or procedures, and can be learned by consulting any good book on play production or scene design.

Blocking Stage Movement

The procedure of *blocking* — that is, setting the actor's movements, crosses, entrances, and exits — is the director's task and responsibility, but the actor should be aware of some of the terminology and difficulties. In the first place, many directors do not block the movement of a play with great precision. They prefer to allow the actors to "feel" their way around, and in the long run the actors thus set much of their own blocking. Secondly, when preparing practice scenes for class, actors often work without a director, and it is reasonable to expect that they should be able to move about the stage comfortably without creating a lopsided picture and without knocking the furniture over or getting into traffic snarls.

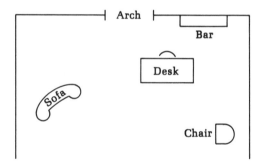

Figure 2.   FLOOR PLAN OF A LIVING ROOM

Let us imagine three actors doing a scene which takes place in a living room (Figure 2). As the scene begins, Matthew is standing between the desk and the sofa, reading a letter. He is in a direct line with the arch. Seth enters through the arch and, making a *direct approach* (Figure 3), stops a few feet above Matthew and greets him. The audience cannot see Seth very well because Matthew is directly in front of him; Matthew is *covering* him. It would have been a simple matter for Matthew to have been in front of the sofa at the start of the scene so that Seth would have had a clear entrance. Or, if it were important that Matthew be standing between the desk and the sofa, Seth could have made a *curved approach* (Figure 4) and brought himself into a clear line of vision for the audience.

Figure 3.   DIRECT APPROACH   Figure 4.   CURVED APPROACH

Matthew gives the letter to Seth, who reads it as he walks to the desk. He stops directly in front of the desk, reaches over to a lamp which stands on a corner of the desk, clicks the switch, and removes his hand. A second later, the light goes on. The audience laughs. Seth, of course, should have left his hand on the switch until the electrician turned the light on, for all the lighting instruments are controlled off stage. Matthew goes to the upstage side of the desk to get something out of the drawer. Now Seth is covering Matthew; but Seth should have prevented this from happening by taking a few steps back toward the sofa as Matthew approached the desk. This is known as *dressing stage*, clearing the way to create a better balance.

Norma rushes in, and Seth meets her near the arch and gives her the letter. Seth leads her to the sofa, where she sits, and he then goes up to the bar to mix her a drink. Matthew moves slightly toward the sofa and starts a long speech explaining the importance of the letter. At this moment, Matthew is being *upstaged* by Seth, who is at the bar. If an actor in the upstage area is busy or moving, the eyes of the audience tend to look past the actors who are downstage or center stage and focus on the upstage actor. Upstaging is clumsy when accidental and deplorable when intentional.

Returning now to Matthew's big speech about the letter, the director, at this moment in rehearsal, may tell Matthew to *take stage*. This means that this actor is free to move anywhere he wishes. The director will have settled the other actors down to listen, and Matthew has our undivided attention. It is his big moment. While he is delivering his speech, Seth and Norma should, of course, be paying close attention. Seth may decide, however, to *steal* the scene by attracting the attention of the audience away from Matthew and toward himself. One way to accomplish this is by intentional upstaging: he might stop listening to Matthew and become very busy at the bar; he might notice a smudge on his drinking glass, pull out his handkerchief and try to wipe it off; naturally the smudge resists cleaning, so he works harder. By this time, the audience has probably ceased to notice that Matthew is even on stage. This is a thoroughly unprofessional tactic; it should win Seth a severe reprimand.

Upstaging is only one way to steal a scene. A determined scene-stealer can accomplish his objective even though he is downstage of the actor upon whom attention should be focused. He simply performs distracting movements or, more subtly, concentrates fiercely upon something which has little or no relation to the scene being played. The audience will usually be more fascinated by his quiet, deep concentration than by the lines being spoken on stage.

To carry this demonstration scene further, perhaps the director wants Seth to be in the down-left chair by the time Matthew finishes his speech. Accordingly, he will direct Seth to *work downstage* during the speech. Over a considerable period of time, Seth will slowly and surreptitiously *ease* his way down, taking a step now as though to get a bit closer to Matthew in order to listen more attentively, then —during a momentary pause in Matthew's speech—taking two more steps down to the desk in order to put the drink down, then—a little later—another step or two to bring himself below the desk in order to watch Matthew. Eventually, in this manner, Seth will have *stolen* his way down to the chair at down left. Stealing in this sense is not the same as "stealing a scene."

When Matthew finishes his speech, Norma crosses to him. If she does so in such a way that they are both on the same line parallel with the footlights, they will be *sharing* the scene. Matthew, however, may *give* the scene to Norma by moving downstage a step and turning his body slightly upstage to face her, thereby giving her the upstage position. If Seth now crosses over to Norma and Matthew, the director may feel that they are all too closely bunched and will direct them to *open up* the scene—that is, to move apart. If their relative positions are too spread out, he will ask them to *close in,* or *close it up.*

The Arena Stage

Directions and denotations for movement on the arena stage, or "in the round," pose a somewhat different set of problems, because such terms as *upstage* or *left stage* are not applicable in a theatre in which the stage or playing area is surrounded by the audience. In blocking movement for a stage of this kind, many directors use either a clock face or a compass as point of reference (Figures 5 and 6).

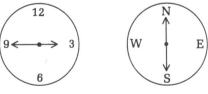

Figure 5.   *Figure 6.*

To illustrate, actors can be directed to move from *six o'clock* to *eleven o'clock*, or from *south* to *northwest*. Personally, I do not employ either of these systems, for I have found that the actors, after revolving around an arena stage for half an act, haven't the foggiest notion of which direction "south" may be. I simply tell them, for example, to go over to the red armchair or move behind the sofa and take a letter from the desk drawer.

Movement on the Arena Stage

At first glance, it might appear that there can be no wrong move on the arena stage. Since the audience is seated on all sides, there would seem to be no such considerations as upstaging, sharing, or giving scenes. But, here again, we find that we cannot simply transplant life to the stage without making some adjustments. The diagrams demonstrate some typical actor relationships and suggest some of the problems which these interrelationships pose with reference to the audience.

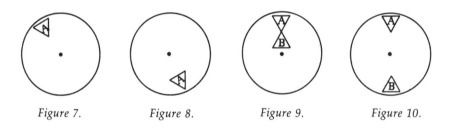

| Figure 7. | Figure 8. | Figure 9. | Figure 10. |

In Figure 7, Actor A's face is exposed to the largest possible number of spectators. As he moves closer to the center of the stage, more and more of the audience will lose sight of his face, until—as in Figure 8—he is presenting only his back to the majority of the viewers.

When two actors, A and B, are facing each other "in the round," each one is necessarily blocking or obscuring the view of the other's face from at least some of the spectators directly behind him. The closer actors A and B are to each other, as in Figure 9, the more blockage or obscuring there will be. When A and B move apart, as in Figure 10, B is still in a direct line with A insofar as some viewers are concerned, but A is now far more "open" than he was in Figure 9. A spectator behind Actor B, in Figure 10, can lean very slightly to one side in his seat and see past B to Actor A; but if Actor B is closer to A, as in Figure 9, the spectators directly behind B cannot do so.

Some directors, when doing plays in the round, introduce an

exorbitant amount of movement because they feel that the actor's face should be seen by as much of the audience as much of the time as possible. They use terms such as "fluid" or "plastic" movement, and they keep the actors in a state of perpetual motion. This is less than necessary.

Consider a so-called "static" scene: one actor is sitting behind a desk, interviewing another actor who is sitting in a chair facing him. They are blocking each other from the view of a certain number of people in the audience. But the tiniest shift in the actors' relative positions—a slight sideways turn in the chair, for instance—will bring the opposite actor's face into view for a large section of the audience. Similarly, the actor whose back is toward a part of the house because he is sitting at the desk need simply turn slightly in his chair as he ponders a question or examines a piece of paper, and he has thereby opened himself up to a new quarter of the house.

Acting in the round demands greater concentration and discipline than does acting on a proscenium stage. The actor in the round can always see the audience through the corner of his eye; light "spills" from the stage area, illuminating the front row of spectators and revealing any distractive movements they may make. Furthermore, the actor can never let his eyes wander, for he is always facing

Figure 11.

some part of the house. And, as in Figure 11, when one actor is holding forth in center stage, the actors on the perimeter must remember that they are practically in the laps of their audience and that the tiniest movement will distract attention from center stage. They must listen, often in frozen silence, without the little naturalistic physical shiftings and adjustments that are sometimes permissible on a proscenium stage.

"Rules" to Be Broken

Many other rules have been laid down to govern the actor's movement on stage, but here I part company with those who solicit our strict observance of them. There are, for instance, concepts of weak and strong parts of the stage, and weak and strong entrances and exits. We are told that downstage center is the strongest part of the stage and that consequently all important speeches and business should be maneuvered to that position. Others areas are supposedly less strong, and upstage right or upstage left is positively weak. This idea harks back to the days when actors declaimed on a bare stage with a painted backdrop behind them. For the actor to get close to the drop would destroy the illusion created by the painted perspective, for he would then appear to be as tall as a house or a mountain. In addition, when the major source of lighting for the stage area was a chandelier of candles hung over the apron, downstage center was the *brightest* part of the stage and therefore the best, or strongest, for soliloquies.

Today, with our modern lighting equipment, the strongest part of the stage is where the spotlight hits. We can focus attention anywhere we please by dimming one area and brightening another. In recent times, many plays have been episodic, taking place in a two-level set. One scene may take place on the right side of the upper level, the next directly below it, followed by another at the extreme left of the lower level—up and down and back and forth. Thus the strong part of the stage moves with the successive scenes.

It is quite possible to take what some people consider to be the weakest area on stage—the upstage corner—and make it the strongest. To demonstrate this, simply put an orator on a soapbox in the upstage right corner and group a number of spectators below him and extending out to his left so that he becomes the apex of a rough triangle. Have all the other actors turned to face him, and he is now in the strongest part of the stage.

Another concept you may encounter is that of the strong and weak entrance and exit. Entrances or exits are supposedly strong when made from left stage to right stage. The explanation offered for this is that we are accustomed to read from left to right; and when a figure forces our eyes to move in the opposite direction, a kinesthetic tension or conflict is created which makes us feel that the figure is somehow strong. Conversely, a figure moving from right stage to left would be drawing our eyes along in the same direction in which we read, thereby creating an easy, harmonious feeling and, therefore, a weaker movement.

I have always been skeptical about this theory because I believe it is the character and the situation which make for strong or weak movements. Following this strong-weak hypothesis to its logical conclusion, we can imagine a set designer studying the script for happy entrances and angry exits and placing the doors accordingly. But what happens, we wonder, when the script calls for a "strong" entrance and, later, a "strong" exit through the same door? And what happens to this theory on an arena stage when for one half of the audience the figure is moving to the left and for the other half of the audience the figure is moving to the right?

Here are some additional enjoinders frequently made to actors:

Face the audience when speaking.
Kneel on the downstage knee.
Rest the weight on the downstage foot.
When starting to move from a standing position, take the first step with the upstage foot.
On an exit line, deliver most of the line as you cross to the door, stop just before going out the door, turn back to those on stage, deliver the last part of the line, and leave.

These techniques are not necessarily wrong, but they are limiting. We have adopted a much more casual and "natural" attitude toward movement on stage; and for the actor always to face the audience when he is speaking could result in stiff and rather formalized postures which would seem out of place in the realistic setting of many modern plays. Of course, there is no reason for the actor to deliberately flout convention by playing the majority of his scenes with his back to the audience. But while the audience should see the actor's face most of the time, an occasional delivery upstage is quite natural and can be effective. These are matters to be determined by common sense and taste applied to the style of the play and the character being portrayed.

The reason for the actor's kneeling on the downstage knee is to "open up" more of his body to the audience and effect a better "picture." In principle, there is nothing wrong with that; and nothing is essentially wrong with the actor's standing with his weight on the downstage foot, or starting to walk with the upstage foot, *if* these techniques truly enhance his grace and effectiveness. But all too often, unfortunately, they only serve to make him self-conscious and ungainly. As for ways of delivering exit lines, these must change with each character. One character may validly storm out the door without a backward glance; another may make six false starts and turns before finally vanishing. Therefore it seems illogical to suggest that there is such a thing as *the* way to deliver an exit line.

There is a sensible middle ground between the application of all the "rules" of stage movement and the license with which some actors amble about the stage. Realism notwithstanding, the theatre is at a remove from life; and it is not unreasonable to ask our actors to assume the artist's responsibility for making his creation just a little more beautiful, a little clearer, and a bit more ordered than ordinary life.

American actors are up in arms when producers in this country import individual actors, or sometimes whole companies, for certain plays; yet the American actors who complain the loudest are usually those who refuse to adopt the practices of their British counterparts by spending hours in acting classes learning to walk, sit, serve tea, doff a derby, and look comfortable and charming with a cocktail glass in their hand. Too many American actors consider these accomplishments to be trifles—mere superfluities—not the stuff of real acting. Americans, they proudly point out, are interested only in the "guts" of the role. As a result, they are severely handicapped when called upon to perform a role in which the social amenities must be executed with some grace and *savoir-faire*.

Marking the Script

Just as there are various approaches to the blocking of a play, so are there several ways of learning or recording that blocking. Some actors learn the blocking as they rehearse and never bother to mark anything down. Others like to have an accurate record of all moves and positions. These are some of the abbreviations used in marking a script:

X: cross

XDL: cross down left

R–1: in old scripts, this indicated the door nearest the audience on the right wall of the set. The door above it was R–2, and so on. This designation may also·be used in modern exterior sets when there are several entrances between wings, or interior sets with several doors on one side of the stage. Thus, if there were two wings on right stage, there would be three possible entrances: R–1, below the wing nearest the footlights: R–2, between the two wings; R–3, above the upstage wing. Corresponding notations (L–1, L–2, and L–3) are used to indicate doors or entrances on the left side of the stage.

A downward arrow may be used to indicate "sit" and an upward arrow to indicate "rise." Special business and props peculiar to the individual play will naturally have to be written out or put down in the actor's own devised shorthand. Actors usually like to devise their own markings for phrasing, stress, and intonation. Here is part of a typical script marked for blocking.

through arch –OR MARYA

(*Enters*) Oh, excuse me.

KLESTAKOV *drop letter on desk*

Sudarinya. *bow*

MARYA

I thought perhaps mamma was here.

XOR to her KLESTAKOV

No, she isn't.

MARYA

I'm sorry to have disturbed you. You have business. *turn to go*

KLESTAKOV *block her exit to arch*

You could never disturb me. A look from you is worth more than any business.

MARYA *back away to door L*

You know how to flatter, you do.

KLESTAKOV *follow her*

It is not flattery when the lady is as charming as you. May I offer you a chair? Ah, but no, you should have a throne, not a chair.

kneel MARYA

I had best be going.

X to door–L–block her way

KLESTAKOV

What a beautiful necklace you have.

MARYA

You're making fun of me . . . because I'm from a small town.

KLESTAKOV *move closer*

How I wish I were that necklace, mademoiselle, so that I might be embracing your neck.[1]

Now that we know a little something about how to get around on stage, our next consideration will be how to fill with life those moments between and during the crosses.

1. From the author's translation of *The Inspector General* by Nikolai Gogol.

three

The actor's instrument

Unlike musicians, painters, sculptors, and other artists who use various instruments with which to shape, mold, or apply their expression, the actor's instrument is his own self: his voice, his body, his will, his imagination. And just as Segovia doesn't play on a cowboy guitar and Picasso doesn't use stiff old brushes, neither can the actor play Hamlet with an impoverished instrument. The artist's instrument is his most prized possession; whether it be a flute or a human being, it must be under remarkable control, sensitive to the artist's will, and capable of the greatest range of expression.

While it is considered perfectly normal for the beginning pianist to play scales before tackling sonatas, most beginning actors expect to plunge right into the playing of scenes. But the playing of scenes is the end, the synthesis of our work, not the beginning. First we must tune up the instrument. We must learn what is expected of it, what we can and cannot do, just how far each of us can stretch our abilities. Then, slowly, one area at a time, we must bring our instrument under the control needed to play a scene sensitively and well.

RELAX!

If you are a fairly normal human being, it is a pretty safe bet that one of the most horrible moments in your life was the first time you stepped in front of an audience to make a speech. Your knees turned to jelly, your mouth felt stuffed with dry cotton, your heart was about to thump through your shirt, and your voice had a hollow sound as though you were speaking in a cavern. And you couldn't think. If you forgot your lines, you were lost—you hadn't the vaguest notion of what subject you were supposed to be talking about.

Why evoke such awful memories? To demonstrate that tension is the actor's greatest enemy. It is the single most destructive force with which we must contend; it inhibits both physical and mental activity. To test this, lift an extremely heavy object and at the same time try to perfom the mental task of multiplying sixty-eight by seven. The physical tension demanded of your muscles will make the normally simple calculation almost impossible.

Tension, as I am using it here, is not to be confused with the few butterflies in the stomach, the excitement which we all experience just before making our first entrance on the stage. This emotional keying differs from tension in that it is not destructive. On the contrary, it is usually valuable, for it brings the performer to a heightened sense of awareness, to a super-alertness. He is healthily and happily charged, ready to go. It would be far worse to have no butterflies at all, to be nonchalant or lethargic about a performance. The word tension, then, is hereafter to be understood as something undesirable.

The actor must be free from all tension so that his creative energies can flow freely. When he is completely relaxed, he can command his body, his voice, and his mind to do anything of which he is capable. You must have noticed how, under tension, your voice rises in pitch due to the corresponding tension in the vocal cords. This tension distorts and fatigues the voice, greatly impairing its effectiveness. The rest of the body is similarly affected. There are two ways, in particular, by which the actor can work to relax and thereby free his creative energy: *by becoming aware of his specific tensions* and *by purposefully involving himself with his role.*

Becoming Aware of Tensions

Among our many human peculiarities is the fact that most of us are usually not aware of our tension.Watch people's hands. Though a person is apparently sitting at ease, his hands are clutching the arms of the chair in a death grip. Tell him to relax, and he will bark at you that he is perfectly relaxed; and the tension will travel from his hands all through his body.

If he is to rid himself of this inability to relax, the actor must first learn to become conscious of his tensions and their location. We all have them in different places: the neck, the arms, the shoulders, the legs. We employ as a check that little part of our consciousness with which we watch ourselves, that tiny bit of awareness that lets us know that our terrible stage battle is only make-believe. Try it. In the midst of an interview, a class, a meeting, or any social occasion, suddenly authorize this corner of your consciousness to make a self-examination. Keep smiling at the old bore with the demitasse cup, but concentrate all your attention on your toes. Are they curled up in your shoes, clutching at something? Let them go, wiggle them freely. Then direct your attention up to your kneecap. Is it flexed? Relax it.

In this manner, keep moving your concentration over your body, consciously relaxing each part. You will be amazed to discover that you have many areas of tension of which you have been completely unaware. After you have done this exercise a number of times, you will become sensitive to the changes in your body, and you will perceive and relax your tensions much more quickly. Until relaxation becomes a habit, however, you must continue this procedure on stage as well. It takes only a second. Choose a moment when you are supposed to be writing or reading or listening to someone else, and make a fast tension check.

Involvement

William James explains that the most important part of our environment is our fellow man; it is our consciousness of his attitude toward us that triggers most of our shames, fears, indignations, and — consequently — tensions. We are extraordinarily sensitive when we are aware of being noticed by our fellow man. This awareness is increased tenfold in the case of the actor, and his thoughts fly out to the audience. Since the human mind, bright as it is, cannot concentrate on several things at once, the actor is therefore left with no support for his work on stage. He must learn, then, to involve himself with his role and the play to such a degree when on stage that there is no concentration left over to be wasted on worrying about audiences or tensions.

CONCENTRATION

Upon what can we fasten our concentration? An object, an idea, a memory. What do we do when we concentrate? Do we simply stare hard at an object? No, this is not concentration. Concentration is an active, selective process. We cannot think "in general"; we must choose some specific activity. We might decide to analyze thoroughly the physical characteristics of a certain object. We look at our watch. It is round, with a silver rim . . . . the silver doesn't shine as it once did . . . . the crystal is scratched . . . . is it glass or plastic? . . . we can feel the scratches with our fingernail . . . . there are particles of dust inside, around the rim . . . . the hands are very narrow and pointed . . . . instead of numbers, there are thin bars of gold — gold or brass — about a quarter of an inch long and a thirty-second of an inch wide . . . . the leather strap is worn . . . . some of the stitching is undone. Thus we explore every facet: the color, the texture, the weight, the size. We are actively concentrating.

EXERCISE

Bring in an object. Make yourself comfortable on stage, and describe the object to the class. Mention as many details as you can possibly extract from this object. The more details you find, the more involved you will be.

EXERCISE

Repeat this process with an object you have not seen before. The instructor will have collected several props and will hand you one before you go on stage.

Now we take these exercises one step further. We deepen our concentration by recalling the circumstances connected with the object. "Where did I buy this watch? Switzerland . . . a rainy day in Berne . . . the street was lined with watch shops . . . . I remember how difficult it was for me to calculate francs into dollars . . . . there it is, the Omega . . . that's the one!" And so on. Try to reconstruct an entire sequence in this way. It may take a bit of work, but one small detail leads to another, and soon you have brought to mind incidents and people you thought you had forgotten. And in the process you have become so involved that you have forgotten to be nervous.

During an exercise of this kind, the recollection of a particular moment may make you smile or frown or feel indignant or whatever. Just let it happen; don't do anything about it. Later on, we will discuss the evoking and handling of emotions; for the present, it is enough that you be aware of the feelings being evoked by your memories without interfering with them. Most important of all, don't try to convey your feelings to the audience. Don't make a little smile into a big guffaw because people are watching you. *Work for yourself. Once you start working for the audience, your acting becomes strained and false.* If a memory brings only a tiny twinkle to your eye, and half the audience cannot see it, fine. First establish the truth for yourself. We'll worry about the audience later.

Stretching the Truth

When you have done these exercises several times with various objects and are able to become completely engulfed in your thoughts, it will be time to start oiling the imagination.

EXERCISE

As before, the instructor will hand you a prop which you have never seen. This time, rather than simply describing its physical characteristics, you will create a fictitious set of circumstances involving yourself and the object.

Stretch the imagination slowly. If you leap all at once to a wildly improbable situation, you will strain your own credulity. Your own faith and belief in what you pretend on stage must be unshakable. Start these exercises with situations you *can* believe in, even though they are not necessarily true. Use bits and pieces of the truth as mortar to hold together the bricks of fantasy.

Suppose you've been given a ring. You start by saying that your wife gave you this ring. You don't have a wife, but you have a girl friend, and it's not too great a stretch of the imagination to picture her as your wife. You note that it is not a wedding ring, so you'll have to invent some other circumstances for the gift. Has something happened recently that warrants celebration? A new job? Another degree? There's the occasion for the gift. Where were you when your wife gave it to you? Perhaps you were out dining. Choose a little restaurant that you've been to, and describe the checkered tablecloth and the dripping candle in the Chianti bottle. Then you recall how, next morning, the fellows at the office admired the ring. Make sure the "fellows" you think of are not abstract names or words; see actual friends of yours in your mind's eye. These are the truthful touches which lend support to your belief in this story. Well now, what might happen next? You lose the ring, and you are terribly upset. You'd like to buy a new one before your wife notices that it's gone. But this ring will be almost impossible to duplicate because . . . and so on. Let your imagination lead you into that remarkable realm of the actor where lies which are believed become a kind of truth.

Detail

It takes a strong discipline to pluck out a mass of details from an object or an event, for most of us would rather take the easy way and merely pick the highlights, the obvious features. It is easy to describe a room *generally:* "It was dingy, old furniture, a lot of junk lying around." It is much more difficult to describe each article of furniture exactly, what kind of fabric it had, where it was torn, and just what "junk" was lying where. But this discipline is vital to the actor, especially when he works on actual scripts and will need to recall and cull out every detail which can contribute to his characterization.

Sense Memory

We remember things through our five senses. Call upon each of them to help you. After you have *seen* everything in that dingy room, try to recall what things *felt* like — the worn, rough fabric on the sofa, the cheap stuffing sticking through, the uneven wooden floor underfoot. What did you *hear*? Was there a radio blaring next door? A dripping water tap? And what about the *smells*? Was there any cooking going on? Was there a musty odor from lack of ventilation? Perhaps you didn't eat anything there, so the sense of taste would not be of service this time.

These exercises, if properly done, will fatigue you, for the brainwork is enormous. But lazy people never become anything but rested.

EXERCISE

Work with each of the five senses, one sense at a time. Recall a place you've visited. Describe everything you *saw*. Describe all the *tastes* you experienced at a smorgasbord. Describe everything you might *hear* at a circus. Describe everything you would *feel* if you were to handle all the objects on your desk. Can you describe the *smells* at the perfume counter? Or the tobacco store?

EXERCISE

As a variation of the above, the instructor can name a place and designate the sense to be worked on: a toy shop — sense of touch. In rapid succession, each member of the class will respond with a single appropriate impression. Keep the exercise going around until the impressions wear thin. You will have to think quickly, for someone else may describe the very same fuzzy teddy bear you had in mind.

EXERCISE

Choose an environment — restaurant, cocktail party, factory — and describe it as completely as possible, using all five senses.

There is much controversy over the use of sense memory, and many actors do not understand its application. They are asked to handle invisible objects, to hear sounds which aren't there, to taste thin air. They are told that in some strange way this will make them better actors, just as studying mathematics was once supposed to make students logical thinkers.

Sense memory requires intense concentration and is capable of involving the actor to a great degree. It also helps him achieve a unique expression rather than the cliché. Ask the amateur actor to go on stage and wait for a bus on a freezing evening. Tell him he has been waiting a long time, and he has not dressed warmly enough. Very probably, he will immediately cross his arms and thrust his hands under his armpits; he will scrunch up his shoulders and stamp his feet; he will make horrible grimaces to show the audience that he is suffering from the cold. All these are the conventional, cliché manifestations.

Now stop and think for a moment about a time you were really cold. The cold hits each of us differently. Some people are never bothered in the toes but get terrible earaches. Others must cover the nose because breathing the cold air causes pain in the nasal membranes. How exactly do *you* react to the cold? Where do you feel it first? If each member of the class were to "wait for a bus on a cold corner," remembering specifically how *he* behaved, there would be an amazing variety of reactions. Moreover, the actor would have greater belief in his reactions, because he would be doing things which he truly does under those conditions.

The practical application of sense memory should now be obvious: It can help us avoid standardized or stereotyped reactions. Isn't it annoying, for instance, to watch a jungle scene in which everyone is mopping his brow the same way? Or to see a group of people supposedly watching an off-stage event, each with the identical stare on his face? We know perfectly well that no one in that group is seeing *anything*.

There will be times in performances when you will be eating applesauce and pretending that it's Beef Stroganoff. Or holding a dead phone to your ear and pretending to hear the dulcet tones of dear what's-her-name. Or swallowing a vial of poison which will put you to sleep until Romeo arrives. Don't just swallow it and make an awful face. Remember the worst medicine or food you ever tasted. Sense memory, if imaginatively employed, can make your reactions more truthful and more individualized.

In the previous exercises we recalled sensory impressions, but the *telling* of them dissipates them somewhat, for we have to hunt for the right word and make sure we are being heard in the back of the room. If we don't bother describing them, we are free to enjoy a greater response.

EXERCISE

As an actor in a play, you must admire a painting which is placed with its back to the audience. The front is blank. Don't make general expressions of approval. Create a picture in your mind's eye. See every detail: the colors, the shading, the carefully rendered folds of clothing. It does not matter that the class has not the faintest idea of what you are seeing. Work for yourself. If you really "see" it, the class will believe that you are looking at a painting. The more details you can "see" in the painting, the greater the variety of responses you will evoke in yourself. Again, don't do any more than you actually feel.

EXERCISE

Pick up a prop phone and listen to someone deliver a long harangue. Don't raise your eyes heavenward to show us how bored you are. Hear what the person is saying. Maybe you deserve to be told some of those things. Maybe some of the things are so ridiculous you almost laugh. In effect, you must practically memorize the speech you are "hearing."

EXERCISE

You are a wardrobe assistant. Pack the Shakespearean costumes (which aren't there) into a trunk. In your mind's eye, you will have to see the size of that cape; you will have to feel its weight and its texture; and then you must fold it neatly. Be careful with the brocaded gowns. Feel the various textures: the silks, the cottons, the heavy wools, the feathers in the hats. This would be no problem if the actual costumes were there on stage; but without them you will have to concentrate intensely. You will find yourself strongly involved.

Now that you have the idea, use your ingenuity to evolve similar exercises for the senses of smell and taste. Then work with heat, cold, and pain. Choose a specific environment each time. Sit in a beach chair on the hot sand or in an off-Broadway theatre with no ventilation. Visit a doctor's office. Localize the pain in your body. Concentrate on the exact spot. What kind of pain is it? A dull throb? A piercing ache?

Will you really *be* cold when you do the exercise of waiting for a bus on a cold corner? Will you really, honestly feel the pain? Of course not. Let us emphasize again that you are training to become an actor, not a candidate for the mental asylum. Obviously, no one in a comfortably heated classroom is actually going to *become* cold, have his fingers ache and his ears turn red. You are learning to strengthen your belief—and the audience's belief—in an imaginary situation. No one will believe you if you stamp your feet and flap your hands around like a dozen other unimaginative actors. But do something which a person really does under the circumstances, and the audience is all with you. Again, you are not becoming cold, you are behaving as you would *if you were cold.*

A SENSE OF TRUTH

Wise old actors will counsel you never to appear on stage with a child or a dog. (If you find yourself asked to appear with both a child *and* a dog, don't even bother to sign the contract; your case is hopeless.) It's not just that children are invariably "cute"; they act with astounding conviction. They have such complete, intense belief in their make-believe world that adults, who have lost that power, can only stare and marvel. Watch children at play. Whether they are playing "house" or "cops and robbers," they are virtuosi of sincerity. To watch a child in a situation which is new to him is particularly fascinating, for his response will almost certainly be a surprise. He is naïve and honest and free. He has not yet learned the "proper" social response, which—more often than not—is an adult convention designed to conceal our true reaction. The child has not yet developed all the little complexes, problems, and defense mechanisms which people in our society are heir to. He has not yet become cynical, disappointed, or inhibited. Consequently, he reacts as a unique individual, with a freshness that is joyful to behold.

If we adults could retain that childhood power of belief, that miraculous ability to thoroughly convince ourselves at will of a set of imaginary circumstances, what acting would there be! Unfortunately, as we grow older, the shell around us gets thicker. We are embarrassed to "let loose"; we worry about what others think of us. Moreover, we are so overwhelmed with financial burdens and other grown-up dilemmas that our imaginations have dried up. In the case of actors, we have all witnessed so many thousands of poor motion pictures and television programs that, when we are asked to perform a scene, we immediately repeat the stereotyped pattern we have seen so often. When the actor does this, he defeats his art.

ACTIVITIES

As a first step in training for acting, we must start with a clear slate. We must learn to do the simplest everyday activities on the stage without faking, forcing, or being overburdened by awareness of the audience. Our motto will be "Do, don't show." That means that if you are asked to go on stage and read a book, you must not make interested faces, turn the pages, and generally "show" us that you are reading. Most beginning actors, after doing this exercise and being asked by the instructor what they have just read, will look blank and then indignant. They have no idea what they have just read. "We weren't reading, we were acting," they explain. But acting is *doing* —doing just as much as demanded by the situation, and no more. And no less.

EXERCISE
Perform a simple activity on stage. Do it thoroughly and specifically, and don't worry about showing it to the audience.

Example: Prepare a list of names of people you intend to invite to a party. Look for the addresses in your address book. Really *look*. Don't *pretend* to flip through the pages and then give a big, phony nod of triumph when you find the right address. You don't do that when you are alone at home, so don't do it on stage. We'll get theatrical later. First be truthful. Write down all the names and addresses. Really write them — not make-believe scribbles. If you do this activity properly, you will be involved and you will be truthful.

EXERCISE
Continue working on simple activities:
  Set the table.
  Study for an exam.
  Pack a suitcase.
  Fix a hem.
  Read your morning mail.
  Write a letter.

You must not rush on to the next phase of our work until you can perform this kind of basic activity on stage with absolute honesty and to the complete belief of your audience. This is the foundation of acting. Start with the smallest truth, and it will give birth to another truth; but fake the smallest detail, and the rest wobbles. If you do not really write the letter, if you merely scribble in pretense, then you do not believe in the letter or in the letter's purpose or in the recipient; you are merely adding empty deceit to empty deceit until you have built a mountain of lies in which no audience will believe because you don't believe in it yourself.

ACTIONS

At the outset, we must distinguish between activity and action. An activity is the smallest unit of work. It is any single task we do. Were we to break our role into its component activities, there would be hundreds of them, scattering our forces and dissipating our concentration. It would be as though we were to break a speech into single words rather than meaningful phrases, or a painting into brush strokes rather than areas of highlight and shadow. Therefore, we must synthesize; we break our part into *actions* and *objectives.*

Every character in every play has a goal toward which he is striving. Perhaps it is his life's ambition, perhaps a particular milestone in his life. Now, no one reaches a major goal or objective in one step. There are many obstacles and detours along the way, many small objectives to be gained first.

Each objective, if realized, brings us one step closer to our goal. But there are many ways of realizing an objective. If our objective is to secure a raise from our employer, we may plead, demand, threaten, cajole. For many reasons, we choose one specific course of action rather than another. *Our action is what we do to reach our objective.*

An action cannot be a vague feeling or an abstract concept. It must be a solid, clear statement, capable of being executed physically. *Physically!* An action is not a state of being. Can you go on the stage and be angry? Or be happy? Certainly not. We are angry about *something,* and we *do* something — take some action — to express that anger. The point is this: it is exceedingly difficult to define our feelings and even more difficult to control and repeat them. Our moods and emotions are fickle, constantly changing in intensity and being triggered when we least expect them to be. But a physical action can be exactly defined, controlled, and repeated. Herein lies the actor's conscious technique. Rather than trust to luck and pray that the right "feeling" will well up within him when he needs it, the actor sets a specific, physical task for himself — an action — which he knows he can do *every single time.* And if he performs this physical action properly — that is, with full conviction and involvement — the moods and emotions will come of their own accord.

By giving physical expression to his actions and by knowing exactly what he is doing every single moment he is on stage, the actor will never commit that most horrendous crime: playing a "quality." The actor who does not know what he is doing in a particular scene will resort to gestures, facial expressions, and vocal tricks in an effort to convince the audience that he is experiencing some emotion. He will push for the effect, for the result, rather than play the action which will truthfully evoke the right results. He will present a vague "quality" of anger or happiness. He will play a "mood" instead of playing the scene.

I am going to harp on this point, for it is one of the most vital tools in the actor's technique. Actors often wonder why they are required to know in such great detail every aspect of their actions on stage, every detail of justification, every last bit of motivation. "Why," they ask, "can't we just get into the feel of our part and then allow our line readings and emotions and everything else to come naturally as they do in real life?" Because in real life none of our remarks or actions comes out of a total void. Those remarks or actions which are not clearly conscious are backed up by our subconscious; and though a particular action may appear strange at the moment, it is, nevertheless, logical and consistent with our character.

On stage, there exists for the character no subconscious which will *automatically* and *correctly* offer the proper response or action. For that reason, the actor must supply a conscious and logical reason for every single action he performs on stage. It is perfectly true that in real life we may blurt out a remark unwittingly (and only much later do we sometimes realize why we said it), but as artists we must be completely witting and aware.

EMOTIONS

One of the most difficult concepts for the acting student to accept is that he need never concern himself with emotions. "Emotion is a state which the actor must never be conscious of," says Jean-Louis Barrault, the brilliant French actor and producer.[1] His only concern is to play his physical actions, and the emotions will be there without any further effort on his part. Does this sound like some sort of heresy — not to be allowed to wallow in emotion, the very stuff of acting? Isn't acting "emoting"? No. Acting is doing. Aristotle advised us that

> Tragedy is an imitation, not of men, but of action and of life, and life consists in action, and its end is a mode of action, not a quality. Now character determines men's qualities, but it is by their actions that they are happy or the reverse.[2]

Barrault puts it thus: " . . . characters never pause for one moment in the middle of their actions in order to offer gratuitous displays of feeling."[3]

1. *The Theatre of Jean-Louis Barrault*, trans. Joseph Chiari (New York: Hill and Wang, 1959), p. 51.
2. Aristotle, *On Poetry and Music*, trans. S. H. Butcher (New York: The Bobbs-Merrill Company, Inc., 1948), p. 9.
3. *Op. cit.*, p. 54.

What all this means is that the actor's performance will be emotionally charged, that he will experience the grip of strong emotions, but he will not "play the emotion" directly. He will *evoke* it. The emotion which the actor experiences is a *result* of other things he does. The direct playing of an emotion (imitating the external manifestations of the emotion) produces "quality-acting," which we usually call "ham."

Well, just what *is* an emotion? There are differing theories, but they all recognize an interplay of two factors: the mental apperception of a stimulus and a corresponding physical manifestation. Whenever we are visited by an emotion, these two factors are always present. For example, you are walking along a street where some construction is going on. Suddenly you notice a heavy beam falling directly overhead. You leap out of the way, your heart pounding madly, your knees feeling weak. We say you experienced the emotion of fright. The mental apperception was the sight of the falling beam and the realization that you might be killed or badly hurt. The physical manifestation was the jumping out of the way, the pounding of your heart, and the weak feeling in your knees. Needless to say, different individuals would display different physical reactions. Some might scream, some might turn pale, still others might faint. But there would always be *some* physical reaction.

Now the psychologists enter the discussion. Some hold that you became frightened because you saw the falling beam and realized that you might be hurt, and as a result of this realization your heart began to pound and you leaped out of the way. In other words, the mental apperception creates the emotion which in turn causes us to react physically. Others believe that the reverse is true. They maintain that, upon seeing the falling beam, you "instinctively" leaped out of the way with a pounding heart, and that the awareness of the physical changes in the body, plus the realization that you might have been hurt, produced a feeling in you known as fear. The experiencing of an emotion is actually, according to this theory, the sensing of our bodily changes.

This "emotion" that we are dealing with is an intangible factor. We *feel* it, we *experience* it. We do not *do* an emotion or *think* an emotion. It does not matter whether you believe, with some psychologists, that we think first and act later or, with others, that we act first and think afterward. What does matter to us as actors is that these two factors are both necessary to a fully realized emotion and, equally important, that these two factors are subject to control. We can think and we can move. We cannot control the vague, fickle feelings we call emotions, but we *can* control the things which *produce* these emotions.

We have said that the two factors which reside in an emotional experience are inextricably bound together, and that one without the other can offer only a half-truth. The poor actor indicates to the audience the physical results of the emotion he is supposedly feeling, and short-cuts the mental process. He leaves out the vital *why* of the emotional experience. Herein lies Delsarte's mistake, which was to chart a series of gestures which imitated only the external manifestations of the emotion. He compounded his error by assuming that everyone reacted in the same way to the same stimulus. And for him who believes, contrariwise, that emotion is purely a "mental state," let him imagine himself in the grip of a powerful emotion and then abstract every bit of physical change which took place within him since the onset of the emotion. What is left? Again, if emotions are purely mental, why is it virtually impossible for even a strong-willed person to conceal a powerful emotion? It is interesting to note that long before the psychologists started theorizing, primitive chieftains urged their warriors to shriek and hop wildly about before going into battle—that is, to manifest the physical expression of rage.

The actor, then, must know what his *action* is. He must physically *do* it, and he must know *why* he is doing it. Having thus supplied the two inevitable concomitants, he will be rich in emotional feelings as a result. Moreover, besides being organic, this emotion will be an individual expression—purely his own—and not an imitation of someone else's emotional expression.

Pinpointing the Action

Suppose you are asked to play this scene: You have been summoned to the Dean's office, and you expect to be expelled for letting your marks slide deplorably low. Of course, the last thing you want in this world is to be expelled. Your parents, who have very little money, took extra jobs at night to earn your tuition. They will be sick at heart when they hear the news.

The actor who flapped his arms around and grimaced to show us how cold he was will now make more mistakes, for an action usually consists of several activities and is attended by a much more complicated set of motivations. This actor, in playing the scene outside the Dean's office, will fidget, bite his lips, smoke many cigarettes, and pace up and down. He will do all the cliché things which show nervousness. The fact is that he won't know what he is doing; he will have no specific action. He will be acting *generally;* he will be floundering about, attempting to create some sort of mood for the audience. However, we can no more act in general than we can paint a picture in general or play the piano in general.

The actor must decide exactly what he will do. Perhaps he will plan some strategy — try to make excuses for his poor marks and attempt to talk the Dean into giving him another chance. Perhaps he will decide not to make any excuses but to throw himself on the Dean's mercy and cry about his poor parents. Or he may have given up any hope of being kept at school and attempt to calm down by distracting himself — thumbing through a magazine or reading the notices on the bulletin boards. Once he has decided exactly what he is doing in that scene, he can control it; he can repeat that action over and over again with added involvement each time.

The Right Word

Once you have decided on your action, you must nail it down with the right word. This is important, for unless you can specifically name the action, there is a danger that your idea will remain vague and loosely defined. What you will do in the scene must be put into a strong, physical verb form — into a word that screams for action. Never use a state of being. Banish the verb *to be* from your vocabulary. To say "I am annoyed" or "I am waiting" tells us nothing. The word you choose should put your whole being into a state of *need*, of *ferment*, into a *compulsion* to take action. This is extremely difficult to do because there is no one "right" word for a scene. The word chosen depends on the actor. Words are highly charged, but very subjective.

Let's take another look at the scene outside the Dean's office. What is your verb here? Yes, you are waiting to be admitted, but is your action *to wait?* Does that tell you anything specific about what you are doing? There are scores of things you can do while waiting. Suppose you've decided to defend yourself and try to be kept in school. You will *plan your attack*: you will take out a term paper for the Dean's inspection because you feel the mark was unfair; you will prepare a list of dates on which you were marked absent in spite of the fact that you were officially excused to go to other colleges with the basketball team; you will put together several newspaper clippings in which you are hailed as the best member of the team. Planning this strategy will keep you actively engaged. After you have compiled the actual papers, you will go over in your mind the remarks you wish to make to the Dean. These things must be said just so; you don't want to annoy him by seeming to brag.

Picture another scene: You are studying for an exam. Is *to study* an action? No, it's too general, too indefinite. Are you simply flipping through your notes to refresh your memory, your feet slung over an armchair and a beer nearby? Or are you frantically pacing up and down, becoming surer and surer that you will never pass? The latter. All right, are you being frantic? Careful! Never play the quality, but the action that leads to it. You must name the action that will *make* you frantic. You are *cramming every single name and date into your head.* If you really supply yourself with notes and *do* this action, you will find it is not very easy to memorize a list of names and dates quickly, and as a result you will become genuinely frantic and jittery.

As still another illustration, imagine that you've broken into a strange apartment to look for a letter. Think a moment before you begin. Will you be very careful to put everything back exactly where you found it so that no one will notice? Or will you just knock everything about without caring how soon the theft is discovered? The first action, *to search without leaving a trace,* tells you exactly how you must behave: you will closely examine the position of every object before you touch it to be sure you can replace it accurately. The second action, *to tear the letter out of its hiding place,* sends another, quite different message to the muscles, and you charge on stage ready to *do* it.

Stating the Action Positively

One further point before starting the exercises: An action should never be stated negatively. Inaction is an escape from action. Remember that your action must always tell you what you are *doing.* You cannot say that your action is *to do nothing,* for then you will simply keep repeating to yourself, "I don't want to do anything." And the scene will dry up. It has nowhere to go. You may be inactive or resting or bored, but there must be a reason behind it. Suppose you are in a sulk. You have thrown yourself onto the sofa and refuse to say or do anything. People are trying to cheer you up; they are suggesting things for you to do. If you have stated your action negatively, you will just sit there like a boulder, occasionally raising your eyes to the heavens, and the vital give-and-take which the drama demands will be gone.

State the action positively: you want *to retreat into nothingness,* to cut all ties with these awful people, to be swallowed up, to vanish. This suggests that you would not be sprawled out on the sofa but rather digging into a corner, burrowing into it, squirming and turning, tucking your feet under you, trying to become as small as possible. As the others pressed you, your inability to escape would become a great frustration, and the scene would grow. It would become more and more organic and alive as you struggled with a positive action.

Perhaps the scene just mentioned occurs in a comedy, and the effect you want is precisely that of a stubborn, motionless character surrounded by wildly gesticulating people. Here, too, your action can be stated positively. You try to become that boulder. You do not want to give these people the satisfaction of knowing that they are reaching you, that you are even aware of their existence. You determine not to react at all to anything they do or say. You will not move a muscle or bat an eye. You will be deaf, dumb, and blind to their entreaties. Try this sometime. You will be surprised how positive—and difficult—this action can be; for you must concentrate on not reacting to anything in the scene, concentrate on not letting any tiny movement betray you.

EXERCISE
The instructor suggests a scene, using very *general* terms. Each student will do the scene, bringing to it his own *specific* action.

Example: The instructor suggests *Getting ready for a date.* A specific action might be *to drag yourself together,* because you are very sorry you ever made this date with that bore. Or you might be 'getting ready *to dazzle* him with your flashiest jewelry and extravagant eye make-up.

Example: Prepare a shopping list. This can be done many ways. If you are terribly broke, you will *painstakingly cut it to the bone,* crossing out items you would like and substituting items you really need. Or the list may be for a party, and you find yourself *relishing every item.*

EXERCISE
Each student brings in his own scene, with a clearly defined action.

EXERCISE
Expand the scenes now, doing an action which has several activities. If you expected your boss for dinner and your action was *to make a superior appearance,* you might engage in several activities: you could get out the best linen and silverware; you could unwrap the expensive bottle of wine you just bought; you could dust off your most "intellectual" books and set a few on the end tables; you could put on that guitar record he likes so much; you could check whether you needed to change clothes.

Playing Ambivalence

One of the most difficult actions to play is that in which someone *tries to make up his mind* about something. Vacillation and ambivalence have two elements: weighing each possibility, then rejecting it—until we finally accept one possibility or reject all of them. The action is not *to make up one's mind* but *to weigh the evidence* or *to choose the best course*—positive actions which can be played. The actor must carefully create all the possible courses open to him: he thinks of one alternative, considers its good points and its bad points, rejects it, takes up another possibility, and repeats the process. He is weighing and judging, and the going back and forth among the various possibilities creates vacillation; but vacillation itself, or ambivalence, as qualities, cannot be played.

Playing Drunkenness and Insanity

Someone is almost sure to try to portray a drunk and here the danger of playing a quality is probably greater than in any other type of scene. A half-coherent speech is assumed, and funny faces are made along with rubberized movements of the limbs. The result is a thumping cliché in which every vestige of action and character is lost. Alcohol affects each of us differently. Not everyone loses control of his articulation and equilibrium. Many people are extremely lucid under the influence of alcohol—indeed, they become wittier and more charming than when sober. Some become nasty or sarcastic, still with perfect control of speech and movements. Some get giddy, others morose. Moreover, people drink for different reasons, and our reason for getting drunk will affect our actions. Also, there are many degrees of inebriation, ranging from slightly tipsy to thoroughly plastered. So you see, there are several variables for the actor to manipulate; there's no need to fall into a stereotype.

Insanity must be approached the same way. We do not want the wild, piercing stare, the quick, darting movements of the head, the maniacal laughter. The actor must know specifically what troubles him, for "insanity" cannot be played. In fact, psychiatry does not even recognize insanity as an illness; the word *insanity* is purely a legal term used to denote a condition in which an individual is no longer considered responsible for his actions.

Psychiatry does recognize, however, many different forms of mental aberrations, each with its specific symptoms. The actor must thoroughly investigate the particular mental illness from which his character suffers and determine specifically what he will do in each of the circumstances of the play. Many a mental patient has perfectly sane moments. Just when do these moments occur? What is it that "sets the patient off"? What circumstances arouse his deepest, though most illogical, fears? An individual experiencing delusions of grandeur will certainly act differently from one who believes he is being persecuted. Find out. Play the action, not the quality.

Reminiscing

It happens very frequently that the weakest scene in a production is the "reminiscence" scene, the one in which a character relates an event which happened to him in the past. The actor gets lost in a nostalgic flight, or "re-lives" an especially bitter moment, and while he thus indulges himself, the play stops dead.

Now one of the special properties of the theatre is that it exists only in the immediate present; the events occur right here and now before the spectators. A novel may take place in the past, we may read about its happenings in the past tense; but a play is concerned with the actions of human beings as they are demonstrated to an audience, and human beings cannot act in the past. They may talk *about* the past, but they can only do so *in the present.*

Do not confuse reminiscence scenes with flashbacks, such as occur in *Our Town* and *Death of a Salesman.* The flashback is a dramatic device in which the entire action of the play shifts in time. The actors then proceed to act in the here and now. They are not *recalling* the past; for them the past has become the present, and they act with all the justification and urgency that they would use if the time sequence had remained unchanged.

This does not mean that the reminiscence scene is invalid as a dramatic technique (although you will rarely find such a scene in the great plays — see Sophocles and Shakespeare), but it does mean that the actor must be especially careful not to fall into the trap of wallowing in the mood of the past while he forgets that he should have a present action and objective every moment he is on stage.

Nor am I implying that the past is an unlikely subject for concern on the stage. It is precisely the past which imbues the present with meaning. The entire action of *Oedipus Rex* has been launched by a past event. But from the moment the actual play begins, Oedipus lives in the present, trying desperately to root out the truth.

The point to be made here is that the actor must find a reason *in the present* for reminiscing. He must play an action here and now which will further develop the play and his character. He cannot take leave of the play and float away down memory lane. Now it may be that his character finds his present life too burdensome and therefore often speaks of the past, which was more pleasant. We sometimes say of such a person that he "lives in the past," but this is an unfortunate phrase and a flat contradiction of facts. A person may *recall* the past, but he cannot *live* in the past — even actors cannot do that. If a person recalls the past, there is an immediate reason *in the present* for his doing so. His action and objective may be *to shut out the present* (objective) by *conjuring up the past* (action). The scene then will have life and spontaneity, for it will reflect the character's despairing state. The play will not stop but will move forward, for the actor is living in the present and every present moment portends for the future.

There are any number of scenes which start something like this: "I remember when I was a kid, things were a lot tougher than they are now." These scenes are deadly actor-traps. Don't get caught. Don't just reminisce; we do not reminisce merely for the sake of reminiscing. *Why* are you telling the other person about your difficult childhood? *How will it help you achieve your objective?*

If you have mastered the principles of the exercises thus far assigned, your scenes should now show relaxation, strong involvement, and sharply defined actions. There will be no more acting generally, no more trying to act "qualities." Art is not accidental; it is ordered and precise.

OBJECTIVES

An action, be it ever so neat and crisp, ever so positive and specific, is still lacking something. Our actions are only physical expressions of our inner needs, desires, drives, and other personal urgencies; what we do, we do for a reason. Without the feeling of want or need that has compelled us to perform a particular act, our actions remain empty gestures. We must give them purpose.

That purpose is the *objective* of the scene, the goal, the end toward which we direct all our energies. The objective remains in the back of our mind at all times; it is the fuel that provides the driving force. The objective colors our actions and gives them intensity and direction. Without a strong and clear objective ahead of us, our actions tend to wander off in all directions.

The actor's objective must be immediate, not far in the future. Our overall objective in the play may be to avenge our father's murder, but there are many intermediate steps. Every successive scene has its objective which is *immediately attainable*. The character does not always succeed in achieving his objective, but it is within his grasp, and he strives toward it. With two characters in conflict, only one can win.

The objective, like the action, must be stated in vigorous, physical terms. Don't be intellectual about this. The stated objective must awaken a challenge to physical action, must create within you an irresistible compulsion to *do*. To say that your objective is *to find out the truth* leaves us with a shrug-of-the-shoulders attitude, with an idea but with no spark to set it aflame. Instead, suppose you say you are going *to tear the truth out of Joe.* The very saying of it makes you grit your teeth and prepare yourself for flailing arms and flying fists. A vivid image is evoked, and you bound on stage with real drive behind your actions. That you will not literally "tear" anything out of Joe does not matter; what is important is the strong feeling aroused, the need which is created. Your actions *may* be quite physical: you may push Joe back into his chair every time he tries to get up; you may grab him and shake him; or you may do it all verbally with a wicked tongue-lashing. Whatever your method, you have added a vital dimension to your action, an invisible undercurrent that propels you unswervingly toward your goal.

Remember that an actor has only a certain amount of energy to expend, and unless it is properly channeled toward a clear objective, this energy will be dissipated in several directions. But narrow your sights, pinpoint your goal, and that same energy assumes a much greater force. The narrower the stream, the stronger the flow.

Which Is Which?

For a time, you may experience considerable difficulty in learning to differentiate actions and objectives, as well as in learning to state each clearly and provocatively. The objective is the result you want, but it does not tell you what you will do to attain it. Always ask yourself, "How do I want this scene to end?" If the situation is a job interview, you want the scene to end with the employer giving you the job. You know that *to get the job* cannot be an action because it gives you no idea what you will *do* to get the job. So getting the job must be your objective. But we still do not know what you will do to accomplish this. Your specific action may be to brag to your prospective employer about your achievements, or you may respectfully place before him letters of recommendation from ten of the most prominent people in your field.

Now suppose for a moment that you are an employer, and you do not want to give an employee a raise. This objective provides no fuel. It gives no clue to what you might do in the scene. Let's say you want to make this employee crawl. There's a strong objective; things immediately start to bubble inside, and quite probably you can now think of various actions which will serve your goal. You might pretend to be oh, so sympathetic, to seem to consider his plea, to assure him that you'd just love to give him a raise but you really can't afford it just now. Or you might make him crawl by sternly demanding to know why he thinks himself worthy of a raise.

I, Not He

Since learning to verbalize your actions and objectives is so important, these matters should be discussed after each scene presentation or exercise. It is helpful to note how other members of the class would have developed the actions and objective you have just performed. In these discussions, never speak of your character in the third person. Don't say *"He* wants." This removes the character and the scene from you personally and weakens your feeling of identity. The discussion then becomes an intellectual activity rather than an organic probing into your own wants and needs. *You* are the one who must be compelled to action, not *he*. When you say "I want" and "I must," your personal involvement deepens.

Urgency and Immediacy

Imagine that we are playing a scene in which we are prowling about an apartment in search of some documents we intend to steal. We are cautious; we are very nervous lest we fail to find them. First, let's tinker with one crucial circumstance: If we know the owners of the apartment are away on vacation, we have plenty of time; we have no chance of being caught, and we have a pretty dull scene. Change that one circumstance: They may walk in at any moment! We must find the documents and get out quickly. Now we have added *urgency* and *immediacy* to the scene, a sense of excitement, of theatricality.

In the theatre, as we have observed, life is heightened; everything is terribly important. As an illustration, no playwright worth his dialogue will write a scene in which the secret list of very important names you are preparing is due next week. No, it is due *right now*. At any moment, Mr. X will knock at your door to pick up the list; and because you were negligent, you've only just gotten around to working on it. In creating any scene, after you have found your action and objective, you simply ask yourself, "Why must what I am doing be done *right now?*"

Urgency, Not Speed

Here a word of caution is in order. After the concepts of urgency and immediacy have been introduced to student actors, all their scenes tend to become frenetic. Actors race about the stage like Keystone cops in an old-fashioned movie. Urgency and immediacy, however, are not to be confused with speed. The actor *may* have to work quickly sometimes, as in the document-stealing scene, but urgency has more to do with the great *importance* the actor attaches to his action and objective. For instance, your boss is leaving for his vacation tonight, and it is therefore vital that you speak to him *now* about that important contract you hope to work out. This scene will have urgency and immediacy, but it need not have speed. The discussion may be quiet and deliberate, which in no way diminishes the pressing motive behind it.

EXERCISE

The instructor will assign to each student one simple physical action, so simple as to be no more than a single activity:

Stand on a chair.

Compile a list of names.

Tear up a letter.

Knock on the floor.

The student will supply his own *objective*. Note that while two students may perform the physical action in much the same external way, the different objective each has chosen will lead to various intensities, emotional levels, and involvements.

Examples: One student knocks on the floor because his parents have just left for the evening, and he is signaling his friend who lives in the apartment below. He wants this friend to help him send "secret" but harmless messages over his ham radio set. Another student is a prisoner in this room and, at the risk of his life, knocks on the floor to signal some fellow prisoners in the cell below that the escape plan has been set in motion. By thus changing the objectives, our two students have created two entirely different atmospheres with the same action.

EXERCISE

This time, the instructor will state the objective, and each student will perform a precise *action* intended to accomplish the given objective. Do one action only. Typical objectives may be:

To save someone's life

To end a relationship

To prove your innocence

To blackmail someone

Each of these objectives can be handled in many ways. There are various actions which will lead to any one of them. Use your imagination. Let's have interesting actions. Writing a "Dear John" letter is not the only way to end a relationship.

EXERCISE

Develop two actions leading to a single objective. The objective may be given by the instructor or chosen by the student. Both actions must be aimed at the objective. One action may lead to another.

Example: You have invited your boss to visit you, and his arrival is imminent. First you polish up the apartment, and then you put out some erudite literature to impress him with your intellectual prowess. Or you may try one action, give it up as hopeless, and try another. You want to contact someone for a job. First you search for the slip of paper on which you have written his name and telephone number. When you realize it has been lost, you start calling people who might know him.

EXERCISE
Perform one action with three different objectives. Choose a simple action, and perform this same action three times — once for each of the three objectives.

Example: Pack a suitcase. The first time, you are packing to go on your vacation; another time, you are going to attend a funeral in another town; and the third time, you are packing to run away from home. Each time, you will have to decide on different things to include; you will place them neatly in the suitcase or toss them into it carelessly; you will move as though you couldn't wait to get out of the room or as though you never want to leave it. As the objective changes, the whole tone of the scene will change.

Environment

Many actors have a habit of marching into every setting as though they had lived in it all their lives, even though they are supposedly entering a particular place for the first time. They don't take things in; they don't allow themselves to react to the new surroundings. And they thus deprive themselves of a rich source of color and involvement. Environments are fascinating. They contain so much to "connect with," to ponder on and wonder about. True, some people float through life seemingly oblivious to everybody and everything around them, but the actor must always be sensitive to his surroundings. The first few moments in a new place are rife with impressions, some of which may continue to please or annoy us all during our stay. Environments are experiences, more grist for the actor's mill. He should learn to use the scene's environment in every advantageous way.

EXERCISE

Develop an action and objective in a changing environment. Choose a simple action: *to write a letter* for the purpose of obtaining a job interview. Do this three times in three different environments.

Example: 1) Alone at home
2) At home, where your six-year-old son is having a birthday party and twenty Indians are attacking the fort.
3) At your office. Don't let the boss know you are applying for another job.

JUSTIFICATION

Just as the objective serves as the motive power for our actions, guiding and keeping them in a straight and narrow channel, so the justification sparks our desire to attain our objective. We may well have decided that our objective is to get a particular job; but if the job is not really vitally important to us, how desperately will we strive to get it? Are we simply looking for a new job because we are bored with our present one? Not very exciting. Do we need the money because we want to pay our tuition to medical school? Or because we must suddenly pay off a gambling debt, or else . . . ? Much better! We must create a justification that will drive us toward our objective — not something we merely want, but something we need urgently and desperately, something we must have or die. This is the stuff of the theatre. People who like to have possessions solely for the sake of having them are perfectly normal, but they do not arouse in us the same excitement as do people who are obsessed with a need.

When we have specified our objective, we ask ourselves "Why? Why do I need it? Why must I have it? Why must I do this?" Keep asking these "Why's?" and arm yourself with strong and numerous reasons. The deeper your need to attain your goal, the more of a stir will you create within yourself and hence the more forcefully will you play your actions and the greater will be your involvement.

We cannot do justification exercises in isolation. After the student has presented a scene, the justification should be discussed, with the instructor asking a series of "Why's?" until the reasons are exhausted: Why do you want this particular job? Why do you prefer working for this employer? Why do you like this kind of work? Why are you willing to settle for less salary? Why does this job have a better future than another? Remember to answer in the first person, creating reasons and needs that are plausible to *you*. The more thoroughly you explore your reasons for wanting your objective, the more likely you are to spark a real desire that will become an organic force. Again you are cautioned not to let these discussions become intellectual chats. The very act of talking about your reasons must awaken an excitement in you, a dynamism. The actor does not speak casually about his wants; he is charged with vitality, he seethes.

You say you need money to pay your tuition to medical school. You are asked why, and you answer, logically, that you want to be a doctor. Again you are asked why. If you shrug your shoulders, your scene is dead. You have no materials for acting. You must be catapulted into a passionate exposition: You have dreamed about being a doctor ever since you were a child. . . . you are fascinated by the intricacies of the human body, the challenge of surgery. . . . to save a human life is the most blessed thing one can do! Carry on this relentless cross-examination until you can barely contain your desire to get on stage and play the scene.

Justification in Farce and Melodrama

Justification is strained to the utmost in the playing of farce and melodrama. Here, the actor is required to pursue objectives which are often quite far-fetched and which we would normally consider frivolous, even absurd. His character may exhibit a monumental fear of a perfectly ordinary phenomenon, or he may show no concern whatsoever in the face of fearful danger. These scenes demand great justification and a deep faith or belief. Utterly improbable though the situation may be, the actor must believe in it completely, lest he again resort to playing qualities, clichés, and generalities.

EXERCISE

Strengthen your ability to justify by creating a series of absurd situations and playing them with complete conviction.

Example: You come home and notice one of your child's toys on the floor. You wind it up and it begins to move about. Soon, you are convinced it has a life of its own and that it is coming after you with deadly intent.

PERSONALIZATION

Personalization is the process by which the actor makes every aspect of the scene or play vitally alive and meaningful to himself. He brings his own personalization to his role, just as the carpenter brings his own tools to his job. If the back porch is properly repaired, the customer doesn't particularly care what kind of hammer the carpenter uses. Similarly, the playwright supplies the allusions, and the actor brings to them his own experiences and observations. If an actor has the line "I went to a night club last night," whether in a written script or one of his own improvising, he must have a specific night club in mind so that the moment is fully alive and personally significant. Each actor, saying the line, will naturally envisage a different night club, but what matter? The important thing is that the actor functions organically, entirely, and does not merely make sounds with his vocal apparatus while the rest of his being is dead. Every word we utter as actors must be backed up by a personal image.

The character may be talking about his sister, but the actor playing the role doesn't have a sister. All right, he must create one. He may use a friend, a relative, anyone at all, but he must have a definite image of his "sister" in his mind when he speaks of her. Perhaps this sounds as though we were overdoing it a bit. Why must we go to all the trouble to create a sister? Why can't we just say the words and be done with it? Because human beings cannot relate anything without accompanying images. We think in terms of pictures, not words. Words are only sounds, symbols which have meaning for us because they stand for ideas or objects. Try describing an experience to a friend, and see if your mind remains a perfect blank. No, your mind becomes a kind of movie screen with a rapid succession of pictures being flashed on it. We "see" these pictures, react to them, and find the words with which to convey our impressions to our listener.

It is only the actor, that very special creature, who somehow manages to say words with nothing behind them, often because, in a given scene, he is thinking of anything but what he should be thinking of. At such moments, his acting is empty and flat. He may be producing sounds that make a certain amount of sense intellectually; but his attitudes, his reactions, his impressions of the things the sounds stand for are absent, and so he is only partially alive, half real. When we speak of something, be it our sister, a visit to a night club, or any other of the countless things we have occasion to discuss, we cannot do so without adding our own personal attitudes; and in the theatre it is the personal attitude of the character that the actor is called upon to project. Machines have been made which can produce speech sounds and recognizable words; the actor must be one up on the machines by filtering those sounds through his personal experiences. By creating for himself concrete images of all the things he has to discuss in the play, the actor assures himself of a rich, vital, and meaningful substructure for his performance.

Personalization, then, is bringing the events of the play as close as possible to our own lives so that we can act and react with the fullest sympathy and understanding. There is, however, a kind of personalization—beyond the call of duty—which is highly controversial and which—in my opinion at least—can lead to trouble. Sometimes personalization is pushed to an extreme degree, with the actor bringing in from his own life certain elements which are quite removed from the actual circumstances of the play. Rather than reacting to the people and events of the play itself, the actor mentally conjures up other people and other events about which he feels more strongly and reacts to them instead. This is called *substitution*.

Substitution

Very few things in this world are entirely black or entirely white, and substitution, too, has its shadings. At the lighter end of its spectrum, there is a simple kind of substitution which can be very useful to the actor. Suppose we are asked to deliver a speech extolling the beauty and excitement of Rome. But we have never been to Rome. By now you know that we cannot say believable words while forcing a false enthusiasm. There are two choices open to us: We can take ourselves off to the library and study pictures of Rome and learn what travelers have had to say about Rome's beauty and excitement. Or we can recall a city we have actually visited—Paris, perhaps. And our spirits—and our voices—will have a genuine glow when we speak of the sidewalk cafes, the parks, and the museums. For our purpose, it doesn't really matter greatly that the people at their sidewalk cafes are speaking French rather than Italian. There are live pictures behind the words, fond memories of a personal visit, and an honest enthusiasm. In order to personalize this particular speech, we have simply substituted Paris for Rome in our mind's eye. This is reasonable enough and usually will not lead to complications.

But now let's move to a darker part of the substitution spectrum. We are playing Torvald in *A Doll's House*. You will recall that when Torvald learns of Nora's forgery, he upbraids her unmercifully; and we understand why, for Ibsen has made Torvald's justification abundantly clear. He has shown us the man's overweening sense of propriety, his belief that women should be sheltered from the affairs of the world and should have no responsibilities. Now, an actor must be a person with a mobile faith, as it were, which he can plant under any suggested situation. If the character he is portraying thinks that women should be treated like dolls or toys, why then so does the actor.

Being a sensitive individual, he will be able to find within himself the means by which he can thoroughly sympathize with Torvald's point of view.

Sometimes, however, an actor finds that he has drawn a blank. Torvald's philosophy leaves him cold; he is indifferent to the character's needs; he finds it impossible to share Torvald's ideas. Thereupon, the actor decides to personalize the situation and find something else within his own experience and mental make-up that will activate him to treat Nora as a toy. This puts the actor on very slippery ground, for personalization is exactly what the term implies —personal—and therefore admits of no outside or objective limitations. If we say that the actor must be personally motivated from within, then admittedly the actor feels justified in calling upon anything and everything that will ignite something within himself. And if the fuel the actor uses does actually burn, to that extent he may be right in using it. Yet the problem is not quite so simple, for in searching for a substitution which will move him in a particular scene, the actor may eventually wind up with something far removed from that which Ibsen intended for Torvald. If we cannot believe in Torvald's attitude, and we find within ourselves a reason to upbraid Nora which is very different from Torvald's reason, the question arises as to whether we are indeed playing Torvald or some other character.

I personally believe that if an actor is to play Torvald, he must be in strong accord with Torvald's motivations. If he substitutes his own justifications for Torvald's, he may achieve a somewhat similar effect, but he is not really playing Ibsen's Torvald; and the fine nuances, the subtleties, and the shadings are lost.

An actress once told me that she found it impossible in a certain play to react with frozen shock to her husband's death. Instead, she performed a sense memory of extreme cold. She was completely "out" of the scene at that moment, yet the audience (so I was told) accepted her behavior as shock. For me, such complete substitution takes the joy out of acting and turns the performance into a sleight-of-emotions trick. I believe an actor must be able to react to a loved one's death; that's what makes him an actor. If his sensitivity, or lack of it, is such that he cannot fully respond to any imaginary situation, I think he should try office work.

There are, of course, prominent and talented people who disagree with me, and because acting is an art and not a science, I cannot presume that my way is the right way—or the only way. When an audience is moved by a great moment of acting, it does not stop to question the actor's method. If you can move an audience to laughter or tears, if you can make it accept you wholeheartedly *as the character the author wrote*, then whatever your means, you are right in using them. I will continue to discuss substitution in order to offer as complete a picture as possible of the actor's technique and because some of my readers may find it useful at times. I will also continue to intrude my bias.

Substituting People

This is a process whereby the actor pretends that the person with whom he is playing the scene is someone else. Romeo doesn't care much for his Juliet, so he imagines his own girl friend in her stead. This is a bad business because a great deal of acting is *reacting* to the person on stage with you, being acutely aware of all her innuendoes and subtle changes. If you have screened her off and are imagining someone else, you have, in effect, pre-set all your reactions. You are not reacting to the live presence of the person right there with you but to some imaginary person. Whatever poor Juliet does will be lost on you; you have cut off communication, set up a wall between you, eliminated the vital give-and-take of acting.

You absolutely must work with your stage partner. It may be that you find her quite unattractive, but following our technique of discovering tiny bits of truth, you can cement together a believable situation. Look at her. Surely there must be something about her that is pleasant; no one is a total mess. Perhaps she has a warm voice or lovely hair or beautiful eyes. You will build your appreciation of her favorable features to the strongest possible extent. You will concentrate on these attractive features until you come to realize that she's not so bad after all. Your stage partners offer you dynamic material for acting; you must not deprive yourself of this rich source.

Emotion Memory

Emotion memory is to modern acting what the Copernican system once was to science. It has been jeered at and sneered at, lauded and applauded, used and abused. It has been the subject of satirical sketches, doctoral dissertations, and violent debates in acting classes. It is standard practice at the Actors Studio; it is sometimes used at the Moscow Art Theatre during early rehearsals, but is strongly disfavored for performances.

That last statement may come as a minor shock, for it is commonly supposed that emotion memory is the very marrow of the Stanislavski system. This is because American actors, when first learning about Stanislavski's method, seized upon emotion memory as the *sine qua non* of their craft. It became their magic key, binding actors together in mystic cults of introspection. However, some

American teachers of acting felt that to use emotion memory in performance was to introduce matters which were extraneous to the play. They believed that the actor must deal—and deal only—with the circumstances of the play.

Briefly, emotion memory, or affective memory, is the recollection of a personal event in which the actor has experienced an emotion analogous to the one he is supposed to be experiencing on stage. By recalling the event, he evokes the emotion and substitutes it in the scene he is playing. Thus, when Antony, distraught, kneels over the bleeding piece of earth that was Caesar, the actor is really recalling his father's funeral a few years before. No doubt the grief thus conjured is real and affecting and involves the actor to a great degree, but grief for one's father is not the same as Antony's grief for Caesar. If we wish to be loose about it and say that grief is grief no matter what the circumstances, then we are, in effect, creating pigeonholes for the actor and filling them with generalities. But there are no pigeonholes in art; each creation must be utterly itself. If our Antony is to be a truly unique characterization, then we—as actors—must be completely involved with thoughts of our friendship with Caesar, our admiration for him, what his loss means to us. Otherwise, we are not playing Antony, and our acting becomes general.

Moreover, if we accept the technique of playing our actions in order to evoke the emotions, then we deny the entire foundation of our approach to acting by using emotion memory in performance. For what action are we playing when we involve ourselves with thoughts of our father's funeral? We are not playing an action of Antony's, to be sure. And if we employ emotion memory fairly often in the enactment of the play, we will discover that very few of our actions correspond to those which Shakespeare wrote for Antony. We are playing someone else.

What is in question here is not the actual working of emotion memory—it is not a theory, it really works—but its application for the actor. We have all experienced emotion memory many times in our lives. While telling a friend a story about a fight we had with someone who wronged us, we begin to repeat the accusations and retorts more forcefully, our vehemence mounts, and soon we are relating the story with full-blown anger. How often have you nearly collapsed with laughter as you once again unfolded the details of a hilarious happening? This happens to all people, actors and non-actors alike; the difference between them is that the actor is one who can summon emotional responses to *imaginary* circumstances. (By the way, when you experience an emotion memory such as we have just described, you are demonstrating the use of actions to evoke emotions: our fundamental technique. For you did not *start* with the emotion; you started by relating certain *events,* and gradually the emotion — willy-nilly — was there.)

Probably one reason why emotion memory has exerted such an influence on actors is that exercises done in class can be spellbinding. An actor is asked to think of a moment in his life which was deeply emotional — a severe shock, an unbearable humiliation, an over-whelming joy. He is then asked to take a seat on stage and describe the room in which this event took place. He may protest at first that it was long ago and he hardly remembers the room; but he need only start with a single detail to discover that one little memory leads to the next and, surprisingly, all the details of the room start coming back. At no time is the actor to say how he *felt*; he must give a purely objective, clinical description of the physical room. If there were people in the room, he tells what they were wearing, the color of the dresses, but never what emotions they were manifesting.

The actor will usually start the emotion-memory exercise in a casual manner, and he will relate the details of the remembered room to the audience. But soon something strange begins to happen. As the details are filled in, as he gets closer and closer to the event he is describing, the actor slowly starts to cross the time barrier, to move into another dimension. He loses contact with his audience and withdraws into himself. The details pile up, and the event becomes more and more real. Suddenly, the last detail is supplied; and the event, as he lived it, has been so vividly recreated in his mind that a spontaneous and overwhelming gush of tears, roar of laughter, or some other appropriate expression of emotion bursts out. The recol-lection of the event has evoked, not the identical emotion — for that can only be experienced once — but an emotion very like it. The whole effect of the exercise is quite startling. Usually the actor him-self is greatly surprised that he is capable of exhibiting such full and deep emotions on stage. And one good by-product of this exercise is that it makes actors more aware of the moments when they are forcing emotions. Having experienced a true and profound emotion on stage, actors are less willing thereafter to settle for phony emo-tions.

Emotion memory can be used during rehearsal as a kind of "psychic tune-up." By recalling analogous experiences and emotions, some actors can put themselves into a more receptive state in relation to the experiences and feelings of the character they are portraying. They feel that they thus create a stronger feeling of sympathy with their role, that they are more strongly "tuned in" to the character's wave length, for have they not both felt the very same things? If this works for you, if it brings you closer to your character, then use it. But I believe it should be used only as a means to an end. Once the emotion-memory exercise is carried into performance, the actor is no longer playing the play.

The argument offered by some of those who use emotion memory—and substitution in general—in performance is that these techniques are to be used only as a last resort. "If the actor absolutely cannot respond to a certain situation in the play," they say, "it is better to substitute something which will at least make the moment organic for him—even though it be alive with the wrong stimulus —rather than force a false emotion." These techniques, they insist, are to be used as crutches only when the actor's other methods are not functioning properly. I can agree with that. If I had to choose between playing a phony quality or substituting something which offered a spurt of vitality to get me over the rough spot, I would choose the latter. It is probably the lesser of the two evils. But only when all else has failed.

IMPROVISATION

There are certain moments in our lives when we live more fully, experience more deeply than normally. All of our concentration, all of our faculties are focused on a single event; there is an excitement, a tension, an especially high level of awareness and involvement. Take the moment a teacher meets his class for the first time. The class has assembled, and a general buzzing prevails. The new teacher walks in, and there is an immediate and total silence. In the next few moments, the pace and quality of the entire term will be divulged. What kind of person is he? Is he tough or easy? How much will we be able to get away with? The teacher, too, is wondering whether this will be a dull bunch or a challenging group. Class and teacher alike are busy sizing each other up, noting tiny things, searching for clues, making pre-judgments. The air is loaded with attention.

If we had to live our whole life at such a high level of involvement, we would be worn out before the first day ended. Happily, old Nature has provided a protective device: We become so familiar with many situations that we are able to function with only a modicum of concentration, sometimes none at all when we perform habitual acts. We also learn social amenities: how to say hello to new acquaintances, for example. Without sapping our imagination for original phrases, we just spew out the old clichés with a pleasant smile: "How are you? What's new?" And if there is an answer, we don't hear it.

Let's return to the example of our opening-day class. After a few meetings, teacher and class have each other pegged. The students continue buzzing when the teacher comes in. They hardly notice him; he gives them only a cursory glance. The ritual of recording attendance is performed automatically, and everyone's concentration is somewhere else. Spontaneity has given way to familiarity, which gives way in turn to detachment, which gives way in its turn to a kind of automatism. Now, this may be restful for ordinary people, but it is death for the actor. The actor is not afforded the luxury of leisure moments alternated with intense moments; his life on stage consists of all the high moments strung together and the low moments cut out. For the two-hour duration of a play, he leads an *intensified* existence, a highly ordered and selected life, a life full of crises and unexpected situations. He doesn't often find himself in an old, familiar situation. This means that the actor must meet each event with a high level of excitement and concentration and must exhibit the spontaneity which informs a first-time experience. The achievement of this kind of spontaneity is our next concern.

What happens when the untrained actor prepares to do a scene? Typically, he takes the script home and learns the lines; he decides when he will display a particular emotion, when he will move or rise or sit. He rehearses the scene with his partner. They run through it several times until they know the lines cold. As a matter of fact, they know the lines so well they hardly have to think about them. They don't even have to listen to what the other one is saying because —having heard it so many times—they already know that, too. They develop a clever little innate sense of timing which tells them just when their partner's speech is ended, and then they pop in with their own lines.

The more familiar they become with the scene, the more detached they become; the movements and reactions are set and are mimicked each time. The scene grows duller and duller, more mechanical and stale. Knowing so well just what his stage partner is going to do, the actor barely notices him; he looks through him rather than at him, and, as we mentioned earlier, he thereby deprives himself of one of the greatest sources of stimulus. He takes it for granted that his partner will say his lines the same way all the time, and he repeats his own responses the same way. And if, on occasion, his partner does come up with a different reading, our actor takes no notice of it and gives his line exactly as he has given it dozens of times before.

Also taken for granted is the environment, and we've talked about that, too—how the actor will walk into a room in which he's supposed never to have been before and totally ignore these new and different surroundings. Instead of walking into a new environment, our actor is walking on stage to play a scene.

The improvisation is an antidote to some of these maladies. Not a cure-all, you understand, but an excellent device for making the actor aware of these errors in his own acting and for giving him a means of combating them. In the following exercises, we shall work in pairs and create our own improvisations. With only the most meager hint of a plot, we shall create our own dialogue as we go along, and let the story develop as it will. We shall not use scenes from actual scripts because they demand characterization, and for the present we are primarily interested in exploring our own selves, our own personal reactions to various situations.

We use our own words because at this stage of our development the words of the playwright only hinder us. When the actor has a tight grip on his actions, objectives, and justifications, he can move on to the handling of formal dialogue. Often, the words set down by the playwright have little or nothing to do with what is really happening in the scene, and the inexperienced actor, taking them out of context, is misled into reciting the words rather than playing the actions. However, when there are no lines or plot to guide him, he is forced to play an action; he is forced to *do* something to get the scene moving. He is compelled to really listen to what his partner says, else he will have no basis for reaction. Improvising in this manner, the actor finds that his concentration is at a much higher level, for he is alert to every contingency; and since he has not previously set his responses (the two actors are literally creating the story as they go along), he is far less likely to play a quality but will rather react spontaneously, fully, and almost always more truthfully.

To test how unimportant words can be compared to actions, let two people memorize these few simple lines of dialogue:

SHE. Well, I thought you'd never get here.
HE. Sorry. I was delayed.
SHE. Obviously. Are you staying?
HE. What do you think?
SHE. I wouldn't know. You're such a mystery man.
HE. You talk too much.

Have the actor and actress go on stage and recite these lines with no preconceived notions. Not much of a scene, is it? Now let them suppose they are lovers. She is not annoyed by his lateness, but is overjoyed to see him; the lines suddenly take on a delicious, teasing quality, and the final line might be said as he stops her babbling with a kiss.

By way of contrast, let us suppose that these two are about to perpetrate a nasty crime. Both are edgy, and he, particularly, is not

1. *Stop the aimless chattering.* Get into the scene immediately and play your action. Don't say anything unless you absolutely must, unless it's bursting out of you, or unless you are compelled to answer your partner. Try to achieve your objective *physically*, saying as little as possible. For instance, you are annoyed because your roommate has never returned that book he borrowed. With mounting fury, you have been looking for the book in the adjoining room and have only just now realized that your roommate still has the volume in his brief case. You storm into his room, march right up to that brief case, take out the book, and turn to leave. There is no need for discussion, your action being merely to get back the book. You will only dissipate the scene by starting to chat. But if you grab the book and start to storm out, your roommate will jump up to stop you, because he hasn't finished using it yet. You will retort nastily that he should have returned it a long time ago, and a strong scene will quickly evolve.

Know your action and come on stage ready to play it to the hilt. Students frequently rationalize a static opening by saying that they are deliberately stalling to feel each other out. It's amazing how many improvisational scenes start with stalling. Now, it's perfectly true that you will occasionally run across a scene in a play in which a character hedges, but that is another matter. For the time being, learn to burst into your actions with all your engines going. That's difficult, because it means you must have a very strong justification and clear and urgent actions and objectives.

2. *Keep the scene going.* Once you have decided on your objective for the improvisation, you must not stop the scene with a helpless shrug because your partner will not give in to you. Only the instructor may stop a scene. The actors are to keep going, no matter how desperate their situation becomes. In fact, the scenes achieve full power only when the actor is so unbearably frustrated in his attempts to attain his goal that he boils over with rage or tears or comes up with a truly Machiavellian scheme. Some improvisations become superb little pieces of theatre by virtue of a powerful conflict fought to the death by two determined actors.

When you are given your objective, you must not jump onto the stage with the first action that comes into your head. Suppose it fails. No, you must go into the battle armed with *several* actions. Discard an action only after you have played the life out of it. Then try another. This change of action will give a new, fresh impetus to the scene. If you can possibly have an ace up your sleeve, a devastating action that will surely turn the tide—blackmail, for example—save it for last. But get on that stage with a searing need to attain your objective. And let nothing stop you.

3. *Begin the scene at once.* If you are alone on the stage, do not wait until your visitor arrives before starting the scene. You are not even supposed to know that a visitor is about to arrive. You are at home or at your office when you receive an unexpected caller. You must have an *independent activity,* a life of your own, something you are doing and would continue to do if you were not interrupted. Inexperienced actors carefully seat themselves on stage and wait nervously for the scene to start, meanwhile casting furtive glances into the wings and wondering why Zachary doesn't make his entrance. Forget Zachary. He doesn't exist. You do not expect him. You are at home. Concentrate on what you are doing. Get busy, get involved. Get involved in something very important, so that if Zachary *should* drop in, it will be difficult for you to give him your full attention because you are working on something else. This is how you can bring life to your scenes. If you are merely waiting for the scene to start, then obviously you have no action; and if you have no action, you are not ready to take the stage.

4. *Do only what you want your stage partner to see.* Don't work for the audience. How many times have we seen an actor stumbling and stammering and swallowing and looking at the floor as he speaks his lines—all to let the *audience* know that he is lying. Does he assume his stage partner is an idiot? Doesn't his partner see all those shenanigans? If the audience can see it, the other actors on stage can see it. If you are lying, obviously your action is not *to betray yourself* but rather *to make your fellow actor swallow the lie.* To accomplish this, you will have to lie with the same forthright earnestness you use in telling the truth.

5. *Remember that you are the actor, not the playwright.* As new and unexpected events are hurled at you in the improvisation, you are faced with a series of choices. How will you respond to what your partner has just said? What should you do? Do not make the choice on a theatrical basis—yet. That is, do not assume the playwright's role and decide what would be more effective dramatically or what would get a laugh. The choice must be made strictly according to the dictates of your inner promptings. Do what *you* would do in the circumstances. Only in this way will you respond fully and spontaneously to the situation. Do not divide your attention and try to be half-playwright and half-actor at the same time. It is not always easy to choose the natural reaction, because we are tempted to do the thing which is more theatrical. But remember that this is an exercise, not a polished performance. We are working for certain techniques now. Later on, our choices will become theatrically effective, and those choices will be all the better for having a foundation of truth.

Using Environment in Improvisation

The importance of environment to the actor, the vast amount of material offered him by his specific surroundings, has already been emphasized. Here are some improvisations for two people intended to develop the actor's effective use of the environment.

EXERCISE
The instructor assigns a specific environment to a pair of actors. They are to create their own situation. The environment is to be fully justified; that is, it must be an integral, organic part of the scene to be improvised. The environment must play a vital role, almost like that of another actor. To have an argument which could take place anywhere is not using the environment. The scene must be such that it could not possibly happen *anywhere but in the designated environment.* Consider the following possibilities:

A locked museum
A deserted railroad station
The top of the Empire State Building
The pressroom of a newspaper
A lighthouse
A restaurant in a foreign country
The star's dressing room
A research laboratory
An archaeological site
A space ship

EXERCISE
Again the instructor designates an environment, and two actors are asked to create a scene in which one of them is at ease in this particular place and the other is uncomfortable. This will make the individual keenly aware of all those things in the environment which work on him — either things which he can comfortably use or things which make him ill-at-ease.

Example: The environment is the posh apartment of an extremely wealthy family. The society lady is interviewing a prospective piano teacher for her daughter. She offers him little trays of tidbits, etc., but the poor teacher knows very little of this sort of life and wonders whether to pick up a morsel with his fingers and how to hold the demitasse cup. Also, he is not quite sure whether that chair with the gold silk fabric is meant for display or for sitting.

EXERCISE

Two actors decide on a strong situation and on their actions and objectives. The scene is then played twice, in two different environments.

Example: An important member of the underground visits the apartment of one of his agents. The visitor informs the agent that a certain individual with whom the agent had become very friendly was in reality an enemy spy and had to be killed. The agent protests, and in the privacy of the apartment the two are able to argue forcefully.

Then the environment is changed to an outdoor cafe where the same two men have met. The same information must be imparted to the agent, who will profess the same disbelief. Now, however, there are waiters passing back and forth, and other people are seated at nearby tables. The important information cannot be shouted. The men must pretend to be smiling, engaged in empty chitchat, so as not to arouse suspicion.

Using Other Actors

By this time, you have probably realized that the greatest adjustment you have had to make in working with another actor is . . . to the other actor. When working with someone else, you cannot sail through your carefully planned actions as you did when you worked alone. Now you are faced with another person who has actions and objectives of his own, in conflict with yours. The relationship becomes a verbal fencing match. You have to adjust, adapt. Give and take. You may not be able to play your action quite the way you imagined it because of unexpected reactions from your partner. Fine. The constant adjusting and adapting to your partner's moods and actions helps bring truth and spontaneity to your acting. Unfortunately, this is too often lost in a performance where reactions are set and soon become lifeless. For this reason, some improvisations are more exciting than some performances.

In our discussion of substitution, we have stressed the importance of looking to your stage partner for clues, of being sensitive to his every subtle change. Try to read his thoughts, anticipate his actions. You cannot work alone on stage; you must establish the closest possible rapport with the other actors. The following exercises are intended to help you establish that rapport.

Two actors are seated on stage, facing each other. No environment and no relationships are designated for them. Each thinks of an independent situation. One is miserable at having failed an exam this morning. The other is looking forward to a special party tonight. They do not tell each other what they are thinking. In the beginning, there should be a few moments of silence to allow the actors to become involved in their thoughts and also to watch each other. Absolutely nothing is to be said in this exercise except that which is taken from or motivated by the behavior of the other person or that which is said in direct answer to the other's question. No one may volunteer information, such as "Gee, I just flunked an exam today." It is for the observant actor to ask, "Why are you fidgeting so?" Don't try to force the dialogue. *This is not a scene; it is an exercise.* At this point, we are not even concerned with actions and objectives. The actor is to speak only when he sees his partner doing something or when he feels he can read his moods or thoughts from his outward appearance or movements. The task of each actor is to take as much from his partner as he possibly can.

The dialogue, which is not based on any relationship or objective, will probably be strange. It might go something like this:

A: Why are you clutching the chair so?
B: I'm not.
A: You are. And you look like a ramrod. Why don't you relax?
B: Why don't you mind your own business?
A (after a pause): You need a shave.
B: So what?
A: So nothing.
B: You need a shave yourself. And your tie doesn't go with your shirt.
A: At least I have a tie. You look like a mess. What're you so gloomy about?
B: You're nosy.

And so on. This exercise can reveal to you the tremendous amount of material waiting for you right there in your partner. The good actor is sending all kinds of signals constantly; you must be ready to receive them. And use them.

EXERCISE
Four people sit in a circle. Again, there is no environment, no pre-established relationship. Each actor will decide on an attitude

toward each of the others: That girl is very cute; I'd like to date her. That fellow has a superior look, probably thinks he's great; I don't like him. That other fellow looks guilty about something; I wonder what his story is.

As before, no one is to volunteer any information. Everyone is to be alert to the moods of the others. Don't strike up a conversation out of thin air, but make sure you are taking some kind of stimulus from one of the other people. You may be itching to talk to that girl, but if she is not "sending" anything, you're out of luck. This is not "give-and-take" but strictly "take."

EXERCISE
Do an improvisation in which there is no basic clash of objectives to start with. You enter the given environment and adapt yourself to the other person by trying to find out what troubles him, what is tickling him, what he is hiding. As you become aware of your partner's problem, you will formulate actions and objectives accordingly.

Example: The instructor announces that A and B are roommates. A is told to come home after an ordinary day. Nothing more. B is already home; he has lost his job because he did something of which he is dreadfully ashamed. He does not want A to know that he has lost his job, but he is horribly upset and cannot completely hide his feelings. It will be up to A, when he enters the scene, to study B carefully and try to pull out what information he can. A's action may become *to cheer B up*, or *to dig out the story*, but whatever he does will depend entirely upon what B is doing.

Warning: A is not coming on stage to do a scene. He is coming from a specific place and has definite plans for the evening. When he discovers his roommate in such a depression, he will drop his first action and objective and adopt others, dictated by the degree of his friendship with B.

IMAGINATION

To say the artist needs imagination is somewhat like saying the tailor needs a needle. The artist must sweep away the clichés, challenge the dull conventions, and present us with his own unique and illuminating expression. For the actor, his entire two hours' traffic on the stage is lived in the world of the imagination. Life on the stage is not real, and it is only by the power of imagination that he can pretend to live there briefly as if it were real.

The actor uses his imagination with every exercise he performs. In choosing actions and objectives, he thinks of every conceivable combination and chooses the one that is not only the most pertinent but the most interesting. When faced with this choice, you should probably automatically reject the first thing that comes to mind, for in nine cases out of ten, it will be a cliché. We moderns are so conditioned by the mass media that we think in cliches in spite of ourselves. I have seen really good actors, in an unaware moment, fall right into this trap. They are asked to play a hard-headed businessman, and they immediately light up a big cigar and begin to bark. But how about the businessman who speaks very quietly and with a polite smile? The next time an idea pops into your head, think of its opposite. You may come up with some interesting alternatives.

The following exercises are designed to stretch the imagination even further. As you work with these problems, don't settle for an easy solution; exhaust every possibility before you make a choice.

Props

EXERCISE
Bring in a prop and create a scene in which you use this prop in many different ways. We've all seen the old movie cliché where the maid puts a feather duster to various uses: now it's a huge powder puff, now a fancy hat, now the rumpled hair of her dancing partner. Do an improvisation we've not seen before.

Example: A tramp is trying to start a fire with a part of his newspaper. When the flame is started, he protects himself from the cold by lining his shoes with another part of his paper, rolling some of the pages around his shins, and placing some other pages inside his shirt. He uses still another part of the paper to swat some unwelcome bugs. Soon it starts to rain, and the fellow uses the remainder of his newspaper as a head covering.

EXERCISE
The actor is given a prop he hasn't seen before and asked to create a scene around it. As in the case of the feather duster, the new prop may be used in various ways, or it may be used as itself.

EXERCISE
Two actors are handed a prop and told they must create a scene around it. Again, make sure the prop is integral to the scene. To

try to sell an object to a pawnbroker is not using the prop within the intent of this exercise, for you could be selling him anything. Get interesting props.

An old carpenter plane

An hourglass

A carved knife from Africa

An ancient map

Obstacles

EXERCISE

Create a short scene in which some obstacle or interruption within the environment interferes with your action or objective.

Examples: You are up to your elbows in cake batter when the telephone rings.

You are normally right-handed, but your right hand is in a sling, and you must fill out some very important application forms immediately.

You are in a desperate hurry to leave the house but have just torn your hem. At first, you can't find a needle. When you finally do, you have trouble locating thread of the right color. By the time you find the thread, you've forgotten where you put the needle down.

Positions

EXERCISE

Two actors are assigned specific physical positions for the start —or end—of a scene. They then proceed to improvise accordingly.

Examples: When the scene starts, one actor is standing on a desk; the other is standing on a table on the opposite side of the room.

When the scene ends, the actors are standing back to back.

Mottoes, Proverbs, and Isolated Words

EXERCISE

The instructor divides the class into pairs and each pair draws a proverb which is to serve as the springboard for an improvisation.

He who laughs last laughs best.
A stitch in time saves nine.
When in Rome, do as the Romans do.

EXERCISE

The instructor divides the class into pairs and gives each pair a line of dialogue which must be the first line uttered in the scene to be improvised. This is not so easy as it sounds, especially when the designated line is something like "And don't ever bring the matter up again!"

EXERCISE

Again, the instructor divides the class into pairs and assigns to each pair a brief line or single word which is to be the last sound uttered in the improvised scene—perhaps something like "Hello."

Note: The scene as a whole need not start or end with the words or line designated in the two preceding exercises; there may be silent action before and afterward. The particular words or line designated by the instructor must be the first or last words actually *spoken*.

EXERCISE

For each pair of actors, the instructor specifies three words which are to appear as basic elements in an improvised scene. The less relation the words have to each other, the better.

fantasy — eraser — telephone
atom — hanger — hat
documents — pipe — lipstick

This exercise will tax the imagination to the utmost, for the improvised scenes must have a sense of order and logic, and the actors must, as always, have actions, objectives, and justifications. The actors may not dispose of a word such as *fantasy* simply by using it in a sentence like "Oh, stop the fantasy, Charlie, and be realistic." Rather, fantasy must appear in the scene as an *element*.

EXERCISE

Two actors are to create a scene in which each is permitted only one line of dialogue of reasonable length—not a never-ending sentence. The line to be spoken must be of the actor's own choosing and may come at any time. For instance, one actor may open the scene with a line, and the other actor may decide not to voice his line until the very end of the scene.

Chain Improvisations

EXERCISE

Develop a chain improvisation which, in the beginning, involves two actors. This is great fun and calls for very quick thinking. Two actors, designated by the instructor, start to improvise a scene; and when another actor in the audience gets a valid idea for twisting the plot by the introduction of a new character, he steps on stage just as though his entrance had been planned. This naturally comes as a surprise to the actors already on stage, and they must adapt very quickly to the new situation, making other actions and justifications. The scene can continue to grow in this way until five or six actors are involved. The one thing which is not permitted is the switching of the plot by the arrival of a telegram or the use of some similar device. The actor who joins the scene must have his own life, actions, and objectives. Any anonymous person can deliver a telegram and leave. That's not fair and does little to exercise the actors' imaginations.

Example: The husband comes home and tells his wife that he has been fired. She is very upset, and he tries to assure her that he will find another job very quickly. The doorbell rings. The husband opens the door, and another actor steps in and says, "Al, I just had to come by to congratulate you on your promotion today. The boss was saying you will be district supervisor by next year." The wife, of course, will want to know why her husband has told her that he had been fired rather than promoted. The husband will have to invent an immediate justification. Perhaps he felt that his wife was spending money extravagantly and wanted to frighten her into being a bit more economical.

When this scene has progressed a bit further, a fourth actor may get an idea. He enters the scene and says, "Al, I had to stop by and say how sorry I am that you were fired today." An entrance and a comment of this kind do nothing to move the situation forward; in fact, they may only tie the development into such a knot that the scene can move no further. The actor must not go against all logic and make the scene ridiculous. He must *advance* the improvisation with his entrance.

EXERCISE

A variation of the chain improvisation is to have two students start an improvised scene. When it is in full swing, the instructor points to a third member of the class, and that actor then steps on stage and replaces one of the actors already there. The newcomer must follow the same line of action that his predecessor has been taking but will bring to it his own justification. When he feels he has played out that particular action, he may introduce his own action and continue with it until he, in turn, is replaced.

PREPARATION

Before the performance starts, the dancer warms up at the bar, the singer vocalizes, the orchestra tunes up in full view of the audience. But we hear stories extolling certain actors who suddenly interrupt themselves while telling a joke in the wings, step on stage, and instantly plunge into a powerful emotion. Nonsense. They plunge into playing a quality and empty histrionics. It takes at least a few moments for an actor to become involved; no one can turn involvement on and off that quickly — not *real* involvement, that is. We cannot strike twelve at once.

Like all other performing artists, the actor needs a warm-up period. He does not magically become transformed into his character as he steps through the door onto the stage. Some actors of the past seemed to know this, for we read that Macready (a famous English actor who performed in the U.S. in the mid-nineteenth century) used to spend some minutes in the wings, working up a rage by cursing *sotto voce* and violently shaking a ladder fixed to the wall. He was preparing. He realized that the life of the character must start off stage, that the audience must see a fully alive person walk on stage, not one in the midst of a transformation.

Just how long a preparation is needed depends on the individual actor and the level of involvement demanded by the scene. If the actor has a strong empathy with his character, and if he is able to trigger his responses quickly, his preparation may take no more than thirty seconds.

By now you should know that purely mental activity — thinking of emotions or trying to talk oneself into a mood — is not the actor's way. His approach is always physical. And preparation is physical. So it is only logical that the actor must be involved with his character and his situation before he steps on stage. This is done simply by extending the situation of the scene backward in time. What would you be doing in those few moments just before you make your entrance? Where have you been and where are you going? If you are coming on stage for an important interview, wouldn't you stop outside the door and check your personal appearance? This takes only a moment, but it gets you going; it starts up the engines. Adjust your clothes, fix your hair, make sure your papers and letters of recommendation are easily accessible and in the right order. When you are satisfied that everything is in the best possible condition, open the door and step in.

Let's suppose you are preparing to enter your girl friend's home and propose to her. In the actual scene which you will play on stage, she rejects you. But you do not know this before you enter. Don't anticipate her rejection. At this moment, you are happy and eager. By way of a prop, pick up a fifty-cent engagement ring from the five-and-dime store. Though it may never be used on stage, it is a valuable prop for your preparation. You don't want to fumble when you present the ring to her; you practice taking the box smoothly out of your pocket, and you flip open the lid. Oh, she'll be pleased! This simple physical preparation starts the life of your character and makes all the difference in your entrance.

The emphasis on physical preparation does not mean that you do not think at all. Thinking can also involve you, provided you think about the right things and do not try to think yourself into an emotion. Suppose you are preparing for that chain improvisation we did a while ago, the one in which the husband comes home to tell his wife that he has just been fired. He is very upset and knows that she, too, will be shocked and upset. He wishes he could put off his telling her forever. He can hardly bring himself to open the door. The actor is thinking not "How unhappy I am!" but "How will she take it? What will she think of me? She'll feel I'm a failure. Well, I *am* a failure! I've let her down. What can I ever say to ease the situation?" These surely are some of the things the husband would be turning over in his mind; and with this real involvement, the actor's entrance and the subsequent scene will have truth and depth. The emotions will come of themselves.

Probably the most difficult thing about preparation is facing the queer looks and flippant remarks of your fellows backstage. Many actors, when they hear their cue, just charge on stage, hardly knowing what scene is next. What happens then is that the scene, instead of getting off to a solid start, flounders weakly about while the actor gets adjusted. He is actually doing his preparation on stage, and perhaps after a few moments he will become involved and the scene will perk up. Unforgivable. If you take acting seriously, you must go ahead and do your preparation and pay no attention to people who call themselves actors but who should've stayed with gardening.

EXERCISE
Divide the stage in such a way that three quarters of it is used for the scene and the remaining quarter reserved as off-stage

space. Create an improvisation in which you will be making an entrance; but first, actually perform your preparation in the "off-stage" area in full view of the audience. When you are completely involved, make your entrance and start the scene.

SUB-TOTAL

This completes the first section — the work on the instrument. We have taken part of the actor's job and have broken it into dozens of bits and pieces. Don't be at all disturbed if you feel as though you had two left feet for a while. All the various techniques we have discussed are fighting for your attention when you do a scene. You are trying to satisfy them all at once, and that throws your concentration off balance. Synthesis is a slow process, but it is a sure one if you have worked steadily and have thoroughly mastered the individual skills involved.

As you continue working at your craft, one after another of these skills will become second nature — in no particular order; it varies with each actor — until eventually, with the complete control of the techniques of your craft, you will be freed to enter that very exciting and unique sphere of the performing artist, that creative twilight zone in which the imagination rides at full tilt and the outside world fades out under the sparkle of a fantasy world made of grease paint, wigs, colored lights, and canvas which, for a few too brief hours, has an all-consuming reality for the actor. (If that sounds a bit romantic, just wait until you make your first entrance to a packed house.)

SELECTED READINGS

History and Theory of Acting

Archer, William. "The Anatomy of Acting," *Longman Magazine*, Vol. XI (1888).
   Famous actors speak for and against "feeling the part."
Cole, Toby, and Chinoy, Helen Krich. *Actors on Acting*. New York: Crown Publishers, 1962.
   Actors, from the ancients to the moderns, discuss their views.
Duerr, Edwin. *The Length and Depth of Acting*. New York: Holt, Rinehart and Winston, 1962.
   History of actors, acting techniques and theories, and criticism from ancient to modern times.
Eustis, Morton. *Players at Work*. New York: Theatre Arts, Inc., 1937.
   Interviews with contemporary actors.

Matthews, Brander (ed.). *Papers on Acting*. New York: Hill and Wang, 1958.

Notes and quotes: Coquelin, Talma, Siddons, Gillette, Kemble, others.

Seyler, Athene, and Haggard, Stephen. *The Craft of Comedy*. New York: Theatre Arts, Inc., 1946.

The philosophy of comedy and the actor's special problems in handling comedy.

Presentational Acting

Bosworth, Halliam. *Technique in Dramatic Art*. New York: The Macmillan Company, 1926.

A manual of external techniques by which the actor can learn to "project his emotion over the footlights."

Coquelin, Constant. *The Art of the Actor*. Trans. Elsie Fogerty. London: George Allen and Unwin, Ltd., 1932.

One of the leading exponents of the anti-feeling school of acting, Coquelin advocates complete technical mastery of the instrument but no emotional involvement.

Coquelin, Constant; Irving, Henry; Boucicault, Dion. *The Art of Acting*. New York: Columbia University Press, 1926.

Discussion, but not agreement, by these three renowned actors.

Delsarte, François. *Delsarte System of Oratory*. New York: E. S. Werner, 1893.

A celebrated system of external signs by which any emotion is supposedly conveyed. If this book is not accessible, Delsarte's principles are set forth by William Bridge in *Actor in the Making*, Boston: Expression Company, 1936.

Diderot, Deniś. *The Paradox of Acting*. Trans. Walter Herries Pollack; and *Masks or Faces?* by William Archer. New York: Hill and Wang, 1957.

Archer attacks Diderot's theory that the actor must not feel the emotions he is portraying.

Franklin, Miriam. *Rehearsal*. New York: Prentice-Hall, 3d ed., 1950.

The actor should express, but not experience, emotions. Gestures are offered for the expression of love, happiness, anger, etc. Exercises are given to achieve different kinds of laughs.

Kjerbuhl-Peterson, Lorenz. *The Psychology of Acting*. Trans. Sarah Barrows. Boston: Expression Company, 1935.

A theory almost diametrically opposed to Stanislavski's.

Mackay, Edward J. and Alice. *Elementary Principles of Acting*. New York: Samuel French, 1937.

The combination of movement and voice gives character and

name to emotion. How to use vocal quality, stress, and inflection, how to weep and laugh.

Representational Acting

Boleslavsky, Richard. *Acting, The First Six Lessons*. New York: Theatre Arts, Inc., 1933.
  Several basic, clearly defined facets of Stanislavski's method. The actor must understand the problem that confronts him and spark his will to dynamic action.
Calvert, Louis. *Problems of the Actor*. New York: Henry Holt and Company, 1918.
  An astonishingly modern approach, based on a full understanding of the character and the actor's complete involvement in the emotions of the role.
Clurman, Harold. "Interpretation and Characterization," *New Theatre*, January, 1936.
  A leading American director discusses involvement in the role and physicalization.
Giatsintova, A. S. "Case-History of a Role," *Theatre Workshop*, October–December, 1936.
  An analysis in depth of the character elements of a role.
Irving, Sir Henry. *The Drama*. New York: Tait, Sons and Company, 1892.
  An organic and creative approach, far ahead of its time.
Lewis, Robert. *Method, or Madness?* New York: Samuel French, 1958.
  Based on a series of lectures delivered to actors in New York by a prominent American director. Dispels some of the erroneous impressions which have been built up about "The Method."
Rapoport, I. "The Work of the Actor," *Theatre Workshop*, October–December, 1936.
  An excellent and succinct statement of the actor's technique, based on Stanislavski's system.
Salvini, Tommaso. "Some Views on Acting," *Theatre Workshop*, October–December, 1936.
  The actor must be moved by the emotion he portrays.
  Salvini made a deep impression on Stanislavski.
Stanislavski, Constantin. *An Actor Prepares*. Trans. Elizabeth Reynolds Hapgood. New York: Theatre Arts, Inc., 1936.
  An elucidation of the actor's internal technique.
———. *Building a Character*. Trans. Elizabeth Reynolds Hapgood. New York: Theatre Arts Books, 1949.
  The means by which the actor physically projects his character.

_____. *Creating a Role.* Ed. Hermine Popper; trans. Elizabeth Reynolds Hapgood. New York: Theatre Arts Books, 1961.

Application of the principles set forth in the first two books to the preparation of specific roles.

_____. *Stanislavski's Legacy.* Ed. and trans. Elizabeth Reynolds Hapgood. New York: Theatre Arts Books, 1958.

Excerpts from speeches and letters of Stanislavski on various aspects of the actor's life and art.

_____. *Stanislavsky on the Art of the Stage.* Trans. David Magarshack. New York: Hill and Wang, 1961.

Stanislavski's views on the actor's creative work. A long introduction by the translator in which he summarizes Stanislavski's system.

Sudakov, I. "The Actor's Creative Work," *Theatre Workshop,* January – March, 1937.

A discussion of inner and outer technique. Stresses the importance of playing actions, understanding the character, and being able to physicalize all character elements.

four

The colors: characterization

The most brilliant script analysis and the deepest understanding of the character one is portraying will be quite useless unless the ideas and character traits are *projected* to the audience. Character, as we have stated, is revealed through action. We are not yet telepathic; we must embody even the most intellectual traits and express them physically.

Character Elements

Characterization is *how* we do *what* we do. Given a certain situation, each of us will behave somewhat differently. Our behavior is based upon a complex *personality,* which we may loosely define as the sum of our physical and psychological characteristics. The actor, in piecing together a personality for his role, tries to find as many distinguishing characteristics as possible. Each identifying feature of his role is another *character element.* Physical character elements might be near-sightedness, a limp, a bald head, a distinctive speech pattern. Psychological character elements might be cowardice, a hot temper, avarice, a penchant for order, aggressiveness. Each element we discover is another color with which we paint our role.

PHYSICALIZATION

Every character element must be projected. It is quite obvious that one's walk and one's gestures are easily projected because they are physical to begin with; but it is not always realized that avarice and cowardice must be just as physical. We'll not believe you are a fanatically meticulous housekeeper merely because you say so. But if we see you, as we see the title character in George Kelly's play *Craig's Wife*, constantly testing surfaces for dust, compulsively straightening things, and snatching articles from tabletops lest they scratch the surface, then one of your traits has been vividly brought to life for us. Your compulsion for neatness and cleanliness has been put into action that we can see; it has been physicalized. (We use the term *physicalization* to mean the translation of a character trait — particularly a psychological one — into its physical expression.) The old adage "Out of sight, out of mind" means, in the actor's case, that if the people in the audience don't see it, they'll not be aware of it.

Masks and Movement

Once when I was directing a summer stock company, I called the character man aside to discuss his make-up for the coming show. Among other things, I thought a trim little moustache would be suitable. "No moustache this week," he informed me; "I wore a moustache last week." With the unshakable conviction of the true character man, he explained that it was his practice when playing a variety of roles in summer stock to alternate his moustache-wearing: one week on, one week off. That in itself would not have been so bad, but unfortunately that was the extent of his physical characterization.

The actor must be physically versatile. We all have our characteristic gaits, gestures, ways of handling things, and so on, but the actor's own walk will not do for every role he plays. He must respond physically as completely and as subtly as he does emotionally. He cannot play Sir Fopling Flutter with the same physical adjustments he would assume for Stanley Kowalski. This is why the actor should study dance; his body must be supple and under perfect control.

We begin our work on physicalization with individual pantomimes. Everything is to be expressed in movement which is bold, sweeping, exaggerated. No subtleties. Gestures are to be large and obvious — *stylized*, if you prefer that term — to a degree which might be called semidance. Thus, if you are tiptoeing across a room, you will heighten the movement by bringing the knee up to the chest, then extending the pointed toe straight out and moving the entire body forward to bring the foot down. Instead of just "glancing" behind you, you will arc the entire body around, with the arms describing a sweeping circle. The actor must feel free and easy on stage. He must be able to move with total abandon.

This is not easy. When we discussed involvement, we examined the pressures which inhibit the actor on stage: the presence of the audience, his own personal little neuroses and timidities, etc. An excellent first step toward the elimination of physical inhibition is the use of a mask. The liberating effect of a mask is surprising. We feel safely hidden behind the mask and are able to move more freely on stage than when we feel we are exposing our own selves. For this same reason, many fine actors are poor public speakers and shun personal appearances. Endowed with his characterization, his make-up and costume, the actor feels secure; he knows that whatever he does on stage will be attributed not to himself but to his character. But when he has no character behind which to hide, when he must face an audience as his own self, he often feels naked and ill-at-ease.

EXERCISE

Get a full-face mask, one with lots of character: a clown, a hag, a pirate. Let the mask dictate the scene. What kind of person is this; what would he be doing? Put the mask on and look at yourself in the mirror. You will get a "feeling" for the character, for the way he would move. Give in to such feelings, for they are the foundation for all the rest of our work in this section. Move about the house, allowing your mask-character to impose its way of doing things on you. Walk, sit, pick up articles. Exaggerate the movements as though you were playing the character for an audience of children.

Now decide on an action for your character which you will do in class. It needn't be a story, just a vignette: the pirate sorting his treasure, the hag preparing an effigy. Emphasize big movements. Use the whole stage; don't cramp yourself. Place your areas of activity as far apart as possible so that your crosses become broad sweeps.

Remember in doing this exercise that your mask has a fixed expression and any reaction you wish to portray must be done solely with the body. We have a tendency to rely too much on facial expressions while the rest of the body sleeps. Get it all working.

EXERCISE

Repeat the previous exercise without the mask. You are now free to choose any sort of character you wish and any situation. Your face is now exposed and you may use it, but only in conjunction with the same exaggerated movements as before.

Physical Adjustments

Physical adjustments are external traits which we assume for our role. The further away the trait is from our own inclination, the more difficult is its integration with our character. A mild-mannered and gentle young man might find it very difficult to assume the coarse mannerisms of Stanley Kowalski. But this is the actor's task: to blend these external traits so skillfully into his performance that they appear to be his very own and not superimposed.

The actor finds physical adjustments in the script, through his own inferences, and by borrowing them from living people. The important part of any physical adjustment is to make it so habitual that you can incorporate it without thinking of it; your concentration must be left free for your objectives and justifications, the real driving forces behind your performance. If your character has a limp, you cannot stop to think which foot it is that you favor; nor can you afford to handle your crutches as though they were just handed to you in the wings when the script plainly indicates that you have been using them for a month. If you are terribly near-sighted, you are *always* near-sighted—your vision doesn't suddenly become normal when you forget your adjustment. The use of a physical adjustment requires a strict discipline.

One way to bring a physical adjustment under absolute control, to make it second nature, is to use it as you go about your daily activities at home. If your character has his left arm in a sling, then try for several days to use only your right hand. At first it will be very difficult, for most of your concentration will be devoted to not using your left hand. But gradually you will develop tricks and techniques of getting things done with the right hand alone and, as this adjustment becomes part of you, your concentration will be freed to deal with other elements of your performance.

It is sometimes difficult to separate the physical adjustment which has a purely external origin from that which is psychologically inspired. Physical incapacity creates psychological problems. But for the sake of our exercises, let us accept a broad definition: an externally imposed physical trait will be any physical condition which is accidental, congenital, or otherwise visited upon the individual, such as near-sightedness, a severe backache, a broken arm, a stiff neck, pigeon-toes. A psychologically inspired physical trait would be the swagger of the self-conscious muscle-man, the downcast eyes of the very shy girl, the constant fidgeting of the nervous woman.

EXERCISE
Choose an external physical adjustment and use it in a scene,

either alone or with a partner. Don't slacken the other elements of your scene: have strong actions, objectives, and justifications.

Your physical adjustment must be so well controlled that you could perform any activity without losing it.

Note: In the category of physical adjustments come speech defects, accents, and dialects, which must be assumed with the same absolute control.

Physicalization of Psychological Elements

Psychological elements are the backbone of your character; they are the keys to his motivations and reactions; they are what make him the person he is. One of the things that differentiate the theatre from written media is that elements of human personality are not talked about or explained with words but are physically projected to the audience by means of actions. After studying your role, you may find that your character is lacking aggression, or exceedingly jealous, or very gullible, or shy, or cowed by authority. Your job is to translate these elements into physical expressions.

A supreme example of the actor's use of physicalization to add to the playwright's intention and to illuminate the character is a bit of business invented by Brecht's wife, Helen Weigel, when she was playing the title role in *Mother Courage*. Forced to make the best of a miserable situation, Mother Courage has become a hard-bitten realist who scavenges odds and pieces in a war-torn land and sells them to soldiers — of either side. There is no room for sentimentality in her world. During the play, she loses her two sons to the war, and near the end of the play her daughter is killed. Though heartbroken at the girl's death, Mother Courage cannot really afford to tarry — business waits, and, after all, death is death and nothing more can be done — and so when two peasants offer to bury the girl, Mother Courage accepts. She opens her purse and takes out some coins. She starts to extend her hand toward the peasants, but stops and looks at the coins in her hand. Then she removes a coin, replaces it in her purse, and gives the remaining money to the peasants. And she is on her way.

So right and so brilliant was this gesture that it has been noted in many books on the theatre and has been copied by other actresses playing the role.

In exploring this facet of our work, we start — as always — with ourselves. We choose a single psychological element and ask ourselves how we behave in a situation when that element is dominant.

What do we *do* when we are shy, aggressive, flirtatious, insecure? Not how we *feel*, but what we *do*. Try to recall a particular situation. What were the physical things you did?

EXERCISE
Choose a psychological character element which is a strong part of your own make-up, one which has functioned in a number of personal experiences. Physicalize this element in an improvised scene by yourself. Make no attempt to introduce other elements; you are working not for a well-rounded character but for the full expression of one element.

Example: Some people, when insecure, try to make themselves as inconspicuous as possible. They avoid others' eyes, they remain in the back of the room, they make no contributions to the discussion. Their entire bodies seem to be trying to become smaller; they are slouched, the hands are jammed into the pockets, or the arms are crossed, hugging the chest. Other people, when insecure, try to fight it by putting on a show of confidence; they stand straight, expand the chest, speak in a loud voice. What do *you* do?

EXERCISE
Now choose a psychological element which is further removed from yourself and physicalize it in a scene. Don't jump to the cliché manifestation of this element but probe into the reasons behind it. Think of all the possible ways in which this particular element could be expressed physically.

Example: You are normally quite reserved, but you wish to explore *aggressiveness*. What does this word mean to you? Pushing forward, making yourself known, never taking a back seat. The aggressive person makes the first move; he doesn't wait to be prodded. Therefore, he must be on the alert for an opportunity to act, always "at the ready," and when he does move in, it is with confidence and boldness. When he speaks, he looks you right in the eye and lays it on the line.

Here are some character elements to be physicalized:

adamant	addled
affected	submissive
hot-tempered	fearful
antagonistic	arrogant
bored	overjoyed

greedy	lazy
slow-witted	egotistical
blasé	nervous
vain	smug
rude	polite
meticulous	careless

It is best to do these exercises alone at first, for when we work with a partner there is a tendency to let our words convey the character element. If you would really physicalize these elements, express them in a silent scene through your handling of props. How does a bored person handle a book? A slow-witted one? A careless one? How does an overjoyed person open a letter? A blasé one? A fearful one?

EXERCISE

When physicalization has been grasped, you may try it in scenes with two people. The instructor will give each a trait and the assignment is to create an improvisation in which each performer will make that trait his dominant characteristic. Don't talk about it; physicalize it.

cowardly — brave
fastidious — untidy
cautious — brazen
domineering — hot-tempered
flirtatious — shy
pedantic — scatterbrained
sedate — informal
vain — hypercritical
prying — secretive

Borrowing Traits from People

Sometimes, when studying a role, it suddenly occurs to us that our Uncle Max's way of waving his hands about would be just perfect for our character. Or our landlady's way of walking. Or a neighbor's peculiar vocal pattern. People, obviously, are the great source of human mannerisms. The idea, however, is not simply to imitate the mannerism but to make it our own. There's a difference. There is no external trait that does not have its corresponding inner response. By understanding *why* a person walks the way he does, we take on not only the physical walk but its psychological counterpart; then it becomes a part of us, properly motivated and under firm control. In this way we are sure to be playing our character and not Uncle Max.

EXERCISE

Do a short scene in which you use a physical trait of someone you've observed. Make sure the trait doesn't stand out like a green cloud; it must be integrated with the rest of your personality. We must accept it as a part of you.

INTUITIVE ADJUSTMENTS

I have an African knife on my coffee table. It has a carved wooden handle and a ferocious-looking curved blade. No one has ever entered my home without picking up that knife, brandishing it aloft, baring his teeth, growling, and acting generally like a cannibal who missed his lunch. That knife does things to people.

So do other things. Our clothes affect us. You've had the experience of getting out of sloppy lounging clothes and into your best bib and tucker, all starched and stiff. You feel — and act — like a different person. Some of us prefer casual clothing and feel uncomfortable in formals; we move stiffly and have to force a smile. Others love to dress up.

Of course you've watched children dress up in their parents' clothes. They are transformed. And this wonderful ability is what the actor must retain. He must have enough of the child in him to play-act with costumes and props and to allow the intuitive feelings which these things inspire within him to take hold and to fashion, almost without his will, mental and physical adjustments.

This is one of the most exciting and creative aspects of our work. In surrendering to these intuitive feelings, the actor experiences a moment — or moments — of disembodiment, of weightlessness, of possession; all the barriers are down, and there is a flood of impressions, memories, and fantasies. These pour in so rapidly that we are hardly aware of individual thoughts but rather experience a blending, a potpourri. When one idea does obtrude itself, we call it "inspiration."

Costumes

You should have access to an old costume trunk. Put on different hats, wrap a cloak around yourself, and see what happens. There is an intuitive change of posture, a new attitude, a new way of walking and gesturing with each kind of costume. You simply cannot feel the same way in tights as you do in baggy pants. Yet the actor must be able to wear either as though it were his normal dress. We often hear it said of an actor that he couldn't handle his costume. If he feels uncomfortable in his costume, he is faced with a very serious obstacle to his performance.

EXERCISE
Choose a costume, or even part of one. A derby will suffice. Let the feeling engendered take possession of you just as you did with the mask. What kind of person are you? What are you doing? Prepare a scene to do in class.

Props

Props, too, have their effect on us. Pick up a sword. Lift a delicate scientific instrument. Put on a pair of heavy horn-rimmed glasses. Try a pince-nez. Unwrap a piece of chewing gum. Take a snuff box out of your vest pocket. Did your little finger pop up when you dipped into that snuff box? Were you aware of it?

EXERCISE
Prepare a grab bag of props. Each student chooses a prop and immediately adjusts to it in an improvisation.

Words

Words do things to us. They can evoke strong feelings. We've talked about the use of words in naming our actions and objectives. Now, instead of searching for the right word to apply to an action, let us choose the word first and then see how we intuitively react. If I say "bouncy" to you, you will not clump around the stage like a bear. You will develop a light step, a jaunty tossing of the head or shoulders; you will spring out of chairs rather than drag yourself to your feet.

Words have intellectual associations for us which costumes and props do not, but try to respond to words just as spontaneously. The intuitive reaction is a short cut to forgotten memories and experiences. If we stop to think about the word, it will probably be a much longer time before we recall anything useful to us as actors.

EXERCISE
Choose a word and respond to it. Or have the instructor throw words at you. Perform an action in the manner dictated by the feelings aroused in you.

acid	brittle
damp	elastic
angular	round

amorphous	expansive
staccato	antiseptic
balanced	sparkling
heavy	light
dry	baggy
stony	dull
airy	slick
andante	mercurial

Music

Perhaps the most affecting stimulus of all is music. The beat of a tribal drum, the drum roll accompanying the walk to the gallows, the military band—all these affect our very heartbeat, the rhythm of our being, and produce strong feelings within us. The value of music for stirring the emotions is well known to the movie makers, who underscore every inch of film with music carefully composed to produce the proper emotional reaction. Often the music itself is primarily responsible for the mood. We've all seen mystery films in which a shot of a perfectly innocent doorknob is accompanied by eerie music that makes the flesh crawl.

In addition to arousing emotions, music creates a feeling of time, place, and character. If we hear a minuet, we jump back through the years to an eighteenth-century ballroom with silken ladies and embroidered gentlemen. There is a feeling of stateliness, orderliness, elegance. If we were playing a character who possessed these qualities, the music of the minuet would make us move very much like our character.

How do you move when you hear a square dance? A honky-tonk piano? Our response to music is irresistible, and different kinds of music make us move in different ways. You are not to dance to this music but to perform practical actions.

EXERCISE
Choose a simple activity such as setting the table. Perform it three times with three different kinds of music (minuet, tango, waltz, for example).

Note: Although you are not to dance, neither are you to allow the music to become simply background while you move about in your own tempo. The music is to dictate the tempo and rhythm of your movements, which may be highly exaggerated if you wish. If you are crossing the stage to waltz music, you may do something very like a waltz step, but the point is you are crossing for a purpose, to perform an action; you are not just dancing aimlessly.

Music is used to help you find external character elements: a walk, a gesture, a manner of shrugging. If you were working on a specific part, you would choose actions which your character does and perform them to appropriate music.

Music does another thing: it is a tremendous stimulus to the imagination. You will be surprised at the flow of ideas you will have when working to music. There is a continuous stream of energy in music which transmits an unbroken flow of internal energy to the actor. This internal energy is a creative force which sparks the imagination. Many actors lack a continuous flow of energy on stage; they come alive for their speeches, and then their energy and concentration droop while they wait for their next cue. They have good moments, but the rest is mediocre. No, the actor must be at full creative level every moment. Working with music helps him realize this continuous flow of concentration.

EXERCISE

Choose an environment and appropriate music. With no preconceived idea, start moving to the music, doing things suggested by the environment. If a little story seems to be evolving, follow it through; but you needn't strive for a plot.

Example: Lazy blues music; a bartender has just said good-by to the last customer. He's tired. He collects the empty glasses — puts the bottles away — takes off the tablecloths — sweeps the floor, etc.

EXERCISE

The instructor will play some music for the class. Each one will decide what the music makes him want to do, or what the environment is, and will then do an improvisation to that music.

EXERCISE

The instructor plays some music and then assigns an environment and roles to several people: an expensive restaurant; a head waiter, waiter, and three individual customers who do not know each other. These people go on stage, the music is played again, and they perform impromptu.

Animals

For centuries people have attributed human characteristics to animals. Feathered and furred folk in fables and children's stories have been made to speak and behave in recognizable human terms: the sly fox, the brave lion, the proud peacock. Now the fact is that almost any animal hunting for food is sly, and bears are as brave as lions, and nobody knows whether the peacock is proud when he spreads that fan or whether he's just opening some vents to let the air in. But these attributes have persisted — so much so that man eventually turned the process inside out and began ascribing to people those characteristics "possessed" by animals! We say someone is as proud as a peacock, as brave as a lion, as meek as a mouse, as slippery as an eel, as clumsy as an ox, as stubborn as a mule.

Has it ever occurred to you that perhaps the mule is not stubborn but afraid? That he digs his heels into the ground and refuses to move because he is a timid fellow and dare not venture out? The outward signs are the same, aren't they? All right then, let's start looking at animals in a fresh way. Try to forget the cliché characteristics with which they've been endowed and really watch them closely. What exactly does the animal do? Instead of reading our traits into him, let us take his traits and see how we can use them.

A long chapter could be written on the misunderstandings and misuses of animal exercises. I personally have been made to jump about like a monkey and walk on all fours like a dog. I practiced the dog exercise at home and thought I was rather good, but I couldn't fool my poodle. She knew who I was all the time.

The object of animal exercises is not to *become* the animal, nor even to *imitate* the animal, but to find something in the animal's behavior which can be translated into human terms. It is another way of stimulating the imagination.

You are playing an elegant society lady at a cocktail party who suffers from congenital nosiness. While trying to maintain a polite and genteel front, you are busy keeping your eye on everyone, checking the new gowns, noting the escorts, observing who talks to whom. Now let's take a trip to the zoo. Look at the giraffe standing there in a dignified sort of way. With his head perched so high he is in a perfect position to see everything about him with just a slight turn of the neck. He overlooks the whole crowd, and with his little pursed lips he seems to look down on others in attitude as well as in physical reality.

Without trying to be a giraffe, you can use certain of his postures and movements. Stand as straight as you can, stretch your neck and try to see above the crowd, turn your head from side to side but don't move any other part of your body. If you feel right doing this, if the movement fits in with the other notions you have of your character, then use the movement, thank the giraffe, and forget all about him. Some actors have the weird idea that they must go through their performance thinking like a giraffe or being conscious of the "giraffeness" of their movements. Ridiculous. We get ideas from any and every source, from anything that will stimulate our imagination. If the actor were to be conscious during his performance of all his sources of material for a single role, he would surely have no room left in his head for thinking of his actions and pursuing his objectives. Again we can see why it is so important that these techniques become second nature.

Another illustration: I was directing a play which took place in a pub in Ireland, and one of the characters was a waitress who came in and out dozens of times, cleaning tables, changing the cloths, picking up tips, and doing all the usual waitress things. As written, she was really not much of a character, and the actress playing her struggled for two weeks to get a "handle" for the role, an adjustment of some sort that would snap her to life. And one day it suddenly clicked; she appeared on stage at rehearsal with a full-blown character. She scurried on with mincing steps, clutching a sponge to her chest with both hands and holding her elbows close to her sides. She looked all about with tiny, jerking movements of her head, spotted a table that needed cleaning, and minced over to it. She picked up a coin, held it up to her nose, squinted at it near-sightedly, and popped it into her apron pocket. She wiped the table with small, staccato movements, all the while looking nervously about to see if perhaps she were neglecting a customer. She made a marvelous character out of that waitress, and she is forever indebted to a squirrel she met in the park.

The best safeguard we have against "being the animal" or playing the quality is to find the right action verb for that particular characteristic of the animal we have chosen to use. It is fine to start intuitively, imitating spontaneously the movement or feeling we get from the animal, but to bring this element under positive control, so that we can repeat it every time, we must make it fully conscious by naming exactly what it is we are *doing*. Then we are performing an action as a human being rather than imitating the animal we used simply to give us the idea. The prosecuting attorney is not imitating the woodpecker when he tap-tap-taps his finger on the railing in front of the jury. He is tirelessly, persistently driving his point home.

EXERCISE

Choose an animal. Watch him carefully and find something that he does which you can use in a short improvisation. Remember that the object is not to make the class guess what animal you are using, but for you to find an interesting, workable character element. You need choose only one trait of the animal: the pacing of the tiger, the authoritative stare of the lion, the dull mooning about of the rhinoceros, the smooth motion of the snake, the sudden scythelike movement of the crocodile's tail.

Two or more people are given an environment and are told to create an improvisation, each one using a different animal.

Examples: Restaurant — customers are a bear and a squirrel; the waiter is a hippopotamus.

Empty apartment with a safe — robbers are a mouse, a bear, and an eagle.

Objects

We say that someone is as stiff as a board, as hard as nails, as solid as a rock, as fresh as a daisy, as limp as a dish rag. Objects may be used in the same way animals were used: we find something about the object that makes us feel a certain way and therefore makes us move a certain way. That's all. This, too, is an oft-abused exercise. I have seen students being alarm clocks, for instance. A student sat in a chair, head down on chest, arms hanging limply at the sides. Silence. Stillness. Suddenly he flung his arms into the air, jerked his head up, stared ahead maniacally, thrust his tongue out of a gaping mouth, and vibrated his whole body to the accompaniment of a long, high-pitched shriek. Just how this helps one become an actor escapes me, though it might possibly help one become an alarm clock.

How do we use objects? Well, suppose you are playing a clerk, stamping papers, sorting correspondence, etc. You have decided that this clerk is very meticulous, a hard worker who doesn't stop to chat or waste time in any way; he keeps going like a machine. Perhaps a metronome. Try doing some of your actions to a metronome and see what happens. There will be a dry, crisp, automated quality to your movements that may be just right for your clerk. Again, as with animals, make sure to find the verb that will tell you what you are doing. Our clerk knows that if he *maintains a steady rhythm*, his speed, concentration, and efficiency will be increased.

Try doing a drunk scene, using a rag doll as a basis for your adjustment. What are you doing? What is the verb?

EXERCISE
Incorporate in an improvisation some mannerism suggested to you by an object. It doesn't matter that no one sees the connection. If an object suggests something to you, use it. Do remember that we're not playing guessing games.

Examples: porcelain figurine, wooden soldier, mercury, rubber band, parchment, weather vane, jack-in-the-box.

Pictures

Pictures of other periods, from classic paintings to engravings to magazine photos, are the finest source of inspiration for make-up and costume. We have already done exercises involving intuitive adjustments to costumes and masks; the psychological effect of the proper make-up on the actor is even greater. He feels a startling transformation when he looks at himself in the mirror, a feeling of closeness to his character which may be the strongest he has yet experienced. This "mask" is not simply superimposed, but a flexible, living part of himself. For the first time he can really see—as he sees other people—this person who has been living within him, whose feelings he has been sharing. Suddenly this imagined being has become an objective, physical reality. The actor is truly in a creative state, and often certain attitudes of his character, or ideas about gestures or movements, which have been hazy during rehearsals will suddenly cohere. It is as though he has burst through the magic looking glass into oneness with his role. For this reason, some actors start experimenting with their make-up early in rehearsal.

Pictures also convey attitudes and an atmosphere of the times. Look at pictures of court life in Europe in the seventeenth century; pictures of American factories in the 1900's; pictures of peasant life in the Middle Ages. These arouse strong feelings of sympathy for the people and the times, they contribute immeasurably to our under-standing, and, most important, they stimulate the imagination. How will we even start to think about our role as an indolent duke if we have no notion of what his life was like—his surroundings, the countless ways he had of pampering himself?

EXERCISE
Find a picture of an interesting character, preferably one in-volved in some action. Assume his pose. Is he a relaxed or a stiff character? How does he move? Capture as many of his physical elements as possible. Infer others.

What is his attitude? Has the artist captured his arrogance, his humility? Why is he arrogant? What is he doing? Create an inner life for him.

The exercise is now performed in class this way: show the picture to the class; then use the actual pose of the picture as either your starting or your ending position. If you start in the pose of the picture, you will have to extend the life of the character forward in time and show us what he is doing. If you start the life of the character before, the pose of the picture will be his culminating action.

Note: Work fully and deeply. Remember action, objective, justification.

EXERCISE

Do the same as above with a picture involving a group of people. The actors concerned will have to decide on their relationships, the environment, what the group in the picture is discussing, etc. Make each of the characters a distinct individual.

Try the caricatures of Daumier, the gentle folk of Vermeer, the boisterous peasants of Brueghel, the shopkeepers in photos of old New York.

EXERCISE

As an added fillip to the above exercise, see if you can find appropriate music to go with the picture you have chosen and do a group pantomime to the music, using the characters in the picture and the activities in which they are involved.

The accompanying illustrations are examples of the kinds of pictures which may be used for these exercises.

Literature

Playwrights down through the centuries have normally been too concerned with getting their plays produced during their own lifetime to worry about the problems which might confront the actors in a translated production 100 years later. Consequently, the playwright usually did not bother to describe in detail, if at all, the countless customs, modes, and trifles of decor which abounded in the particular milieu of which he was writing. The actors and director of his play, being themselves part of that milieu, would quite naturally infuse the production with all the proper local color.

For example, have you ever read stage directions of a play in English translation which instructed the actors to place a lump of hard sugar under the tongue or in the cheek before sipping their tea? Probably not. A playwright years ago would have considered it absurd to tell his actors how to do an ordinary thing like drink tea. Yet if we were doing a play today which took place in old Europe, we

MISTRESS AND MAID

1. Is the note from a casual caller, or is there some intrigue involved?

2. Is the maid eager to be part of the plot, or is she afraid?

3. Does the mistress seem to be hesitant about accepting the note?

4. What was the mistress doing before the maid arrived?

5. How close is the relationship between the two women?

6. Are you quite sure that you know which is the mistress and which the maid?

THE MARRIAGE CONTRACT (below)

This can be a delightful scene played by seven people. Determine actions and objectives for each character.

1. Which is the girl's father and which is the young man's?

2. Is the young man disinterested—nervous—hopeful but shy?

3. What business has the scribe whispering in the girl's ear?

4. The man at the window is holding a plan of the new building being erected. What is he doing here at this time? What does he have to do with the scene?

5. Whose room is this?

THE HOUSE OF CARDS

1. The young man should probably be otherwise engaged, for his apron and his tied hair tells us that he is a servant. Yet he appears to be devoting his full concentration to this seemingly insignificant occupation. Justify this.

2. Where is he?

3. If he is not in his own room (and the game table suggests that he is not), the cards probably do not belong to him. Why, then, has he taken the liberty of folding them?

THE MONEYLENDER AND HIS WIFE

1. What transaction has taken place — or is about to take place?

2. In the time in which this picture is set, wives rarely took part in their husband's affairs. Justify her presence here.

3. Why is she referring to the book?

MALLE BABBE

1. Is she really a witch? Or do the townspeople merely think so?

2. Is the owl a pet — or a familiar?

3. Give her a specific environment.

EL MEDICO (below)

1. Who are the boys? Apprentices? Curious neighbors?

2. The Medico has two books open at his feet. Does this mean that he is preparing something he has never done before? Or that he is new to his profession and doesn't remember the basic formulas? Or simply that most formulas are too complicated for even an experienced Medico to remember?

3. Why is he outdoors rather than in his laboratory?

4. Exactly what is in the bowl, and what specific cure is being prepared?

5. Is the Medico deeply concerned over the patient's welfare, or is this a routine case?

would have to ferret out this kind of information, for the use of pulverized sugar would be an anachronism.

When a play is re-created in another land or at another time, the actors must search outside the script for these details. Unless the actor flavors his performance of the Restoration gentleman with many little details culled from the behavior of that period, he will simply remain a twentieth-century man in a seventeenth-century costume.

So we read the literature, both fiction and nonfiction, of the period during which our play takes place. We learn about the predominant attitudes of the times, the social conflicts, the economic pressures. We read descriptions of the daily lives of people of all classes, what they wore, what games they played, how they warded off the devil. We add these touches which the playwright has not made explicit and thus enrich our characterization.

In the analysis of *The Anniversary* it will be shown how literary sources can be used for a specific role, and the section on MOVEMENT IN PERIOD PLAYS offers many examples of customs and mannerisms of various periods.

Playing historical characters presents the actor with an especially delicate problem. Our tendency is to study the biographies of the person we are to portray and take our character elements from those sources. But very often the playwright has taken liberties with a historical figure and wishes to satirize him or present him in a certain light. Shaw, for example, includes among his *dramatis personae* Shakespeare, Napoleon, Julius Caesar, and Joan of Arc. But they are all more Shaw's creations than reflections of historical characters. In *The Dark Lady of the Sonnets*, Shaw characterizes Shakespeare as a simple fellow who goes about with quill and ink jotting down the clever sayings of other people to get material for his plays. History does not support this characterization. We must, therefore, employ the character elements of the play and portray Shaw's Shakespeare. We may, though, discover certain things about Shakespeare in our outside reading which would enrich our performance with character details but which would not impinge upon Shaw's character.

If our character is not historical, we are at somewhat more liberty to borrow traits from characters in fiction, as well as from the historical accounts of the lives of the people in a certain period. The description of a character by a Tolstoy or a Gogol, his activities, his thoughts and motivations, can be far more penetrating than that afforded us by the playwright, who cannot spend quite so much time with each character. Again, it must be emphasized that we may not adapt character traits or bits of business simply because they appeal to us. They must *complement* the playwright's character.

Find a historical description of a specific segment of life; for example, the daily routine on a feudal estate. Choose one of the people described and do a solo scene incorporating some of his activities.

Choose a character from a short story or a novel and do a solo scene using the character elements and the actions described. In this exercise you will be playing the character as written by the author.

Do an action and character of your own invention using one or more traits borrowed from a fictional character. You may just borrow his walk, his squint, or whatever. You may remove him from the eighteenth century and put him in the twentieth.

Caricature

Caricature is the extreme use of physicalization for a role. All our resources are brought to bear upon the delineation of one dominant character element which must be reflected in our costume, our make-up, our walk, our speech, our every activity, to the near or total exclusion of all other character traits.

Miserliness is a popular characteristic for caricature. Dramatic literature offers us a generous supply of misers. How shall we go about caricaturing miserliness?

The miser is unable to spend money. He enjoys more satisfaction from having the money itself than from the things the money could provide. This suggests that he does not even treat himself to new clothes, and we often see stage misers in ragged clothing. But some actors stop there and do not go on to make further inferences. If the miser never buys new clothing for himself, it is imperative that he make his present — and perhaps only — suit of clothes last as long as possible by being scrupulously careful in his treatment of it. Before sitting down, he may carefully dust the chair; he may use a bib while eating; after removing his coat, he may fold it neatly and cover it with a dust cloth.

Miserliness could be reflected in the make-up. If the character is completely concerned with his hoard to the exclusion of personal considerations, he probably takes no pains with his grooming. His hair and beard might be neglected. This unkempt appearance would be at odds with his finicky treatment of his clothes and would thereby serve as a humorous note. And these character elements are both consistent with miserliness.

How would his movement be affected? He probably spends a considerable amount of time checking his various repositories, perhaps polishing his gold pieces, and he would certainly want to be sure that he was not being spied upon. After many years of locking doors and closing shutters in order to gloat over his wealth in secret (all the while suffering from apprehension that someone might discover his hiding places), he has developed a habit of moving in a stealthy and furtive manner. He would walk very gingerly when coming home after collecting some gold pieces due him, because he wouldn't want anyone to hear the money jangling in his pockets.

The inventive actor will find many movements and bits of business which will further his exaggerated picture of miserliness. The miser, for example, has spied a coin lying on the street. Some people are standing nearby. He sidles over to the coin and places one foot on it. He must have the coin, but he is afraid to stoop to pick it up lest one of the people notice him and claim the coin. What torment! To walk away and leave the coin on the ground is unthinkable. Can he perhaps pretend to tie his shoelace and surreptitiously capture the coin?

How would the miser's speech be affected? Misers are often teased by other people; sometimes a character tries to goad the miser into giving away his hiding place. The miser would speak deliberately and guardedly so as never to let anything slip. Fearful of saying too much, he might exhibit an extreme economy in his speech.

EXERCISE

Choose a trait to be caricatured and express it in every imaginable way. This exercise is an extension of the previous one in which we physicalized a psychological trait, for now we must show how this trait bears upon our choice of clothes, our hand props (do we carry a cane, wear a big ring?), and our attitudes, which will be expressed through our actions.

Surprise Elements

This is a very entertaining exercise and one which helps remind us to avoid the cliché. The actor must keep the audience interested in him; once the spectators get ahead of him, they lose interest. Suppose an elegant-looking couple come on stage and take their seats at a table in an expensive restaurant. The gentleman's dinner dress is impeccable, as are his manners. He holds the chair for the lady, arranges her wrap, orders the dinner with the ease and confidence of one used to such surroundings. Then he takes out a pack of Bull Durham and rolls a cigarette, pulling the tie-string closed with his teeth. That's a surprise element.

Here's a true experience — one which happened in class recently. I was sitting in the back of the room in order to listen to the speeches of my Public Speaking class. A student had just taken his seat, and we were discussing his speech. The door opened and a maintenance man walked in; he was wearing work clothes and carried a pail and sponge. Seeing no one in front of the class, he must have assumed that the meeting hadn't started yet, for he proceeded to wash the blackboards. When he was through, he turned and said, "You have just seen a demonstration of the art of blackboard-washing." His voice was deep and resonant and his diction flawless. He sounded much more like a dean than a maintenance man. The class laughed, which encouraged him to tell a few stories. He left to applause. An excited discussion followed about this most interesting and unusual character. He certainly was not what one expected. And he's hard to forget.

EXERCISE
Choose a character and an environment and do a short improvisation using a surprise element.

Please remember, now, that this is only an exercise meant to nudge your imagination and to suggest another way of thinking about your character. Under no circumstances should you pull in a surprise element just for the sake of doing so, or for a laugh, if it does not go with your character. You will find greater opportunities with characters which are poorly filled in by the playwright. You may be playing a cleaning woman who finds herself alone on stage at one point. You might put down your broom, put on your glasses, and sit down with a copy of T. S. Eliot's poems. Again, understand that any example I offer may be ridiculous in the context of a specific play; it is the director's job to decide whether your inventions are in keeping with the rest of the play. But by all means bring them in. Try everything. It's the only way to make your part grow. (Grow deeper, that is; not longer.)

ASSIGNMENT
As a culminating exercise for this section, choose a role in a period play and do a complete character report. First, tell as much as you know about the character from the facts of the script. Then read literature of the period and describe how the information you gather may be used to help you create your role.

Include pictures that would help you with make-up, costumes, gestures, or any further understanding of the people and the times. Are there any props that would help you? Discuss any of the other techniques — intuitive adjustments, surprise elements, the use of animals — that you might use.

THE ACTOR AS COLLECTOR

When the history professor, preparing the next day's lecture, has forgotten a date, he marches over to his bookcase and looks it up in the appropriate volume. The writer always has a good thesaurus and a dictionary on his desk. The seamstress has a score of colored threads and a box of odd buttons. People need materials with which to work.

We have said that the actor's material is the play; but in a larger sense the actor's material is the whole world — all the people he sees, the places he visits, the books he reads, the accumulated impressions of a lifetime. And that's a lot to remember. How often have you seen a hilarious drunk or met some marvelous character at a party and said to yourself that you must remember that individual and use him sometime in a play? It happens all the time. But we seldom remember. We should, though, for these things are the actor's data. The actor doesn't do his studying only in libraries but everywhere he happens to be. He is doing research as he rides on a train, waits in a doctor's office, or strolls in the park. And he should take notes. He must become a collector of ideas, impressions, and even props — anything and everything that might come in handy some day.

I use a scrapbook, a file of 3×5 cards, and a shoe box. In the scrapbook I collect all sorts of pictures for make-up ideas, hair styles, and costumes. I have pictures of old faces with wrinkles and shadows, of clowns, of gents with moustachios of all shapes and sizes, of hats through the ages — just anything that strikes me. I have no system for choosing; if I happen to be thumbing through a magazine and spy an interesting picture, I clip it out. Many will never be used, but there's no harm in having them.

The file is arranged alphabetically and includes character elements, occupations, activities, and sundry little categories which have meaning only for me. There are all sorts of things to observe and note. Have you ever noticed the different things people do with a cigarette? The way they hold it: between index and middle finger, between index finger and thumb, cupped inward with the lighted end toward the palm, between the first three fingers with the palm up in the continental manner. The way they rid it of an ash: a snap of the index finger, a flick of the wrist, a rolling of the ash in a tray, a puff of breath. A card labeled "Smoking" will help you recall special ways of handling cigarettes which you have observed. Other activity cards will depend on your own observation: the way people handle newspapers, telephones, dinnerware, eyeglasses; the way they walk, sit, dance, behave at cocktail parties. Next time you dine in a restaurant, don't let the waiters remain nonentities. Watch them and you'll probably find something worthwhile to jot down on your "Waiter" card.

Character elements may be broken down according to their various manifestations, using a separate card for each:

"Shyness — in speech"

"Shyness — in dress"

"Shyness — in mannerism"

These are just suggestions to get you thinking. Note-taking and note-keeping methods are highly individual. Make up your own system of filing or note-keeping, just so long as you remember how to find what you want when you need it.

five

The actor's material

Henry Lewes in *On Actors and the Art of Acting* (1878) discusses the question of Hamlet's insanity. Is he mad or isn't he? It doesn't really matter to Mr. Lewes, who concludes: "The actor is by no means called upon to settle such points." But these are precisely the points which the actor must determine. Else how will he play the part? Should he recite the words in a general sort of way and let the audience guess?

The actor's first duty is to the playwright, to create the character he wrote. He must make an exhaustive analysis of the script to find out exactly what the playwright had in mind. The actor starts with the tangible, accessible facts of the script and gradually works toward the intangible, toward the inner life of the character which the actor will create from within himself.

The Text

A play must be read several times, each time for a different reason. An actor cannot grasp everything at the first reading; now he is trying to understand the theme, now he is looking for clues to his role, and so on. And, being somewhat egocentric, he can often manage to read a play and end up knowing nothing about it but the opportunities for histrionics which his own part offers. That is why the play should first be read aloud to the assembled company. When an actor reads a play to himself, he is busy "acting" his part, but when he hears it read to him, he can react to the whole play and place his own role in proper perspective. The first impression of a play is most important; there will be surprises and fresh reactions which can never again be experienced in quite the same way, and these first impressions can be the basis for imaginative work later on.

After the text has been read to the company, you can read it yourself—this time just for the story. Make an outline of the facts, of the series of incidents as they occur, with special reference to what your character is doing in each scene. Note where and when each scene takes place, the kind of room, the weather, the action that occurs, and any other pertinent details. (This and the following points made in the discussion of script analysis are exemplified in the analysis of the model script at the end of this section.)

You will begin to have an understanding—or feeling—of the underlying concept of the play, its theme. Sometimes the author's purpose is obvious, as in certain social satires or plays about class struggles, such as *The Weavers,* Hauptmann's play about a group of weavers who rise up against their tyrannical employers. Other times the theme is less obvious or is subject to interpretation. It makes a great difference whether you decide that *Hamlet* is a play about indecision which leads to destruction or about a dynamic Renaissance prince who has to perform an odious task and is just waiting for the right opportunity. Now it is perfectly true that audiences will take what they please from a play and that people seeing the same performance will quarrel over its meaning. Witness most productions of the so-called Theatre of the Absurd. But the actors and the director involved cannot be undecided. They must choose, and the meaning or theme they decide upon will affect everything about the production. Critics have been in despair over most American productions of Chekhov. Played with a heavy hand—all gloom and doom, without humor—they have been entirely different plays from those Chekhov wrote.

Your Character

In an actual production the director will decide on the theme or point of view. However, the student actor will have many opportunities to interpret themes of plays he uses for scene work in class. When you have decided on the theme, you must then find out how your character fits into the playwright's conception. How does your character help illustrate the theme? What side are you on? Why is your character necessary?

Now read the play for clues to your character. Jot everything down. You are not trying to receive a general impression but to list exact details with which to work. Here are examples of the kinds of questions you must ask yourself:

1. What are you? What do you do in life?
2. What do you want out of life?
3. What do you do to get it?
4. What is your relation to each of the other characters? (Relation means more than "brother," "son," etc. You may love your brother or you may hate him. We are interested in the emotional and psychological relation.)
5. What do others say about you? Are they speaking truthfully? Why do they react to you as they do?
6. What are your likes and dislikes?
7. What do you say? How do you express yourself? Are you forthright or vague? Are you honest?
8. What actions are implied in your lines?
9. What are your beliefs and convictions?
10. Are there any special stage directions which offer clues to your role?

These questions are only the beginning. The play itself will suggest many more. If you are a character in *The Cherry Orchard*, you will have to understand your position in the class system then in existence, your social ambitions, your attitudes to members of other classes, and so on. Drain the play of every clue, but *stick to the facts*. Don't make inferences yet. List every single detail that pertains to your character, for this will be the basis for your imaginative work which follows. Start with too much, and then prune away the less essential elements.

What Are Your Objectives?

Now read the play again, this time to list all your scenes and to determine the objective in each one. Usually, by this time, you have become aware of your major goal, what Stanislavski calls the "super-objective." If this is not yet quite clear to you, get to work on the individual scenes. By finding the objective for each one, you will begin to see a pattern emerge, for the objectives of all your scenes add up to your super-objective. Each scene must take you one step closer to your main goal. For each of your scenes you must know the following:

1. Where am I coming from?
2. What was I doing there?
3. Why did I leave?
4. Why have I come here? And why right now?
5. What will I do here? What do I want?
6. Whom do I know here?
7. What is my relationship to the people here?
8. Have I ever been here before?

What Are Your Actions?

You will also write down your actions for each scene. Sometimes, in studying a scene, you will find that your action is clear but your objective obscure. No matter. Either one may be discovered first. In determining your actions, remember that very often people do not say what they mean. This is why scenes cannot be studied out of context. For example: the text of a scene may indicate that a boy and girl are fighting violently and hate each other, but if we knew the whole play, it would be quite clear that they are very much in love. How often do we find a character rambling on about irrelevant matters when his real action was to dig out certain information? Our action is what we do, not what we say.

What Is Your Justification?

When you have discovered your actions and objectives, you must prepare your justification for each scene. This is one area which will grow in rehearsal, for as you work on your part and get to know your character more intimately, your involvement and personalization will deepen. Of course, the amount of personalization you will need will depend on how thorough the author's justification has been and how strongly you respond to it. For now, list as much as you can find of the author's justification, for you will need this as a base when rehearsal begins. From what he tells you of your character, justify each of your scenes as fully as possible. You must be able to justify every single one of your actions and objectives, and this requires an absolute understanding of the play. There will be scenes or individual lines which will challenge your comprehension. This may be the playwright's fault, but it will most probably be yours. In either case, the meaning of the scene or line must be unearthed, else you will never be able to justify it. Refer back to our discussion of justification in chapter three.

Facts, Facts, Facts

You have now read the play many times and have become thoroughly acquainted with the facts. You must not be in a hurry to do anything with these facts—that is, to draw inferences or to expand them—for if you lay the foundations flimsily, your superstructure may collapse on top of you. There is also the danger, in letting your imagination get to work too soon, of distorting the given facts. Sometimes the actor's desire to play a character in a certain way causes him to overlook facts or to read into the play things which aren't there.

This is not to say that you must be completely detached during the early stages of study; impressions and intuitive feelings are important and valuable. Sometimes we feel a strong rapport with a character on the very first reading of the play; we feel we know him so intimately that we could perform the role the next week. Often such feelings are quite correct. Upon further study we find that we have intuitively grasped the character. But the further study must never be neglected. For it may also happen that we have intuitively grasped a character that is not exactly the one the playwright wrote.

To summarize thus far: the play itself is the ultimate source of your super-objective, your actions, objectives, and justifications. The degree of justification will vary according to the excellence of the play, but it must always be drawn from the play.

Finding the Character Elements

The previous chapter was concerned with the translation of character elements into physical expression. Now we must learn to find specific character elements in the written script.

As always, start with the facts in the script. Make a list. Characters are usually described by the author on their first entrance, though this description is often a superficial account of a few obvious features. Go through the play carefully and note what the character says and what is said about him. Again you are cautioned to be wary when examining statements made by other people in the play. You must weigh the other character's motives; his description of you may be quite objective and therefore valuable to you, or it may be utterly biased. Would you base your portrayal of Hamlet on what Polonius says of you?

You will be able to determine many of your physical characteristics by the things you do in the play—whether you are extremely active and full of energy or always tired; by your occupation—construction workers are usually more tanned and muscular than office workers; by references to your present health or past illnesses. The part of the country, or world, you come from, plus your educational background, will help determine your speech pattern. Good authors are careful to use different speech patterns for each of their characters. When you have discovered other elements such as aggressiveness or shyness, you will want to realize them in your speech pattern —a loud or a soft voice, a hesitant or a decisive delivery.

You will, of course, make careful note of your beliefs and convictions and whether you argue them passionately or simply hold them because they are the proper things to believe in your circle.

Don't skim the play. Read carefully, word by word. If your

author is a Chekhov, every line you utter contains clues. You must not let a single line go by unless you understand exactly what you mean by it and why you say it.

Inferences

No author can tell us everything about our character. The novelist has the advantage over the playwright in that he can take us inside the head of any character and expose his thoughts. The playwright has a limited amount of time and must share it with a half dozen or more characters. He tells us what they say and what they do, and that is all. Hours, weeks, years elapse between scenes, often with only a suggestion as to what has happened to us during that time. Sometimes we have only one scene to play and appear on stage from limbo. We are not told where we came from or where we are going, yet we must create a whole human being. Often, in plays by lesser authors, our character is a standard type with little individuality.

It is the actor's task to create a whole character, and if the playwright offers only 60 per cent, the actor must contribute the other 40. He goes to work with his imagination and fills in all the areas the author has left out. He infers things about his character from the facts at hand. If we are concerned only with our life on stage, there are great gaps in our knowledge of our character. The more we fill in, the fuller a life we create for ourselves, the more we will believe in our character, and the more ideas we will have for portraying him. We should know our character so well that we could play him in any given situation, not only those in the play.

Some people have misinterpreted this to mean that the actor should "live his part" in the wings. Not at all. With the exception of the few moments of preparation, the actor is free to relax in the wings. It is during the rehearsal period that he must, for example, wonder about what his character has been doing off stage, because that information will provide a springboard for his behavior in the next scene.

Start making assumptions from the facts of the script. A small piece of business which the author suggests for you may lead to a special mannerism. A note on the tidiness or sloppiness of your desk will suggest the manner in which you dress and eat your meals as well. A pet phrase or twist of speech can be the basis for a speech pattern. The mere mention of your occupation by the author should set off a train of inferences: do you carry anything around with you that you use on the job—a light meter, a marking pencil, a kneadable eraser, a notebook, a flashlight? Perhaps you toy with these things abstractedly at odd moments. Are you on your feet all day at your job? That makes a difference in your behavior when you enter your own home. Perhaps you're studying ballet. Have you ever noticed the walk of a ballet dancer — the straight back and turned-out toes? Would you, as the town gossip, come into someone's home and look into her eyes as you spoke to her — or would your eyes be roaming all over her house in search of new tidbits? If your character is always arguing about politics, might not your pockets be stuffed with periodicals and clippings?

Sometimes there are very few facts upon which to base our inferences. You may be playing a neighbor who drops in for one short scene, offers "feed" lines to the other characters, and vanishes. Unfortunately, there are many playwrights who use characters to advance the plot without giving them any human substance. Here the actor must be inventive. Instead of being a neighbor who appears from limbo, bring some attitudes with you. The kids have been driving you crazy and you just had to get away for a breather — or you left some things on the stove and must get back quickly. The most insipidly written messenger boy can be colored with a few character elements. Naturally, the shorter a time one spends on stage the less he can show. But he can surely know whether he's awfully tired from delivering messages all day, whether he's pleased with his tip, whether his new boots hurt his feet.

This doesn't mean that we should take a three-line part and try to blow it up to major proportions; we should always be aware of our place in the play and the weight of our character's contribution. But this does not preclude our making him human. Some actors are afraid to do anything that is not specifically stated in the script, but this puts extreme limitations on their performance. The written part is only an outline which the actor fills in with his own body, his experiences, passions, and imagination.

Sources Beyond the Script

Aside from the script itself, there are other sources which will stimulate the actor's imagination. Dig into the period of the play, if it is other than modern. Newspapers and magazines of the times will show you hair styles, clothing, jewelry, postures. Literature will disclose the life of the times — a rich source of ideas. Suppose you are to play Hirin, the clerk in *The Anniversary*. There are marvelous short stories by Gogol (as well as by Chekhov, who wrote the play) which offer penetrating insights into the lives and habits of petty government officials of that period. You will learn many things about these people which you would otherwise have no way of knowing: how they handle snuff boxes, fans, pince-nez; how they bow, curtsy, kiss hands. Very important, too, is the whole atmosphere of the times, the major issues of the day, the social struggles. Absorbing this atmosphere will help you understand more fully your place in the play and your relation to the other characters. But remember: Use only those elements which will complement the author's character.

One further note. The man who spends a great deal of time doing his own home repairs is in a better position to judge the house he is thinking of buying than is the man who doesn't know how to change a fuse. So the actor can pick up some tips for character study by learning something about the playwright's craft. By knowing some of the things that guide the playwright in creating his characters, the actor knows what to look for. Again, this is especially helpful in weak plays. For instance, the good playwright will always provide strongly contrasted characters. He will never write a scene with a group of people in which the speeches could be interchanged. In weak plays, if you cover the names of the characters, you no longer know who is speaking. Use the tiniest clue to establish contrasts between yourself and the other characters. Look for differences, however small, and build them: different views, different temperaments, different modes of expression.

The playwright also knows that drama is movement, change. The revelation of character consists not only in telling us the facts of a man but in showing how he changes under the circumstances that befall him. No well-written character is the same at the end of the play as he was at the start. He gets better or worse, but he cannot remain static. A man may appear to hold the same convictions over a long period of time, but look closely: either his convictions have deepened or they have become superficial. If you are having trouble in a weak play determining your character's direction, or movement, examine the ending. How does he wind up? This will suggest what to look for in the beginning. The greater the difference from the end he manifests at the start, the greater will be his change and the more interesting your performance. Note, also, that great changes are not wrought suddenly. The worm doesn't turn with a presto-chango but goes through a series of minor changes, slowly evolving to his final position. His attitudes in successive scenes might be:

Meek acceptance
Timid attempt to be heard
Resignation
Frustration
Annoyance
Strong attempt to be heard
Anger
Aggression

With such a series of changing attitudes, the character grows before us; he is organic. We believe him because we see him struggling and changing under various pressures and we understand his motivations. We cannot believe in a character who, with no warning, suddenly changes his entire personality.

Summary

Here is a brief outline of the steps involved in analyzing a play:

1. Read the script for the story and theme.
2. Outline the scenes in chronological order with special reference to what your character is doing in each.
3. Find your character's relation to the theme, his purpose in the play.
4. List all the facts about your character: his attitudes, beliefs, wants, occupation, prejudices, etc.
5. Write down your actions, objectives, and justifications for each scene.
6. List all the character elements for your role which are actually in the script.
7. Make inferences about your character from the facts you have.
8. Fill in the gaps in your character's life.
9. Consult other sources to deepen your understanding of your character and the period.

Now read the play that follows. Then we will illustrate the above techniques.

THE ANNIVERSARY

by Anton Chekhov

translated by Jerome Rockwood

CHARACTERS

ANDREI ANDREEVICH SHIPUCHIN, *Chairman of the Board of Directors of the Bank*

TATIANA ALEXEEVNA, *his wife, about 25 years old*

KUZMA NIKOLAEVICH HIRIN, *an elderly clerk*

NASTASYA FYODOROVNA MERCHUTKIN, *an old woman*

MEMBERS OF THE BOARD OF DIRECTORS

BANK CLERKS

PLACE. *The office of the chairman of the bank.*
(*The chairman's office is furnished ostentatiously. The trappings are expensive but not very tasteful. A door at the left leads to the counting house. In addition to the chairman's desk, there are two writing tables. HIRIN is alone on stage. He wears overboots.*)

HIRIN (*shouting through the door*). Send over to the chemist's for a few kopek's worth of valerian drops and bring some fresh water in here! How many times do you have to be told? (*He goes to one of the tables.*) Ough, I'm exhausted. Haven't closed my eyes for three nights—my fingers are worn to the bone with writing. From sunup to sundown I work here, and from sundown to sunup I work at home. (*Coughs*) I ache all over, and I think I have a fever. Numbers are dancing before my eyes. That pompous ass of a chairman will read his report today to the meeting: "Our bank. Present and Future." A regular Tartuffe. (*Writing*) Two . . . one . . . one . . . six . . . zero . . . six. . . . He wants to make his mark so I have to work here like a peasant. I work for days preparing his report and he does nothing but stick in a few poetical touches, may he fry down below. (*Writes*) One . . . three . . . seven . . . zero . . . two . . . he promised me a little something for all this. If it all goes well and he manages to pull the wool over everybody's eyes, he promised me a gold medal and a bonus of three hundred. Well, we'll see. He'd better come through, I'll tell you, or else watch out! I have a temper, you know; oh, yes indeed.

(*Sound of applause off stage. The voice of* SHIPUCHIN *is heard:* "Thank you, thank you. I am deeply touched!" SHIPUCHIN *enters. He is in his mid-thirties, wearing formal attire and a monocle. He holds an album which has just been presented to him.*)

SHIPUCHIN (*appears in the doorway, still speaking to the people in the counting house*). I shall cherish this present, dear friends, to my death in remembrance of the happiest days of my life. Once again, I thank you! (*Waves a kiss, turns to* HIRIN) My dear Kuzma Nikolaevich!

(*While* SHIPUCHIN *is on stage,* CLERKS *enter now and again with papers for him to sign.*)

HIRIN (*rises*). I have the honor to offer you congratulations, Andrei Andreevich, on the occasion of the fifteenth anniversary of our bank, and I hope. . . .

SHIPUCHIN (*clasping his hands*). Bless you, old father, bless you. In honor of this momentous moment, this shining anniversary, I think we might exchange a kiss. (*They kiss.*) I am so happy! Thank you for your fine work, for all you've done. If I have managed to accomplish anything at all as chairman of the Board of Directors, I owe the greatest debt to my colleagues. (*Sighs*) Yes, old father, fifteen years. Fifteen years, just as sure as my name's Shipuchin! Well now, how about my report?

HIRIN. Only five pages left.

SHIPUCHIN. Excellent. Then it will be ready by three?

HIRIN. Yes, if no one bothers me. There's not much left.

SHIPUCHIN. Superb, just as sure as my name's Shipuchin! The meeting is at four. Listen, give me the first half, I'll check it through. Quickly now, give it here. (*Takes the report*) I expect fine things from this report, it's my thunder. Thunder, just as sure as my name's Shipuchin! (*Sits down to look at report*) I'm beastly tired, though. Had another attack of gout last night, and on top of that I was running around all morning attending to things, and now all this excitement . . . presentations . . . quite fatiguing.

(*Off stage* TATIANA *laughs, followed by a man's laugh.*)

SHIPUCHIN (*looking to the door*). She's bothering the clerks. (*To* MERCHUTKIN) This is mighty peculiar. Your husband must know where to apply.

MERCHUTKIN. He doesn't know anything, Your Excellency. All I get out of him is, "Go 'way, it's none of your business!"

SHIPUCHIN. Once again, madame, your husband was in the Army Medical Department. This is a bank, a strictly private, commercial establishment.

MERCHUTKIN. Yes, yes, I understand, yes. Therefore, Your Excellency, tell them to give me at least 15 roubles. I'll take that much on account.

(SHIPUCHIN *groans.*)

HIRIN. Andrei Andreevich, at the rate I'm going, I'll never finish this report.

SHIPUCHIN. A moment. (*To* MERCHUTKIN) There's no getting through to you. Don't you see that to come here with this petition is as ridiculous as going to a chemist with a divorce petition.

(*Knock at the door.* TATIANA'S *voice:* "May I come in, Andrei?")

SHIPUCHIN (*calling*). Just a moment, my dear. (*To* MERCHUTKIN) You have not received satisfaction, I know, but what can we do? Besides, my dear madame, today is our anniversary, and we are very busy . . . people will be arriving any minute . . . excuse me.

MERCHUTKIN. Oh, Your Excellency, take pity on a poor old woman. . . . I'm a weak, helpless woman . . . I'm worried sick . . . my boarders are taking me to court, I must look after the house, I have to take care of my husband's business, my son-in-law is out of a job. . . .

SHIPUCHIN. Dear madame, I . . . No! No, I am sorry, but I cannot talk with you! My head is spinning. You are interfering with our work and wasting our time. (*Aside, sighing*) She's an idiot, just as sure as my name's Shipuchin! (*To* HIRIN) Kuzma Nikolaevich, would you please explain to Madame Merchutkin . . . (*Waves his hand and leaves the office*)

HIRIN (*goes to her, sourly*). Well, what is it?

MERCHUTKIN. I am a weak, helpless woman. Maybe I look strong to you, but if you examined me you wouldn't find a healthy bone in my body. I can barely stand on my feet, I have no appetite . . . I didn't even enjoy my coffee this morning.

HIRIN. So?

MERCHUTKIN. Let them give me fifteen roubles, and they can give me the rest in a month.

HIRIN. But you have been told in very plain language, this is a bank.

MERCHUTKIN. Exactly. And I can show them a medical certificate.

HIRIN. Is that a head between those ears, or what?

MERCHUTKIN My good man, I am only asking for what is mine. I don't want someone else's money.

HIRIN. I'm asking you, madame, if that's a head between those ears? Listen, I can't waste my time with you, I'm busy. Please leave.

MERCHUTKIN (*with surprise*). But what about the money?

HIRIN The fact is that thing between your ears is not a head, but this . . . (*Knocks on the table*)

MERCHUTKIN (*insulted*). What!? Here now, do you think you're talking to your wife? My husband is a provincial secretary! You'd better behave!

HIRIN (*with quiet menace*). Get out!

MERCHUTKIN. Here now, here now! Watch out!

HIRIN (*low*). If you don't get out this minute, I'll call the porter. Now move! (*Stamps his foot*)

MERCHUTKIN. No, sir! You don't scare me. I know your kind, you old weasel.

HIRIN. In my whole life I have never met a nastier woman . . . ouf! You make me dizzy! Now I'll tell you once again, and listen. If you don't get out of here, you old witch, I'll mash you to a pulp. I have a brutal temper and I might cripple you for life. I'll commit a crime.

MERCHUTKIN. All bark, no bite. You don't scare me, I know your kind.

HIRIN (*desperate*). I can't stand the sight of her! I can't stand it, I'm actually sick. (*Sits at his table*) They turn loose a mob of females in here . . . I can't do the report . . . I can't.

MERCHUTKIN. I don't ask for someone else's money. I ask for my own . . . for what's legally mine. Oh, the disgraceful old man, sitting in a public office with his boots on. Pig!

(*Enter* SHIPUCHIN *and* TATIANA.)

TATIANA (*following her husband*). . . . and there was a party at the Berzhnitski's. Katya was in a light blue dress with delicate lace and a low neckline . . . and I did her hair myself, piled up high, it looked wonderful . . . when she was all dressed, with her hair done, she was breath-taking.

SHIPUCHIN (*suffering from a severe headache*). Yes, yes, breath-taking! They may walk in any minute.

MERCHUTKIN. Your Excellency!

SHIPUCHIN (*wearily*). What is it?

MERCHUTKIN. Your Excellency . . . (*pointing to* HIRIN) this man here, this here man pointed to my head and then knocked on the table! You told him to help me and all he did was say nasty things to me. I am a weak, helpless woman!

SHIPUCHIN. Fine, madame, fine . . . I will take care of it . . . I will act . . . but later. Now go away! (*Aside*) My gout is about to attack.

HIRIN (*goes to* SHIPUCHIN). Andrei Andreevich, send for the porter and let him throw her out.

SHIPUCHIN (*alarmed*). No, no! She'll start yowling . . . and there are too many offices in this building.

MERCHUTKIN. Your Excellency!

HIRIN (*tearfully*). I've got to work on the report . . . it won't be done in time. . . . (*Returns to his table*) I can't!

MERCHUTKIN. Your Excellency, when will I get the money? I need it today.

SHIPUCHIN (*aside*). A fantastically pesty woman! (*Low, to her*) Madame, as I have told you, this is a bank . . . a strictly private, commercial establishment.

MERCHUTKIN. Be gracious, Your Excellency. Be a father to me! If the medical note won't do, I'll get a statement from the police. Tell them to give me the money.

(SHIPUCHIN *sighs profoundly.*)

TATIANA (*to* MERCHUTKIN). Grandma, you've been told that you're interfering here. That's not nice of you.

MERCHUTKIN. My lovely lady, no one will side with me. I might as well stop eating and drinking. I didn't even enjoy my coffee this morning.

SHIPUCHIN (*worn out*). How much do you want?

MERCHUTKIN. Twenty-four roubles, thirty-six kopeks.

SHIPUCHIN. Fine. (*Hands her a note*) Here is twenty-five roubles. Take it . . . and go!

(HIRIN *coughs angrily.*)

MERCHUTKIN. Thank you so much, Your Excellency.

TATIANA. It's time I went home . . . but I didn't finish my story. It will take just a minute to tell you the rest, and then I'm leaving. Something horrible happened. Well, we went to this party at the Berzhnitski's . . . it was so-so; gay, but not spectacular. Naturally, Grendilevski, who's after Katya, was there. Now I had talked with Katya; I cried . . . I tried my influence. But she had had a to-do with Grendilevski that same night and had rejected him. So, thought I, all has worked out for the best. I had put mamma at ease, I had saved Katya, and now I could relax myself. And guess what? Just before dinner, Katya and I were walking in the garden . . . all of a sudden . . . (*excited*) all of a sudden we hear a shot . . . no, I can't talk about it! (*Fans herself with handkerchief*) I can't!

(SHIPUCHIN *sighs*.)

TATIANA (*crying*). We ran into the arbor, and there . . . there lay poor Grendilevski . . . with a gun in his hand!

SHIPUCHIN. No! No more! I can't bear it! I can't bear it! (*To* MER-CHUTKIN) What else do you want?

MERCHUTKIN. Your Excellency, could you find another job for my husband?

TATIANA (*crying*). He had aimed right at his head . . . here . . . Katya fainted, poor dear . . . and he was lying there very frightened and . . . and asked if we would send for a doctor . . . and a doctor came and saved the poor man.

MERCHUTKIN. Your Excellency, could you find another job for my husband?

SHIPUCHIN. No, I can't bear it! (*Weeping*) I can't bear it! (*To* HIRIN, *in despair*) Get rid of her! I beg you, get rid of her!

HIRIN (*goes to* TATIANA). Get out!

SHIPUCHIN. Not her! This one . . . this wretched woman . . . (*points to* MERCHUTKIN) this one!

HIRIN (*not understanding, to* TATIANA). Get out! (*Stamps*) Get out!

TATIANA. What? What's the matter with you? Have you lost your mind?

SHIPUCHIN. Oh, this is monstrous! I'm ruined! Get rid of her! Get rid of her.

HIRIN (*to* TATIANA). Get out! I'll pummel you! I'll grind you to dust! I'll commit a crime!

TATIANA (*running from him,* HIRIN *chasing her*). How dare you! You rude beast! (*Screaming*) Andrei! Save me, Andrei! (*Screams*)

SHIPUCHIN (*running after them*). Stop, I beg you! Quiet! Spare me!

HIRIN (*now chasing* MERCHUTKIN). Get out! Grab her! Smack her! Cut her throat!

SHIPUCHIN (*shouting*). Enough! Stop! I beg you! I beseech you!

MERCHUTKIN. Holy saints! Holy saints! (*Squeals*) Holy saints!

TATIANA (*screaming*). Save me! Aaaah! I feel faint . . . I feel faint . . . (*Jumps onto a chair, then falls onto the sofa in a swoon*)

HIRIN (*chasing* MERCHUTKIN). Smash her! Let her have it! Kill her!

MERCHUTKIN. Oh! . . . Oh! . . . Holy saints! I'm dizzy! Oh! (*Faints in* SHIPUCHIN's *arms*)

(*There is a knock at the door and a voice: "The Committee."*)

SHIPUCHIN. The committee . . . what a pity . . .

HIRIN (*stamping*). Get out, damn my soul! (*Rolls up his sleeves*) Let me at her! I'll finish her!

(*The committee enters, five men in dress coats. One holds the address in a velvet binding, another a chalice.* CLERKS *look in through the door.*

TATIANA *is on the sofa,* MERCHUTKIN *is collapsed in* SHIPUCHIN'S *arms, both women are moaning.*)

COMMITTEE MEMBER (*reading*). Dear and most respected Andrei Andreevich! As we peruse back retrospectively through the years, making a mental calculation of the progress of our financial establishment, we receive an extremely satisfying impression. It is true that in our green years the limited amount of capital, the negative consummation of negotiations, and the vague quality of our policy brought to the forefront Hamlet's question, To be or not to be? And there was a moment when voices were heard in favor of closing this bank. But then you took the reins. Your wisdom, your vitality, and your distinctive tact have been the reason for our superlative success and transcendent prosperity. The reputation of our bank (*coughs*) . . . the reputation of our bank . . .

MERCHUTKIN (*moans*). Oooh! Ohhh!

TATIANA (*moans*). Water! Water!

COMMITTEE MEMBER. . . . the reputation (*coughs*) . . . the reputation of our bank has been elevated by yourself to such a peak that we may now rival the leading foreign establishments. And so, our committee . . .

SHIPUCHIN. Our committee . . . what a pity . . . As a summer evening drew its cloak . . . Two friends strolled and wisely spoke. . . . Say not that thy youth is marred . . . By my jealous love forever scarred. . . .

COMMITTEE MEMBER (*in confusion*). . . . and so . . . er . . . objectively scrutinizing the present we, dear, deeply respected Andrei Andreevich . . . (*Lowering his voice*) Perhaps later . . . we had better return later. . . . (*They leave in confusion.*)

CURTAIN

ANALYSIS OF "THE ANNIVERSARY"

What's It About?

This is a play about the ridiculous situations into which our foolish vanity can force us. It has been called by some people a "savage" satire against the practices of private banks in Russia during the 1890's. But this seems to be reading more into the play than Chekhov put there. Chekhov was not savage; he loved people and wrote about their foibles with gentleness and compassion. He loved to tell funny stories, and most of his short stories and one-act plays are really no more than padded anecdotes.

If Shipuchin were an evil man who did considerable harm to others, we might have a "savage" satire; but poor, silly Shipuchin does no serious offense to anyone and manages only, through his pomposity and vanity, to get himself into a fearfully aggravated state. If he connives a bit and tries to hoodwink his associates, he is doing no more than thousands of minor officials of his day who are struggling to survive and get ahead in a country being smothered with red tape and petty bureaucratic restrictions.

For those who like the theme to be wrapped up in a neat little phrase, we might say something like *He who sets traps for others falls in himself.* But these little maxims do not always conveniently suggest themselves, and the important thing is not the search for the right phrase; rather, the company must discuss the play and arrive at a mutual understanding of and agreement on its fundamental premises. Moreover, the proverb, or maxim, is restricting when applied to the work of a great playwright. Often the propaganda play can be fitted out with a slogan, but great authors take mankind for their theme and have many things to say about the human condition.

The following analysis is from the point of view of an actor who is going to play Shipuchin. This is not intended to be understood as *the* interpretation of this role, but as one possible way of playing it. "Subject to interpretation" is not necessarily an escape phrase used by actors who are not sure what is going on in the script. The greater the writer, the more are his characters subject to interpretation (witness the reams written about Hamlet), for once having been infused with life, they refuse to be pinned down like cardboard figures. They insist on behaving as human beings, which means being ambivalent, ambiguous, and contradictory at times. This in turn means that their behavior is "subject to interpretation."

It is possible, of course, so to misconstrue an author's purpose as to come up with a seriously distorted interpretation. However, it is usually not a question of a "right or wrong" analysis, but of a valid or invalid one. A character analysis is valid if:

1. All the actions of each scene lead to the objectives of that scene.
2. All the objectives add up to the super-objective.
3. All actions and objectives are consistent with the character; that is, they are consonant with his character elements.
4. The character, his actions, and his objectives are not at odds with the theme which has been chosen for the particular production being worked on.

This last, of course, invites the question: Is the whole analysis wrong if we have misinterpreted the theme? Not if our analysis is *consistent* with the theme which has been chosen. *Death of a Salesman* may be a character study of a man, or it may be concerned with the effects of the capitalistic system on the poor working man. It has been produced successfully both ways.

Outline of Scenes

The first thing we will do is get an overall view of Shipuchin's actions in the play by preparing an outline of the scenes. Not just *his* scenes, but all the scenes in the play. Modern authors usually designate scenes by a change in locale or by a passage of time. The earlier way of designating scenes was to start a new scene with the exit or entrance of any character. Since *The Anniversary* has only one setting and no break in time, it will be more convenient for us to use the latter method.

PLACE. My office.

TIME. About 1 P.M.

SCENE 1. I offer thanks to my colleagues for their presentation to me.

SCENE 2. Alone with Hirin. I express my thanks to him and express my happiness at my own success—fifteen years at the helm.

I mention my gout attack last night and say that I'm beastly tired.

I check with Hirin on the report: will it be ready by three? I look over what he has already finished.

I reprimand Hirin for chasing his wife and sister with a knife.

I explain the importance of putting on a good show, of making a good impression—even to the extent of writing my own dedicatory address and buying my own presents.

I complain about Hirin's appearance.

I admit that I would have preferred my wife to have stayed away a few more days, since I've planned an outing tonight and she will be demanding my attention.

SCENE 3. My wife enters. I try to be pleasant, but she chatters a great deal. I try to send her home because she is interfering with my preparations, but she insists on staying and telling me about her trip.

SCENE 4. Madame Merchutkin enters. She has a petition on behalf of her husband and demands a cash settlement. My wife is bothering Hirin with her stories, and I send her into another room. I try to explain to Merchutkin that she is in the wrong place and I cannot help her. But she will not be persuaded to leave. I am getting more and more nervous because the commit-

132

tee will be here soon. I finally lose all patience and leave the office, telling Hirin to explain things to her.

SCENE 5. Hirin and Merchutkin alone. She badgers him until he becomes very rude and tries to throw her out. She refuses to budge; he stamps and shouts.

SCENE 6. I re-enter, followed by my wife, who is still chattering. By now I have a severe headache and feel an attack of gout coming on. Merchutkin starts on me again, but I am too exhausted to fight back. I give her a twenty-five rouble note and tell her to go. Tatiana continues her long, emotional story — she is weeping now and I am frantic. Merchutkin is still here; now she wants me to get a job for her husband. She and my wife are carrying on at the same time; I am distraught. I shout to Hirin to get rid of Merchutkin. He starts to chase my wife instead, shouting rude things to her. There is screaming and confusion. Hirin is now chasing both women with murderous intent, and I cannot stop him. Tatiana faints on the sofa; Merchutkin faints in my arms.

SCENE 7. The committee enters. One member starts to read the prepared speech. But I am too far gone to know or care what is happening. I recite poetry. They leave in confusion.

This brief run-down of the play is especially helpful at the beginning of our study, for it is sometimes difficult to keep all the events and their proper order in mind. A glance at our outline shows us how our character stands in relation to the entire play, his movement, or line of action, and where we will need preparation for entrances.

Our Character

Now let's find out what we can about Shipuchin and see how we can use the information. Our very first clue to our man is the description of his office, for a person's taste in decor is surely a reflection of himself. It is, of course, possible for an executive to move into an office which has been previously furnished, but we know that Shipuchin has been chairman for fifteen years and in that time he must have made some changes. We also remember his remarks to Hirin about the importance of making a good impression, of keeping up appearances. The "ostentatious" and "expensive" trappings support this attitude. But we are also told that the furnishings are not very "tasteful." Shipuchin, then, knows the value of impressive surroundings but unfortunately has not the good taste to do a really fine job.

Our next information about Shipuchin comes from Hirin's

remarks about him in the opening soliloquy. Hirin calls his chairman a "pompous ass," a "Tartuffe"; he lets us know that Shipuchin has him working overtime with only the promise of "a little something," that he, Hirin, is writing the report for which Shipuchin will take the credit, and that Shipuchin is preparing to "pull the wool over everybody's eyes." At our very first reading of the play, we would have no right whatever to accept or reject Hirin's remarks, for we would not yet know which side his bias is on. However, Shipuchin's actions during the play indicate that Hirin's estimate of him is essentially correct.

Now Shipuchin enters. The author tells us that he is a man in his mid-thirties, dressed formally, and wearing a monocle. The formal attire is normal in view of the occasion, but what about the monocle? An affectation? Wouldn't ordinary eyeglasses do as well? Not for Shipuchin. Eyeglasses are not so imposing as a monocle. And we usually associate monocles with dukes and barons and other elegant people of high estate. In a very short time Shipuchin is emerging as pretentious.

After thanking the clerks off stage for their presentation, Shipuchin turns to Hirin, thanking him profusely and saying that whatever has been done in this bank is due to the fine work of his colleagues. Is Shipuchin sincere? No sooner are the words out of his mouth than he turns briskly to the business of his report. Will Hirin have it ready on time? And a few speeches later he says, "I must take credit for building the reputation of this bank." We can safely attribute Shipuchin's opening remarks to empty formality. These are the things one says to be polite, to fill in the gaps, to display a false modesty. Or to flatter and cajole someone.

Similarly, his concern over Hirin's personal affairs is insincere. If he were truly interested, he would pursue the matter and really try to help; but he drops the issue quickly in favor of a little speech about himself. Shipuchin probably makes the rounds of his clerks every so often, inquiring into their affairs and pretending to be the benevolent father figure, but it is doubtful that he ever hears or remembers anything they say to him. Under cover of his pretended paternal attitude, he exacts as much work from his clerks as possible. Note how he has Hirin working day and night on his report and how brusquely he demands part of the report when he wants to check it through: "Quickly now, give it here."

Gout. After taking the report, Shipuchin reveals that he had an attack of gout last night. Here's a meaty bit of information. First, we look up gout and discover that it is an acute paroxysmal arthritis which causes severe pain in the joints, especially the big toe, ankle, and knee, which are usually attacked first. Chekhov, being a master comedy writer, knows that gout is a much funnier disease than the somewhat stereotyped ulcers, for to see a pompous character clutch his big toe in agony is more ludicrous than to see him press his stomach. We learn, too, that gout usually attacks men over thirty-five and that, while its cause is unknown, predisposing factors seem to be heredity and alcoholic and dietary excesses. What could have caused Shipuchin's gout? Since we are not told exactly, we will have to infer what we can from the facts offered. Several speeches after he mentions his attack of gout, Shipuchin says, "I may let my hair down at home . . . I may eat and sleep like a hog, I may drink myself into a stupor. . . ." At this point Hirin interrupts and asks Shipuchin not to insinuate. But Shipuchin claims that he is not insinuating, that at home he may let his manners "slide . . . but here everything must be *comme il faut.*"

There is enough reason to believe that Shipuchin is actually speaking about himself and not insinuating about Hirin, for if we choose to believe that Shipuchin's behavior at home is as exemplary as it is in his office, then we must also assume that his gout is hereditary. For Chekhov to have made his gout hereditary is pointless, since he would have lost an opportunity to tell us something more about Shipuchin's character. Instead, he draws a man in his mid-thirties who has been attacked by gout and admits to alcoholic and dietary excesses.

What drives a young man to such excesses? Shipuchin has been chairman for fifteen years, which is quite a feat in a society that is all wrapped up in petitions and red tape. We must admit that Shipuchin has some sort of ability to have kept himself in that position all that time, but we wonder whether that ability doesn't consist primarily of manipulating and hoodwinking people, as Hirin suggests. If he were truly liked by all his clerks, would it be necessary for him to buy his own presents and write an address in his own honor? And he is certainly in a nervous state over the arrival of the committee. A person who owes his position to the constant juggling of "deals," to the maintenance of a proper "front," must surely go home at the end of each day and breathe a great sigh of relief that he has not yet been found out. Having been wound up all day, he must feel a strong need to let go, to shed all the polite, forced smiles, the insincere bows and remarks, and to indulge himself thoroughly. Would a chairman with a completely clear conscience need the constant escape which heavy drinking offers?

We have another clue to Shipuchin's business dealings. Hirin reminds Shipuchin about a "disgraceful" thing his wife did: before strangers she blurted out, "Has my husband really bought the Dryashko-Pryashky shares? He was so concerned about them!" We don't know what these shares are, but we certainly know that Shipu-chin didn't want anyone, not even his own wife, to know he had bought them. An honest purchase on the open market would have been known by everyone, and Tatiana's remark would not have been embarrassing.

Shipuchin has much to say about his having raised the reputa-tion of the bank, but note the factors he considers important: pol-ished doorknobs, uniformed doormen, properly dressed clerks. Now surely these things add "class" to a bank, but if a chairman were boasting about his excellent management, might he not also take credit for having made some wise investments? With Shipuchin, all is appearances; we hear nothing about his managerial wisdom. Yet he never hesitates to pat himself on the back. Why the conspicuous omission of his financial genius?

. . . *just as sure as my name's Shipuchin.* This recurring remark is not only another indication of Shipuchin's egotism; it tells us how it should be said and suggests an accompanying physical gesture. Most of us have a pet phrase or two which we repeat frequently and notice seldom, if at all. But this phrase of Shipuchin's would hardly be "thrown away"; Shipuchin is too conscious of himself, too eager to make an impression. He would announce his name every time with pride, making a little production of his announcement, and he would undoubtedly punctuate the words with a gesture. He might jab the air with his forefinger on each word, as though driving in its impor-tance; he might point a forefinger toward the sky as speakers tend to do when making great pronouncements; he might incline his head very slightly forward as when making a token bow.

While we're on the subject of Shipuchin's egotism, take another glance at the speech he wrote for himself, which is delivered by a committee member at the end of the play. No modesty there.

Wife and women. In just a very few lines, Chekhov gives us some very revealing information about Shipuchin's character. Hirin says it would have been much better had Shipuchin not invited women to the dinner. At first, we assume that Shipuchin has invited the wives of the committee members, but two lines later we read: "You'll ship in a whole roomful of them just for appearances. . . ." So Shipuchin has invited women as company for his colleagues! A time-honored device for making a party successful and for keeping the conversa-tion away from business and avoiding prying questions from board members. As if this weren't enough, Shipuchin goes further and admits that he is not "overjoyed" at his wife's imminent arrival; in fact, "it would have been better if she had stayed at her mother's another few days," because Shipuchin has planned a little "outing" after dinner!

When Tatiana does arrive, Shipuchin tries to get rid of her as quickly as possible. He is plainly not interested in her trip or her stories. Nor can we blame him. Tatiana is a dreadful bore. She goes on with her interminable story, completely insensitive to the fact that her husband is in a nervous state and has important matters to attend to. Moreover, she reveals herself as being thoroughly tactless when she blurts out in front of Hirin, "Do you remember that wonderful speech you wrote for the committee? Are they going to read it to you today?" Then she describes her flirtation on the train with several young men.

We are forced to wonder why Shipuchin married her. In the absence of any evidence whatever, we might assume that this is a marriage of convenience. As head of a bank, Shipuchin must do a lot of official entertaining at his home, and wives can be pretty gossipy about bachelors. Tatiana gives Shipuchin's home the proper air of respectability. A family man is usually considered more "settled" and responsible than a single man, and these things are important factors when climbing up in the business world. And Shipuchin, being the pretentious bore that he is, could hardly have attracted a very sensible woman. Brainless, giddy little Tatiana probably thought it would be marvelous to marry the head of a bank and to have a comfortable allowance for herself. Shipuchin's relationship to Tatiana seems to be one of tolerance which leans over into annoyance when he has more important things to do.

The Merchutkin offensive. Under the onslaught of Madame Merchutkin, poor Shipuchin gradually crumbles. The old woman slowly pulverizes every vestige of patience and strength in him and, together with Tatiana's babbling, helps reduce the unfortunate man to near idiocy. We must give Shipuchin credit for trying to be a gentleman at first; he is courteous and respectful. But he is under pressure, and his courtesy doesn't last long. We can hardly blame him, for Merchutkin is an awful pest. Shipuchin digs into his own pocket and gives the old lady twenty-five roubles, but she is still not satisfied. She continues to plead her case, and when Hirin aggravates the situation by losing his mind and murderously chasing both women about the office, Shipuchin finally accepts defeat. When the committee enters, Shipuchin is powerless even to acknowledge its presence. He retreats from the ghastly reality of his situation into the fantasy of poetry.

The Physical Shipuchin

We have now examined the facts of Shipuchin as offered by the script. We have made a few inferences. What impression do we have of this man? What image begins to form as we put the pieces together?

What is he like physically? Whom shall we cast to play him? We are told only that he is in his mid-thirties, wears a monocle, and suffers from gout. No other physical characteristics are even suggested, and there is nothing in the story or character relationships which strongly implies a specific image. Shipuchin may be tall and thin, short and fat, balding or curly-topped. Do we have a right to assume that he is funny looking because he is the central character in a farce? Not necessarily; after all, he does in his person represent the bank, and it is doubtful that the board of trustees would choose a man who cuts too ridiculous a figure. We might assume, however, that he is not the perfect picture of health and robustness, since gout is due to overeating or overdrinking or both.

What else can we assume about him physically? Is he lethargic or brisk in his movements? We have inferred previously that Shipuchin must be under considerable tension as he manipulates people and contracts in order to maintain and better his position. Today, particularly, he is under much pressure; he is nervous about the committee's visit, the report is not finished, and he is harassed by his wife and Merchutkin. He does say in the beginning of the play that he is very tired, but his is not the sort of tiredness which will permit him to slow down and relax. He is tired because he has been racing around all morning trying to get things in order for the meeting; the rushing about has increased his nervous tension, and his tiredness causes him to be irritable. He probably cannot sit still for a minute at a time. On the whole, then, his movements would be quick and jumpy.

Now here is a complication. Despite the nervousness and tension which Shipuchin's movements betray, he is a man who is careful about his carriage. He is very concerned with proper appearances. He has uniformed doormen, and he berates Hirin for "ruining the *ensemble*" by sitting around in overboots and a faded jacket. Surely Shipuchin would not slouch around in an ungainly manner but would hold himself erect, with poise and dignity. That is, with as much erectness, poise, and dignity as gout, nervous tension, and tiredness would permit. Besides, he wears a monocle, and no one who affects a monocle is sloppy in his comportment. This is an interesting physical problem for the actor, for as the play progresses and Shipuchin becomes more frantic, he would lose much of this poise, yet we must constantly see Shipuchin struggling to maintain his dignity. Here lies much of the play's humor; we see a stuffed shirt vainly trying to remain upright as the starch is dissolved.

What of Shipuchin's speech? Again we must remind ourselves of his responsible position and his numerous contacts with the public. And surely he must have had a fairly good education even to qualify for his post. He has a knowledge of poetry, as we see in the final scene, and Hirin says that when the report is done Shipuchin will add some lyrical touches. Moreover, anyone so concerned with proper appearances would surely be aware of the importance of good speech in making an impression. Our chairman is probably too aware; since he is pretentious in other things, we can reasonably assume that his speech is somewhat affected — the articulation just a little too precise, the inflections just a shade too dramatic. He likes to be effective, just as sure as his name's Shipuchin!

These are some of the broad assumptions which can be made about Shipuchin's physical character elements. You must have realized by now that we have crossed the line into psychological character elements and that most of the inferences have actually been based on the physicalization of psychological and emotional characteristics. By delving further into Shipuchin's psychological elements and thinking of ways to physicalize them, we can discover more shadings and subtleties.

The Psychological Shipuchin

One of Shipuchin's major characteristics is obviously his pretentiousness. The decor in his office, his pretended interest in his clerks, the gifts he buys for himself, the speeches he writes for himself, his repeated phrase, all point to pretense and pomposity. We have suggested that his pretension would broadly manifest itself in his affected speech and dignified comportment. What further refinements can we infer? How else might "pretension" be physicalized? Surely in his dress; the monocle is a clue there. Shipuchin's clothes would be beautifully tailored, and he certainly would not stint on the accessories: a large flower in his buttonhole, a gold watch chain, a diamond stickpin, cuff links, and don't forget the walking stick that gentlemen carried in those days. And, of course, spats.

These accessories would have to be carefully chosen, for while Shipuchin is pretentious, we also learn from the description of his office that his taste is rather banal and ostentatious. The stickpin would be just a little too large, the watch chain a bit too heavy. The walking stick would have a huge gold knob, and Shipuchin would handle it with a little more flourish than actually necessary.

Shipuchin is also meticulous. He keeps reiterating the importance of having everything appear *"comme il faut . . .* impressive, smart, down to the last detail." Chekhov offers a perfect stage direction while Shipuchin speaks these lines. He instructs him to pick up a bit of scrap paper from the floor and throw it into a wastepaper basket. This little bit of business can be the springboard for much more. Shipuchin's desk must be a gem of orderliness, and just as he is compelled to pick up stray scraps of paper, so must he feel the urge to constantly tidy his desk—and probably he tidies Hirin's desk as well, which would annoy the old man—and to pick lint from his clothes.

Also, there is a stage direction early in the play which we should not forget as we go on reading: just as Shipuchin makes his first entrance, we are told that clerks enter now and again with papers for him to sign. What a marvelous opportunity for business! And for character revelation. Some clerk will have an untidy sheaf of papers which will occasion a disgusted look from Shipuchin. Then, when he goes to sign them, he will dip his pen carefully and sign his name in a neat script with a pretty little flourish at the end. He surely wouldn't scribble the name of Shipuchin in a careless manner. And imagine how upset he would be if he got some ink on his fingers!

Another element is his apprehension. Shipuchin is nervous, tense, and expectant from the moment he enters the room until the moment the committee enters. How does "apprehension" manifest itself physically? For one thing, it divides one's concentration. Shipuchin's mind is on the door through which the committee will walk momentarily; he can hardly bear to listen to his wife, and he has no patience with Madame Merchutkin. He probably watches the door as he talks to these two. He is also anxious about his report and looks over Hirin's shoulder every few minutes to note his progress. He cannot relax or stay seated in one place even for a few moments; tension has tightened his whole body and he feels a need to move about. He very probably has some pills which he takes to help him relax, and these would be, of course, in a fancy pillbox on his desk. At the height of his nervousness, Shipuchin might even develop a tic.

We have suggested that Shipuchin's attitude toward his clerks is hypocritical, that he is not truly interested in them, and that he doesn't really mean a bit of what he says about owing a great debt to his colleagues. Shipuchin's hypocrisy in this respect is consonant with his egotism and pomposity; with so much of his attention going to himself, there is little left for other people. There are only a few lines in which Shipuchin addresses some personal remarks to Hirin, but he can clearly either show genuine interest—by going to Hirin and giving him all his attention for a few moments—or occupy himself with his desk or with polishing his ring while he tosses his remarks to Hirin over his shoulder. The same is true of his reactions to his wife; does he stand and listen with any interest, or is his attention elsewhere?

Part of Shipuchin's character is his *savoir-faire*. Despite his pretensions and his egoism, he is not an ox, a loud-mouth, or a coarse individual. He knows how to do things with grace and dignity. He is gentlemanly. He doesn't grab papers crudely or sprawl in chairs; he takes his wife's suitcase and hangs up her raincoat. He may do things with just a bit too much flourish, but he does the proper things.

These have been examples of what one person finds to be some of Shipuchin's psychological character elements and how they might be physicalized. Individual actors working on the part would bring their own experiences to it and would make further refinements. There are many ways to physicalize "meticulous," and different actors would make different choices. The important thing is to be sure that the element you have chosen is consistent with the playwright's character and that you express it physically — project it.

The Super-Objective

Shipuchin is clearly aiming for the highest position he can attain. He wants recognition and prestige in social and business affairs and enough money to purchase the luxuries of life. But these are far-off goals which are not directly attainable in this play, and so we must limit our super-objective to the one major goal which Shipuchin is aiming for now. Everything is centered on the arrival of the committee, and Shipuchin's main concern, his super-objective, is *to make this meeting a success.*

Actions and Objectives

Each of our objectives must lead to the super-objective; all together must add up to it. At this point it would be helpful to look at our breakdown of scenes and get a quick overall view of Shipuchin's actions in the play. We can see a few main threads: he is anxious to have the report finished; he prepares himself for possible objections from the committee by restating some of his basic notions to Hirin; he tries to get rid of his wife and Merchutkin, both of whom get in the way and slow down his preparations. All of these are steps one would take to ensure the smooth running of a meeting.

We must now divide the play into exact scenes for the purpose of defining our objectives; we cannot have a few loose objectives scattered throughout the play. And these scene divisions will not necessarily be the same as those we used to outline Shipuchin's activities at the start of this analysis. That was an arbitrary division based on nothing more than entrances and exits. Within those scenes there may be changes of actions or objectives, or one objective may carry through several entrances. Opinion will sometimes differ as to just where the dividing line should be drawn, but I would say that the first scene consists of the action from Shipuchin's entrance to Tatiana's entrance. (Assuming, of course, that we are playing Shipuchin. For Hirin or Tatiana the division of scenes would be different.)

Now a lot is going on in this scene, and there may be a tendency to slice it up into several smaller segments. The reason I choose to make one single scene out of all this activity is that I believe there is an overriding objective which is far more important than any of the little segments, and we must always aim for a strong line of action which leads to our goal. If we break our actions and objectives into many small pieces, there is a danger of having a choppy performance that does not cohere, does not make a whole.

How do we tie all the seemingly disparate actions in this scene into one singly motivated objective? We have already said that Shipuchin's solicitude for his clerks is not very sincere, so this cannot be a major concern of his in the scene. Either he is pretending an interest for some special reason, or it is just his way of making chit-chat while he attends to more serious matters. But why is he so warm and enthusiastic toward Hirin when he enters — praising him and kissing him? That becomes clear in a moment: contented clerks are more likely to turn out reports on time. But if he wants his report turned out on time, why does he bother Hirin by boasting of his accomplishments? Surely he must realize that chatter will only interfere with Hirin's work; in fact, he sends Tatiana out of the room for that very reason when she is telling her story to Hirin. We must look for another reason for his blather. He must be talking in spite of himself; he must be compelled to talk. He admits to Hirin that he has been called "trivial" for putting such value on appearances. This is obviously one of the things the committee has criticized in the past, and now he needs to bolster his own convictions by practicing the arguments on someone else. And he does indeed hold these convictions, for in the midst of it all he berates Hirin for his untidy appearance.

All these actions add up to one thing which propels Shipuchin through this scene: his objective is *to make last-minute preparations for the meeting.* Taking this as an objective, the actor will not be side-tracked into stopping his preparations to chat with Hirin about his wife. No, he has no time for that; he is at his desk checking through the report at that moment.

Now what are the specific actions Shipuchin does to accomplish his objective in this first scene? The first time we see him, he is offering profuse thanks in all humility and modesty to his colleagues.

A moment later he is lavishing the same on Hirin. His action seems to have something to do with expressing his gratitude, but it is not quite so simple as that. And besides, we want a stronger and more compelling term. There are so many ways to express gratitude that the phrase gives us nothing to do. Suppose we say his action is *to melt his colleagues with love and gratitude*. This gives us a very definite feeling for the action; we know we will have to pour it on thick and heavy to accomplish our purpose. Since it is almost impossible to speak of actions without their attendant justifications, let us consider why Shipuchin does this. Suppose his clerks were in an antagonistic mood when the committee arrived; one or two complaints and our chairman is in a lot of trouble. Moreover, as we have previously noted, the report is not yet finished, and Hirin can be spurred on with honey more easily than with vinegar.

His second action is *to check the report*. Here is an instance, much more common in plays than many actors realize, in which the words and the action do not match. Look at the script and see what Shipuchin is *saying* as he looks through the report. If the actor plays the words in this scene, we have a benevolent chairman who has stopped his business to have a friendly chat with his clerk. The play stops. But if the actor sticks to his action of examining the report and speaks to his clerk casually while keeping his attention on the pages, we realize that the report is far more important than the clerk.

Shipuchin now launches into a little soliloquy in which he justifies his concern with appearances. This action is a difficult one to nail down. It appears that Shipuchin is simply boasting about his accomplishments. But we have said that one of the major character elements of this man is his apprehension of the committee's visit. He repeats over and over again that he is terribly nervous and must force himself to "be steady," his increasing apprehension supplying the mounting tension—and humor—of the play. His action here might be *to arm himself with arguments* should the committee criticize him, or *to quell his nervousness* by reciting some of his positive achievements.

Now let me turn around and repeat something I have said before: There is no one-and-only way to play a scene. Several interpretations may be correct, provided they are consistent with the character and the actions and objectives clearly add up to the superobjective. You may have decided, for instance, that Shipuchin's egotism is so great that it overpowers his apprehension at this point. After checking the report, he starts to re-create in his mind the presentation he has just received and thinks, too, about the one he is going to receive. He speaks to Hirin about these gifts. He is so pleased with himself. He rambles on about his achievements at the bank. He *basks in his glory*. Suddenly, he finds himself face to face with Hirin, who is dressed most inappropriately, and Shipuchin is jolted out of his pleasant self-flattery into the nerve-wracking reality of the impending committee visit. Playing it this way could be very funny and, more important, just as consistent with the character.

Now look at Shipuchin's speech just before Tatiana enters. It is almost pure exposition, and I have heard dozens of inexperienced or lazy actors explain away a speech of this nature with, "It's just there to further the story." But that is no answer for the character whose life in the play must be a solid continuum. Characters do not stop their personal pursuits to tell part of the author's story to the audience (except in a frankly theatrical or presentational play like *Our Town*). What happens at this moment in our play is that Hirin suddenly reminds Shipuchin that his wife is due at any moment. This is a serious problem, for his wife's presence will surely dampen the evening's activities. You will recall that there is an "outing" planned for the gentlemen of the committee with several women who are not their wives, and undoubtedly one of these women is Shipuchin's "friend" for the evening. How will she react when he marches in with his wife? Shipuchin's action now is *to beat down this new obstacle*. This scene becomes much stronger if the actor plays it not as though he were simply telling Hirin that he would have preferred his wife to have stayed away a little longer, but as though he is really thinking aloud to himself, his brain swirling with possible ways to get rid of his wife and save the evening.

This problem, hurled at him on top of all the other pressures, almost proves to be too much for him. He can no longer think straight and his nerves are about to snap. In those last few lines of his speech before Tatiana enters, he has another action, which is *to pull himself together*. This is the most perfect statement for an action, for this is what he literally does; he straightens up and steels himself against collapse.

The next scene, as far as Shipuchin's objectives are concerned, starts with Tatiana's entrance and extends to Merchutkin's entrance. There is no mistaking his objective here: *to get rid of Tatiana*. This will not be easy and must be done with tact. Shipuchin's first action is not, as the words seem to indicate, to welcome her and to inquire about her trip, but rather *to come up with a means of getting her out*. If you prefer, *to stall for time*. He makes polite conversation, but he is silently reaching for ideas; and he is abruptly pulled away from his private thoughts by Tatiana's "But you don't seem glad to see me." Suddenly Shipuchin gets an idea which he immediately puts into action. He *plays on her feminine needs*. He knows women have a desire to look attractive, especially when meeting new people, and so he tells her that the committee will be coming soon and she is not dressed. When that doesn't work, he tries *to appeal to her better instincts* by suggesting that she not interfere with Hirin's work.

Now Merchutkin barges in. This scene continues until Shipuchin's exit, and his objective is as simple as the last one: this time it is *to get rid of Merchutkin*. He tries to convince her that she is in the wrong place. His initial attempts are tempered with efforts to be polite; but Shipuchin is under too much pressure and Merchutkin is a very annoying character. His temper grows short, and he finally gives up in despair and turns her over to Hirin. To say that the action is *to convince Merchutkin that she is in the wrong place* is quite right but quite colorless. Moreover, it doesn't help us build to the extremely frustrated state which causes Shipuchin to burst out of the office. We need actions that will compel this mounting tension and desperation.

Let us use the action *to convince Merchutkin that she is in the wrong place* only for the first few lines. But as she proves obstinate, let's strengthen the action to *to pound some understanding into her* — starting with Shipuchin's speech, "We cannot do anything for you, madame." This is still useless; Merchutkin seems unable to comprehend an iota of what Shipuchin is saying. She pushes him to the point of exasperation by asking for fifteen roubles on account. According to the script, Shipuchin groans at this request, and were I playing his role I would want to shake her so that her brains rattled and throw her bodily out the door. A good action at this point, one that would provide much meat for the actor, would be *to force himself not to lay hands on her*. Shipuchin might restrain his impulse to throttle the old lady by clasping his hands behind his back. He would repeat what he had said, spitting it out slowly through his clenched teeth. Finally, unable to stand it any longer, he *escapes* from the situation in order to save his sanity and to avoid committing mayhem.

It is important to use several actions in a scene of this sort or we run the risk of letting the scene become static. One action would tend to dissipate the rising movement, whereas several actions of increasing intensity give strong direction and greater interest to the scene. And more color to the character.

Shipuchin's final scene starts with his re-entrance and goes to the end of the play. By now his headache is so severe and his nerves so strained that he is very nearly disabled. He is a drowning man, too worn out to struggle much any more but still desperately trying to hold on. He is willing to compromise, to surrender, to do anything, if only he can *survive long enough to meet the committee*. In this objective, poor Shipuchin fails and falls apart.

Specifically, in order to survive, he tries first *to appease* Merchutkin by assuring her that he "will take care of it," and when this fails, he *surrenders* and offers her twenty-five roubles. When the twenty-five roubles fail to move Merchutkin, he *surrenders abjectly* or, better, *prostrates himself* with, "What more do you want?" He is willing to do anything in the world if only he can get rid of the old lady. When she persists in her demands, he breaks down and *orders Hirin to get rid of her*. This action backfires when Hirin mistakenly tries to evict Tatiana and then winds up by maniacally chasing both women. Shipuchin tries to salvage the situation by *pleading* with Hirin to stop. This action may be translated into physical terms in various ways. Shipuchin may run after Hirin to try to stop him, or, being too paralyzed to move, he may stand in the center of the whirlwind and plead with clasped hands half to Hirin, half to Heaven.

Shipuchin's final objective is a slippery one. The bedeviled man seems to have lost his mind, and this kind of scene offers the strongest temptation to quality-acting. Unless we decide on a specific action and objective here, we will fall into the old trap of rolling the eyes heavenward with a stupid grin and reciting the poem in a "mad" sing-song. Let me suggest as his objective *to shut out this horror*, and the action with which he achieves this is *to recite his favorite poem*, which always affords him solace. And so, rather than play the cliché madman, I would have Shipuchin look into the distance with a wistful and peaceful expression as he recited his poem with deep feeling and meaning. The result for the audience will be quite the same: they will assume that Shipuchin has lost his marbles.

Justification

Much of Shipuchin's justification has already been interwoven into our previous discussion of his psychological character elements, his actions and objectives. The justification and personalization are areas which will grow during rehearsals. Our reasons become stronger and more deeply rooted as we get to know our man. And, of course, they will differ somewhat according to the personal needs of the actor playing the part.

Preparation

Shipuchin will need two preparations—one for his initial entrance and one for his re-entrance in the middle of the play. His first preparation is uncommonly easy, for Chekhov has actually written it into the play. Actors hardly ever get such a good break. There is the sound of applause and then Shipuchin's voice thanking his colleagues. The applause will have to be provided by a few actors and stage managers in the wings while the actor playing Shipuchin stands at a slight distance, fondling his album and giving his speech of thanks. He then backs up a bit and continues his speech in the doorway, this speech constituting his actual entrance on stage.

When Shipuchin makes his second entrance, he is followed by Tatiana, who is in the middle of her story. These two actors must, of course, do their preparation together. Tatiana simply starts the story off stage, and Shipuchin, who is not listening, is fighting down the impulse to tell her to shut up. Or perhaps Shipuchin has picked up some papers in the counting house and is bringing them back to his desk. He is trying to concentrate on these papers as Tatiana's verbal cascade flows on.

Other Colors and Sources

People's posture has changed through the years for the very good reason that our clothes have changed. When vests went out of fashion for a while, men no longer had little pockets into which they could hook their thumbs. Instead, they could thrust their hands into their back pockets, a feature which trousers of long ago did not have. Pictures of Russian gentlemen in the 1890's (the period of *The Anniversary*) will show you how they handled themselves in the clothing of the day, how they held their monocles.

You may have no trouble with Shipuchin's expansiveness as he boasts, but if you do, you might watch the peacock. The head reaches upward as the fan spreads out in a slow, smooth arc. This can be nicely translated by the actor whose arms spread out as though to encompass all the fine "touches" which Shipuchin has provided in the bank.

Now let's read some books of the period. Very prominent in histories of Russia during the latter part of the nineteenth century are discussions of the social hierarchy. We learn that the tsar was all-powerful and that the nobility was a strong and privileged class, completely separate and distinct from the mass of the nation. The peasants were at the bottom of the ladder and the bourgeoisie made up the huge middle. The nobility was either hereditary or personal. The personal noble was one who was appointed to the nobility from another class. His son did not inherit the title. Every government worker in Russia was assigned a rank, and upon reaching the eighth rank a member of the bourgeoisie could petition for acceptance to the nobility.

We learn further that some commercial banks were directed by a board elected by the merchant class but were presided over by a government nominee. Shipuchin, then, may very well be a government employee with a rank. It adds greatly to our justification if we suppose that he is but one rank away from eligibility to the nobility. How tantalizing! What a fine thing to strive for! Shipuchin would give his eyeteeth to be a noble, and every successful deal, every positive meeting with the committee, brings him one step closer to his dream. This is excellent material for the actor, strong, driving forces which make his objectives more important and more meaningful.

But Shipuchin is not a noble yet. He is a member of the bourgeoisie. Perhaps we can place him more accurately. The bourgeoisie was divided into several classes: merchants, respectable citizens, citizen burghers such as skilled artisans, freemen such as discharged soldiers, emancipated serfs, and workmen. It was possible for one to pass to a superior position if the community legally and officially accepted him. The community also could exclude a member if he was condemned for a crime or if he was a notoriously bad character. So there were pressures within the bourgeoisie itself in addition to the pressures exerted by the deference owed to the nobility.

Now one way to become a respected citizen was this: through the social position of one's father one could acquire the right to attend the university, and upon successful completion of one's studies one petitioned the government to be included in the class of respected citizens. Education was far from universal in those days. In the city of St. Petersburg (Leningrad), 300,000 of the total 900,000 inhabitants could neither read nor write. The government did not particularly like the idea of popular education, and there was no allowance for independent thought. Books were strictly censored and textbooks were carefully prepared so that only the "right" ideas were disseminated. The educational system was narrow and restrictive. If one did eventually get through the university and become a respected citizen, he had a great deal to be proud of. Shipuchin is certainly proud and vain; perhaps he takes great pride in his status as respected citizen and in the fact that he has had an education. He would also be proud of the fact that respected citizens had privileges; they were exempt from certain taxes, from recruitment, from corporal punishment, and from having their heads shaved when arrested. All this would give Shipuchin ample reason to feel proud and also superior to someone like Hirin, who is only a worker.

By reading on we find sound justification for Shipuchin's "deals" and attempts at hoodwinking. There were thousands upon thousands of minor officials with very small pay. And this situation bred bribery. A Russian proverb of the time was, "If you are going to talk to an official, you must talk roubles to him." With petty officials struggling to rise in rank, with mistrust and suspicion rampant, we can imagine the ulcers, the gout, the shredded nerves that must have been common. One learned to act on the defensive, to take in others.

Other random bits of information can suggest behavior or can suddenly explain details in the script. For example, the peasants showed extreme servility to the noble, bowing to him until their foreheads touched the ground. This was called *chelobitie*, and the custom was so firmly established that the very word for "petition" has become *chelobitnaya*. Between persons of less extreme classes, such as two members of the bourgeoisie, the depth of the bow indicated the degree of subservience. Now we can visualize Merchutkin's greeting of Shipuchin. She would probably make a lower bow than need be in order to flatter him. And she calls him "Your Excellency," which is again flattery, for he is not a noble. We notice, of course, that Shipuchin never objects to being called "Your Excellency." It must give him a delicious foretaste of what's to come some day.

Here is a note for Hirin. The miserable climate compelled people to stay indoors most of the time. The water was undrinkable and the food bad. Decent food could be obtained but not on Hirin's salary. The national drinks, tea, kvass, and vodka, did not have the nutritional value of, say, England's ale. Anemia was prevalent. No wonder old Hirin is bundled up, shivering and coughing.

This is only a start; it is not meant to be exhaustive by any means. It is only an indication of some of the things you can find by digging into the history of the period. By enriching your understanding of the times, you can add to and deepen your justifications and find many little touches which will add much to your characterization.

six

Speak the speech, I pray you

A story is told of a famous screen star who applied to Lilian Baylis, founder of the Old Vic, for the position of leading man in the company. When asked if he was *good* in Shakespeare, he answered that he adored Shakespeare and practically slept with a copy of *Hamlet* under his pillow. "That's not the point," persisted Miss Baylis. "Can you say his lovely words?"

Speech is one of the actor's tools. It must be extremely flexible and under strong control. It is an important character element, used to establish regional or foreign background, educational level, class distinctions, occupation (as in the use of jargon), age, physical condition, emotional state. It is used to render nuances and subtle distinctions in meaning as well as to convey the broad, pulsating rhythms of tragic poetry.

The general improvement of voice and diction should be undertaken diligently and over a considerable period of time. And with a good speech teacher. This chapter is not intended to be a compressed speech course but rather to call to your attention certain problems in the speech area which are of special importance to the actor.

Projection

First of all, the actor must be heard. This is so obvious that it is almost embarrassing to write it, but some actors speak on stage as though only the people in the first ten rows had come to hear the play while those in the back of the theatre had come to watch a pantomime. Being heard and understood, says Jean-Louis Barrault, is a matter of "elementary politeness." to one's audience. Anyone can make himself heard simply by shouting, but projection is not shouting. It is possible to project the voice to the balcony of a large theatre without straining or shouting.

Projection involves an adequate and controlled breath supply, resonance, and clear enunciation. Most people breathe very shallowly and speak with a minimum amount of air in the lungs. Their speech has no vitality, no force. Some people use too much breath and expel it too quickly, thereby producing a tone which does not project well.

For a strong, clear tone, the air must be expelled with sufficient steady pressure so that the vocal cords vibrate without quavering or fading at the end of the breath. Proper diaphragmatic breathing will ensure an adequate supply of breath in the lungs, and practice will enable the actor to expel that air slowly and firmly and achieve a clear, sustained tone. Be careful, after taking a deep breath, not to pour it all out with the very first sound you make. You must learn to hold it back and control the flow. Try to sustain the sound "ah" for a count of ten. Don't use any more breath for the first count than for the last, and don't let the tone quaver.

By learning to take a full breath and to control the rate and energy of exhalation, the actor not only improves his projection but increases the amount of sound he can make before taking a new breath. This need is not great in much modern drama that uses the short, broken sentences of our daily speech; but in poetic drama the actor is often confronted with considerably longer phrases which cannot be broken at his discretion. The actor should break the poetic speech into phrases and make certain that he can manage the longest phrase without gasping for breath. The actor breathes through his mouth; a quick, sharp intake of air through the mouth will fill the lungs adequately, and in far less time than it would take to inhale the same amount of air through the nose.

Read the following speech with full voice, pausing for breath at the slant marks.

Wherefore rejoice? What conquest brings he home? /
What tributaries follow him to Rome
To grace in captive bonds his chariot-wheels? /
You blocks, you stones, you worse than senseless things! /
O you hard hearts, you cruel men of Rome,
Knew you not Pompey? / Many a time and oft
Have you climb'd up to walls and battlements,

To towers and windows, yea, to chimney-tops,
Your infants in your arms, / and there have sat
The live-long day, with patient expectation,
To see great Pompey pass the streets of Rome: /
And when you saw his chariot but appear, /
Have you not made an universal shout,
That Tiber trembled underneath her banks
To hear the replication of your sounds
Made in her concave shores? /

Marullus, *Julius Caesar*: I; i.

Also important to projection is resonance, a phenomenon of sound which occurs when a vibrating body sets one or more other bodies into sympathetic vibration. Perfect resonance is attained when the auxiliary bodies are set to vibrating at the same frequency as the initiating body. In speech, the vibrating vocal cords produce a sound which then enters the resonating cavities — the throat, mouth, and nose — and sets in vibration the air in those cavities. These resonating cavities act as an amplifying system and transmit the sound with renewed energy. If the sound is obstructed, either by inflamed mucus membranes or by a lazy jaw which remains half closed, the tone is *damped* and loses clarity and energy.

Exercises for resonance call for the speaker to articulate vigorously, opening the mouth as fully as is necessary for each sound. Sounds should be directed toward the front of the mouth and the hard palate, which serves as a sounding board. Do not swallow the sounds or muffle them with loose jaws and an inactive tongue.

Finally, good projection demands clear enunciation, which should not be confused with pronunciation. Pronunciation is concerned with syllable stress and sound substitution; whether one says "advertisement" or "advertisement," "creek" or "crick" are matters of pronunciation. Enunciation, however, involves the clear articulation of each sound. If you say "prob'ly" for "probably," "reco'nize" for "recognize," "gimme" for "give me," your enunciation is poor. Muddy enunciation severely hampers projection. This does not mean that you should overarticulate to the point of being affected. Your speech can remain natural and yet be enunciated with vigor and clarity. Enunciation is particularly important when playing dialect parts, for if, in addition to new pronunciations and various sound substitutions, the enunciation is sloppy, the audience will understand very little of what is said. The character being played may be uneducated and may say "Whyncha look where ya goin'?" but the actor must enunciate the line clearly so that the audience hears exactly that.

A Standard Stage Speech

In the United States there is no one standard speech which is assumed to be correct for everyone. Rather, there are several standards for different parts of the country. The speech of the educated Southerner will differ in certain respects from that of the educated New Englander, but both will be considered correct. This presents a problem in the theatre, for what happens when a group of actors from different parts of the country are hired to play members of the same family? A mixture of dialects would be ludicrous. It would also be less than desirable to have American regionalisms creeping into a play by Shaw or Shakespeare.

The problem of a standard stage speech has been met by actors who have adopted a speech somewhat similar to Southern British while avoiding pronunciations which are peculiarly British; for example, they will not say "secret'ry" for "secretary." The American actor who follows this practice will not usually flap his *r*, but he will, as in some Eastern speech, drop the final and preconsonantal *r*. Some actors adopt the broad "ɑ" as in *father* for words like *ask — chance — demand — class*; but most actors use "a", the sound heard in the Bostonian's pronunciation of *Harvard*, for that group of words. A substitution frequently used is "I" for "ə" in certain unstressed syllables. The sound "I" is the vowel sound in *bit*, and the sound "ə" is the unstressed sound heard in the first syllable of *above* and in the final syllable of *sofa*. The substitution, in stage speech, of "I" for "ə" occurs generally in unstressed suffixes. One reason for this is that the sound "I" projects better than does "ə." Say the following words with the usual American ending "ə," and then pronounce them with "I."

necklace	coaches	basis
mountain	actress	artist
pirate	packet	limit
pointed	Alice	definite
chicken	solid	lettuce
minute	palace	curtain
bridges	habit	solace

A full and excellent treatment of stage speech may be found in *Applied Phonetics*[1] by Claude Merton Wise. And there are two guides to pronunciation which every actor should own: for American speech, *A Pronouncing Dictionary of American English*[2] by John S.

1. Englewood Cliffs, N.J.: Prentice-Hall, Inc., 1957.
2. Springfield, Mass.: G. & C. Merriam Company, 1953.

Kenyon and Thomas A. Knott; for British Standard, *An English Pronouncing Dictionary*[3] by Daniel Jones. Both volumes use the International Phonetic Alphabet (IPA), which the actor should learn. (Jones uses a few slight variations which are explained in the key.) A knowledge of the IPA is not only necessary to interpret these dictionaries but extremely useful for the study of foreign accents.

A final note on stage speech for the American actor. The process involved is a sort of negative one. The actor must try to eliminate his regional dialect so that he cannot instantly be assigned to a particular section of the country.

Dialects and Accents

A dialect is a variation in pronunciation of a language; there may also be some words which are different or which are used differently, but usually not to a degree to make the dialect incomprehensible to one who speaks the same language. Southern, Eastern, Midwestern, Cockney, and Irish are dialects of the English language. An accent is the result of sounds and stresses which are carried over from another language and which are alien to the language being spoken. If a Frenchman carries the uvular *r* into his speaking of English, he is speaking English with a French accent. He may also put the stress on the wrong syllable in many words.

When faced with a role requiring a dialect or accent, many actors tend to overdo it. They try to make all the sound substitutions possible, and they end up with a caricatured accent or one that is barely understandable. The actor must realize two things: one, that a little suggestion in the theatre goes a very long way — it is not necessary to pour on a thick accent to create a character; and two, that there is no such thing as, for example, *a* Cockney dialect. There are dozens of gradations, depending upon the person's education, the part of London he comes from, the trouble he takes with his speech, and so on. One has only to spend a day in London to hear a bewildering variety of Cockney dialects.

An actor can no more have a stock supply of dialects to be used for any part that comes along than he can have a stock supply of emotions. A dialect or accent must be measured for the specific character. Surely every character will not make every single sound substitution; an educated speaker who has learned a second language will have mastered many sounds in that language and will carry over only certain substitutions.

And please do not learn your dialects and accents from other

3. New York: E. P. Dutton & Company, Inc., 1937.

American actors; this practice encourages a cliché, vaudeville accent. Many American actors would be surprised to learn that the Cockney does not say "die" for *day*. The sound he makes is not one we have in our American speech, and it is difficult to imitate; and so most actors reach for the nearest thing, which happens to be the sound in "die." Pay close attention to the Cockney dialects used in British films and develop a critical ear.

There are a few dialect manuals available[4], but most of them use our own alphabet with distorted spellings to convey the sounds. This offers the student only a very crude notion of the pronunciation. It is impossible to spell sounds which we do not have in our language by using our own alphabet, but by using the IPA it is possible to note exactly any sound made in any language. I refer you again to *Applied Phonetics* by Wise, which is the best book on dialects and accents I know. Using the IPA, he records accurately the sound substitutions made in a number of English dialects and foreign accents.

Yet even this book should be used only as an auxiliary to the learning of an accent or dialect. The most important part of an accent cannot be rendered in a book, and that is its peculiar melody. Without the special lilt, or intonation, unique to each language, the most perfectly executed sound substitutions will fail to be totally effective. Indeed, it is possible to use no sound substitutions at all and successfully convey the feeling of the accent by its melody alone. This is ear training; the actor must listen to speakers with authentic accents. Also, it is important to note that a major factor in creating an accent or dialect is the special idiom used — word substitutions and grammatical changes. These are usually written in by the author and are largely responsible for conveying the flavor of the accent — sometimes more so than the actual sound shifts.

Using the Voice

Amateur actors are fond of making radical changes in their voices. Young people called upon to play old people squeak and cackle and sputter in ways that no respectable old person would ever dream of. They do not realize that these extreme changes produce a voice which is not only not believable in itself but is usually out of harmony with the physical presence of the actor. It is far more effective to capture the slower pace, the effort required to speak, imposed by the shallower breathing of the old person.

Years ago, radio actors did fantastic things with their voices; but

4. A typical one is: Lewis and Marguerite Herman, *Manual of Foreign Dialects* (Chicago: Ziff-Davis Publishing Company, 1943).

voice was all they had to convey absolutely everything about their characters. On stage the actor is seen, and he is at a far greater advantage. His voice does not have to carry the entire burden. A suggestion in the voice, coupled with his make-up, costume, and physical characterization, will permit the audience to participate with their imaginations in the creation of a thoroughly believable character.

There are many ways in which the actor can vary his own voice and neither strain it nor produce an improbable voice. Several factors contribute to the total effect of one's speech. There is *pitch*, determined by the rate of vibration of the vocal cords. To put it simply, the voice gets higher or lower as the vibrations increase and decrease. There is *tempo*, the speed with which we speak. There is *intonation*, the pattern of rising and falling cadences. There is *duration*, the length of time we hold certain sounds. There is *intensity*, the force with which we expel the air from our lungs and cause the vocal cords to vibrate. There is *loudness*, a correlate of intensity; as the intensity increases for a given frequency, the loudness increases. There are *enunciation*, *pronunciation*, and *resonance*, which have been discussed. And finally, there is *quality*, or *timbre*, which refers to the total effect of the sound produced, its distinct and unique combination of all the foregoing which makes it different from any other sound similarly produced.

With so many variables it is easy to see how the slightest adjustment can effect an appreciable change in the actor's speech. The entire quality of the voice can be changed by making it slightly nasal, or harsh, or breathy; and yet the actor needn't depart so far from his normal voice that he becomes uncomfortable.

Try reciting the alphabet with as many different combinations of vocal factors as you can manage. Raise the pitch slightly and slow down the pace; quicken the pace and increase the intensity; lower the pitch and increase the loudness; etc.

Prose Versus Verse

When dealing with modern prose dialogue which clearly resembles our own speech, the actor has considerable leeway in interpretation. There is no meter, no rhythm, no rhyme to impose itself upon his reading. On the contrary, there are usually many dots and dashes which indicate broken sentences, interrupted thoughts, and half-utterances, and whether the actor pauses for a count of two or three will make little difference to the meaning. Moreover, the meaning, in nine cases out of ten, lies not in the words themselves, as we have discovered, but in the subtext underneath the words. The actor must find his actions, which often are at variance with his words. How limited is the actor, really, by this speech?

True? Yes, I suppose — unfit somehow — anyway . . . so I came here. There was nowhere else I could go. I was played out. You know what played out is? My youth was suddenly gone up the water-spout, and — I met you.

Blanche, A Streetcar Named Desire: Scene 9

The prose of a playwright such as George Bernard Shaw is more formally structured and demands more of the actor. Shaw's speeches are finely balanced; words and phrases are set off against each other like mathematical equations. His lines are packed with meaning and words are not wasted. In his case, there is less subtext and more direct meaning riding on the words themselves. If the actor is to make Shaw's speeches intelligible, he must dissect them very carefully, being aware of the points and counterpoints, the phrases which must flow together, the words which will poke out to support or attack an idea. Compare the following speech with the previous one:

The government of your country! *I* am the government of your country: I and Lazarus. Do you suppose that you and a half dozen amateurs like you, sitting in a row in that foolish gabble shop, can govern Undershaft and Lazarus? No, my friend: you will do what pays *us*. You will make war when it suits us, and keep peace when it doesn't. You will find out that trade requires certain measures when we have decided on those measures. When I want anything to keep my dividends up, you will discover that my want is a national need. When other people want something to keep my dividends down, you will call out the police and military.

Undershaft, Major Barbara: Act III

Poetry presents a still greater challenge to the actor, for the meaning of a poem, or a speech in verse, not only resides in the words themselves but is organically interwoven into the entire structure. John Ciardi's excellent book on poetry is entitled *How Does a Poem Mean?*[5] Not *what* but *how*. How does the poet combine the elements of poetry to achieve his effect? How do the words, the sounds, the pace, the images, the rhythm all blend into a single force which not only is inseparable from the meaning but *is* the very meaning itself? The reason a poem cannot be paraphrased, explains Ciardi, is that "the *way in which* it means is *what* it means." Consider the following passage:

5. Boston: Houghton Mifflin Company, 1959.

O all you host of heaven! O earth! what else?
And shall I couple hell? O, fie! Hold, hold, my heart
And you, my sinews, grow not instant old,
But bear me stiffly up. Remember thee!
Ay, thou poor ghost, while memory holds a seat
In this distracted globe. Remember thee!
Yea, from the table of my memory
I'll wipe away all trivial fond records,
All saws of books, all forms, all pressures past,
That youth and observation copied there;
And thy commandment all alone shall live
Within the book and volume of my brain,
Unmix'd with baser matter. Yes, by Heaven!
O most pernicious woman!
O villain, villain, smiling, damnèd villain!
My tables—meet it is I set it down,
That one may smile, and smile, and be a villain;
At least I'm sure it may be so in Denmark:
So, uncle, there you are. Now to my word.
It is "Adieu, adieu! Remember me."
I have sworn't.

Hamlet: I; v.

Shakespeare has taken twenty-one lines to say what easily could have been said in two or three; after all, the speech means nothing more than that Hamlet swears to remember his father. But who would dare try to paraphrase this passage in a few lines of prose? It is obvious that the raw, intellectual meaning is only a small part of the total emotional effect achieved by the building of images, the repetition of sounds (A*nd* thy comma*nd*me*nt* a*ll* a*lo*ne sha*ll live*), and the mounting rhythm (O villain, villain, smiling, damnèd villain!). The impact of these combined forces produces an experience which is far more important and powerful than the mere "message."

Actors who go to extremes in reading verse, who either read it as pure prose or sing it, show little understanding and appreciation of the poet's means of expression. The old worn-out phrase still applies: if the poet had meant it to be read as prose, he would have written it as prose.

Surely any good writer chooses his words carefully, but the poet is especially finicky for he knows that words, apart from their meaning, produce very different feelings when they are uttered. Various kinds of muscular activity go into the production of a word; the very sounds blend or clash. "Feel" the words as you read the following aloud:

Bloody, bawdy villain!
Remorseless, treacherous, lecherous, kindless villain!
Hamlet: II; ii.

The use of plosives and affricates in the above lines lends a harsh, biting quality. Compare the feeling you have when you read:

It is my soul that calls upon my name:
How silver-sweet sound lovers' tongues by night,
Like softest music to attending ears!
Romeo: II; ii.

There are no true synonyms in our language. Most of us use words interchangeably because we are not sensitive to the distinctions between them; but the poet chooses in each instance, from the entire realm of words, the one word which is right for his purpose. No other word will do. The actor, then, must not be content merely to "get the idea across" but must conjure up the specific image which that word, and that word alone, can evoke.

The use of rhythm as an emotional stimulus dates back to antiquity. War dances and chants, rhythmic battle cries, the beat of ceremonial drums, and working chants affected men strongly. Where there were words, those words were incidental to the overriding grip of the rhythm. And since rhythm is such an important factor in the creation of mood and emotion, the actor who sacrifices the rhythm of the verse to the meaning of the words not only is doing the poet a great injustice but is depreciating his performance considerably.

The poet uses various techniques to establish rhythm. He can manipulate the internal pauses, the end-stops, the run-on lines; he can displace an expected accent or insert an extra syllable; he can impede or accelerate a line by the placement of stresses; he can establish a serene mood with a regular, gentle rhythm, or he can create excitement by sudden changes of rhythm. Note how the following lines convey a sense of joyous vigor. The words flow smoothly, and there is a lilting rhythm which lends lightness and excitement.

Oh, speak again, bright angel! for thou art
As glorious to this night, being o'er my head,
As is a wingèd messenger of Heaven
Unto the white-upturnèd wondering eyes
Of mortals that fall back to gaze on him
When he bestrides the lazy-pacing clouds
And sails upon the bosom of the air.
Romeo: II; ii

Compare the foregoing with the broken, choked rhythm, the words which stick and refuse to flow, the harsh sounds of the following:

> Blow, winds, and crack your cheeks! rage! blow!
> You cataracts and hurricanes, spout
> Till you have drench'd our steeples, drown'd the cocks!
> You sulphurous and thought-executing fires,
> Vaunt-couriers to oak-cleaving thunderbolts,
> Singe my white head! And thou, all-shaking thunder,
> Smite flat the thick rotundity o' the world!
> Crack nature's moulds, all germens spill at once,
> That make ingrateful man!
>
> *Lear:* III; ii

This is indeed heightened expression, distilled and intensified to a far greater degree than much of the muttering put into the mouths of many modern realistic characters. The actor reading this sort of verse does not have the liberty to stretch his pauses, to vary his readings, to work around and under his lines as he does with realistic prose dialogue. He must now work directly through the lines themselves; he must capture the pace, the rhythms, the rich imagery of the words. He must rise to his material and match the poet's vision and bravura.

seven

Nor do not saw the air too much with your hand

THE QUESTION OF STYLE

One of the curious things about discussions of style in the theatre is the careful avoidance of any attempt to define the word. As a budding director years ago, I would gather my production crew about me and very sagely say, "I've decided to stylize this play," praying that no one would ask me what I meant. I had some vague feeling that a stylized play was more artistic or creative than an unstylized play. Fortunately, my crew shared my lack of knowledge. Everyone nodded enthusiastic approval, and I imagine that each one, deep down in his heart, felt dismayed at being the only one in the group who didn't really know what style was.

"Stylize the set, Herby. And Mildred, let's get some real style into those costumes!"

And Herby and Mildred would dash off to put together the weirdest bits of nonsense you ever saw on a stage. But we were all pleased because it was quite different from anything we'd ever seen before and we assumed it was the epitome of style.

The actors were immensely pleased to learn that I had decided to stylize the play. They strutted and fluttered and posed and came up with extravagant line readings. They had a marvelous time. The performance was wretched.

What, then, is style? Style is a way of presenting reality. Not the superficial reality of the "real" furniture on stage, but the heart of the play, the real meaning beneath the surface appearances. Affectation, a certain veneer, may give an appearance of finesse, but this is not style. Style is a subtler thing, a deeper thing; style penetrates to the essence, the spirit, the inner truths. To capture the style of a play is to present its reality in its very own way, not by imposing our own or some other reality upon it.

We make a serious mistake if we think that our way — our modern way — of presenting plays is more truthful than other methods in past eras. The Greek audience was as convinced of the truth of *Oedipus Rex* as modern audiences are of *Death of a Salesman*. At one time it was felt that the only way to present truth on the stage was to create a physical environment made of real items from the outside world, an environment so naturalistic that the audience could not fail to be struck by its truth. But such productions were not more truthful than those of Shakespeare's theatre, which used a bare stage and no settings. Truth does not reside in a sofa but in spiritual values, personal relationships, insights into our human condition. If we find these things in a play and express them in the unique manner in which the playwright formulated them, then, and only then, have we found the style of the play.

Does this mean that style is something which belongs to other periods but not to our own? Assuredly not. We are not aware of our own style because most of us persist in thinking of style as something which can be abstracted and superimposed on a production. If we perform a play in our present-day realistic mode, we are playing it "straight," and if it's "straight," it has no style. It's a matter of not seeing the forest for the trees. People a hundred years from now will discuss the "style of the sixties" just as surely as we discuss the Restoration style.

The drama of a particular age is affected by the wants and fears and philosophies and mores of its people, the shape of the playhouses, the technical means of production, the rules or lack of rules of playwriting, the prevalent theories of acting, the audiences who pay to see the plays, and a few dozen other factors. The combination changes in each age, and so the dramatic product can never be quite the same. Each age finds new truths by which it lives and derogates the old truths as old wives' tales. Now God shapes man, now man shapes man, now environment shapes man. The "truth" sways with the times, and the artists in each age strive to present its truths, seeking new forms for their new content. If audiences accept the reality of the artist's statement, then that mode of presenting the truth becomes the dominant style of the period.

Eventually, as values change, the old style is pushed into the background to become history. As it retreats further and further away from us, the details become harder to discern; we only see the major colors, the broad outlines. We copy these, thinking we are re-creating the style of the period, but alas! we have lost the insides. The shell—the sets, the costumes, the poses of the actors—may be exquisitely imitated, but if that is all we have, then we have mistaken the period for the style. Indeed, all we have is a caricature of the period; without the soul of the period, there will be no style.

This is why styles cannot be mixed. If they are, the reality of the play is sacrificed. Shakespeare in modern dress may be a novelty; it may be amusing, even intriguing; but it is no longer what Shakespeare wrote. If a play is truthful, it is because every single one of its elements is inextricably interwoven into the entire scheme. Just as the meaning of a poem cannot be separated from the way in which the poem is constructed, so the meaning of a play rests in the fusion of its elements. And we cannot introduce elements of one period into a play of another period without creating disharmony. The rationale behind such experiments as Shakespeare in modern dress, or Molière in the Victorian period, is usually that the "updating" of the play will make it more meaningful to modern audiences. It is quite the contrary; these productions succeed only in losing the truth of the original drama. If a play has survived the ages, it must be because the truth inherent in it is constantly re-acknowledged by the people of each generation. The play speaks to us because it is precisely what it is. Why change it?

In 416 B.C. Greek audiences saw the first production of *The Trojan Women* by Euripides. Two thousand years later this scathing indictment of war still screams at us with all its original force. The chorus is composed of Trojan women whose city has been ravaged by the Greek armies. The exalted poetry, the rhythmic chants, and the concerted, formally patterned movements of the chorus are as far as possible from our realistic mode, but the wailing lamentations for lost sons and husbands strike profoundly to the hearts of a modern audience. More profoundly, indeed, than if the women were dressed in modern clothes and lamented the loss of loved ones in one of our own recent wars. Yes, there would be a certain truth in such a modern version, but it would be a small truth, the truth of a particular group of women and a particular, personal war. By keeping Euripides' style intact, we reach a higher truth, a purer, more universal statement: the anguish of the Trojan women becomes the anguish of all women of all times bereft of loved ones by the pointless, vicious insanity of war.

Style and the Actor

How does the actor approach the problem of style? Through the character. There is no such thing as a role which does not have to be characterized. The actor must discover the life of his character and not substitute his own reality or meanings for those of his role. Style is the *result* of a fully realized character, a character who lives and breathes within his own specific environment, who is motivated by the whims or pressures of his own society and his inimitable self. The process cannot be reversed; the actor cannot start with style, *he cannot play a style*. Style is that intangible quality we feel about a performance when absolutely everything has clicked into place. The actor achieves it by working with the very tangible aspects of characterization.

Sometimes the actor misses something somewhere along the line. Perhaps his vocal ability does not match the verse, or he does not wear his costume as comfortably as his character should. Occasionally a twentieth-century gesture slips into a sixteenth-century play. It is thus possible to have some characterization without style, but it is not possible to have style without characterization.

Style is not slipped on like a suit. To decide in advance that we will act in a certain style suggests that it is possible to learn a set of conventional gestures or a way of inflecting the voice and impose these mannerisms on every part we play which happens to fall within a certain period. We thereby reduce every character we play to a common denominator instead of searching out the *differences* between characters and creating a unique individual each time.

As an example, an actor learns a "Restoration bow." He practices it until he can do it smoothly and naturally. He will then use this bow every time he appears in a Restoration play. Does this mean he is acting with style? Of course not. Does every person you know shake hands the same way? Isn't it just as absurd to suppose that every character in a Restoration play bows the same way? Does the stern old man bow the same way as the young gallant? Does the gallant bow the same way as the fop? It is the individual characterization which is important, not the blanketing of the performance with mannerisms assumed to be style. If the actor has created his role thoroughly, if he has immersed himself in the period, if he knows how and why his character dresses, talks, and thinks as he does, if he has learned the customs and social graces of the times and does them *as his character would do them*, then his characterization will have style.

In the finest discussion of style I have read, Michel Saint-Denis asks whether the good realistic actor can be a good classical actor.[1] The question is not one of different types of actors, he answers himself, but of different levels of acting. The actor playing Oedipus is not a different kind of actor from the one playing Stanley Kowalski.

1. *Theatre: The Rediscovery of Style* (New York: Theatre Arts Books, 1960).

Both actors need a physical and vocal technique, imagination, sensitivity, an understanding of the psychology of the role. Oedipus is torn with inner conflict, obsessed with a need to find out the truth. The actor playing him needs to understand his drives just as much as the actor playing Kowalski needs to understand his. And surely both actors must be clearly heard by their audience. If one uses cultured speech and refined gestures and the other uses substandard speech and crude gestures, it is because Oedipus is a king, educated and polished, and Kowalski is coarse. Both actors are creating the roles written by the playwrights. Neither one has inherently more style than the other.

Now it cannot be denied that Oedipus is the more difficult role. But there is no reason why a properly trained actor could not play both. Greater demands are made upon the actor playing classical roles. It is easier to slouch about in modern clothes than to wear a king's robes with convincing majesty. And it has already been observed that the reading of verse demands a far greater discipline than the reading of our modern prose. The talented actor with a weak voice may be quite successful in modern roles, but he will not be able to meet the challenge of King Lear's tirades or Oedipus' anguish. Again, it is not that he works differently or is a different kind of actor but that he cannot reach the higher level.

As an illustration of the differences in acting levels, let me describe a moment in the brilliant production of *The Trojan Women* directed by Michael Cacoyannis at New York's Circle in the Square Theatre in 1964. Andromache, having recently lost her husband in the war, had just been told by the Greek messenger that her small son was to be taken from her and killed. The tears and shrieks of despair which might be expected of any mother dealt such a blow would not have been in keeping with the style of this production. A purely "realistic" reaction would have been out of harmony with the formal chorus, the heightened verse, and the direct lines of the tragic action, stripped of all inessential elements, which lifted the tragedy far above the little realities of everyday life. Andromache emitted a series of three wails. The first started as an almost inaudible moan and slowly rose in pitch and intensity. The second started where the first had stopped and rose still higher, a smooth, ascending torment. The third started at the peak of the second and threatened to split the rafters. It was not the cry of a woman; it was bestial, primordial, the consummate expression of the deepest grief of all the world's women together. To express such grief is more difficult than to weep as an individual woman. It does not necessarily require more understanding of a mother's love; it requires a bigger and more fearless technique, a grander level of acting.

MOVEMENT IN PERIOD PLAYS

The actor's movement in a particular play will depend on several things:
1. The style of the play
2. The physical costume
3. The psychology of the costume
4. The manners and customs of the period
5. The character being portrayed

The Style of the Play

While period is almost always a contributing factor to the style of a play, it is not a corollary that the style reflects the period. It is possible for a play about our modern life to be naturalistic, expressionistic, or severely formalized. Likewise, a naturalistic play can be written about the present period or the medieval period.

Compare the style of *Oedipus Rex* with that of Chekhov's *The Sea Gull*. Chekhov's play is filled with the little realities and activities of everyday life. While people are engaged in conversation, they are also sipping tea, setting tables, filling pipes, cleaning spectacles. The actor's movements will be many and varied as he imitates the actions of real people. The action of the Greek tragedy is different. It is abstracted and distilled so that only the quintessence of the conflict remains. Further, it is elevated by the verse and formalized by the use of the chorus. The physical environment does not play an important part as it does in the Chekhov play; the actors in a Greek tragedy are not surrounded with furniture, nor do they involve themselves in side activities while delivering their lines. There is no place for idle, casual movement, for small hand gestures and shrugs. Characters in Greek tragedy are in the midst of stupendous crises from which all superfluity has been shorn. The actor's movements, then, will be sparse and carefully selected, just as the playwright has carefully selected only the most crucial aspects of his story. (This by no means is meant to imply that the portrayal of a Chekhov character requires less selectivity; but the actor in a Chekhov play has a greater variety of realistic detail from which to choose and will also include many, many more movements and activities.) Movement in Greek tragedy will be big and strong to match the majesty of the characters and the bigger-than-life events.

The Physical Costume

If period costumes are made properly, they can be an enormous aid to the actor. Clothing can inhibit or free our movements, affect our posture, our walk, the way we sit. Women in huge farthingales cannot sink into plush sofas, and steel corsets keep the body like a ramrod. Stiff, outsized ruffs make turning the head nearly impossible; men in high heels do not get about as friskily as men in boots; and it is not easy to cross one's legs when wearing padded breeches.

It is important for the actor to know what kind of costume was worn and how it was managed, for the bows, curtsies, and other gestures of a period grew in part out of the nature of the costume.

The Psychology of the Costume

Clothing has rarely been purely functional—that is, simply a protection against the elements. People bow to Fashion more readily than to Rain. Clothing is worn to show rank, status, wealth; it serves the interests of modesty; it encourages sexual attraction. Today, the President of the United States, a wealthy businessman, and a book-keeper all wear similar-looking suits of clothes. In times past, the difference between the clothing of the privileged class and the clothing of the working class was striking. Veblen, in *The Theory of the Leisure Class*, speaks of conspicuous leisure. The leisure class wore clothing which not only was made of the most expensive material, bejeweled, and gorgeously tailored but was designed to show that its wearers did no work. And so the dress of the leisure class became more and more restrictive, as though to *prove* that its members could not *possibly* work. Balloon sleeves hindered arm movements; ruffled cuffs which extended past the hand put manual work out of the question; and hoops and trains allowed women to do little more than stand about and look pretty.

An actor playing an Elizabethan noble or a Restoration wit or an eighteenth-century dandy would stand and sit so that his clothes fell in the most graceful lines. If his cuffs were made of the finest foreign lace purchasable, he would never be caught with his hands behind his back. He would find little things to do—waving a handkerchief, sniffing a rose--which would bring his cuffs into prominence. In short, the actor who knows *why* he is wearing his costume will be on the right track toward discovering how to handle it and how to move in it.

The Manners and Customs of the Period

It is quite possible to get lost in the mass of information available on manners and customs of any given period. The actor must bear in mind that much of what may be historically accurate may also be totally incomprehensible to a modern audience. This does not mean that anachronisms should be introduced but rather that the

The Stage Curtsy

This curtsy is excellent for any period in which the actress is wearing a wide skirt which conceals the leg movement. The effect is a smooth and graceful sinking and rising, but in order to achieve this, the legs wind up looking very like a pretzel. It is used with beautiful effect when an extremely deep curtsy is desired, such as one might make to a queen (or on a curtain call).

The hands are outstretched at the sides, or, if a farthingale is worn, the fingers rest lightly on top of the skirt. With the weight on the left foot, slide the right foot well behind and to the left of the left foot. Sink down, gradually transferring the weight to the right foot until you are sitting on the right leg. The thighs will now be crossed, the left thigh on top of the right. Rise by transferring the weight to the left foot and bringing the right foot back in place. During this entire movement the left foot remains fixed (Figure 2).

THE MEDIEVAL AND TUDOR PERIODS

The Spirit of the Times

The feudal system created a large body of serfs who had all they could do to keep body and soul together. Their life was one long drudgery; they worked hard, and, when given the rare opportunity, they played hard. Thanks to the toil of the serfs, the nobles were freed to hunt and ride and feast and display their finery. The rules were clear-cut and uncomplicated: it was master and servant; and while there was a very great difference between the two, life on the whole was simple and hardy for both classes.

The plays of the period are direct statements without flourishes or entanglements. Characters and situations are drawn with bold strokes and bright colors; subtleties are left for later periods.

The Dress

In the early Middle Ages, dress seemed to be confined to its function as protection against the elements. The accent was on practicality. Men and women wore long, loose robes which permitted freedom of movement. Men who were active—servants, riders—wore knee-length tunics. Often the sleeves either were pushed up from the

Figure 3.

wrist or were short, reaching only halfway down the forearm (Figure 3).

In the later Middle Ages (fourteenth and fifteenth centuries) differences in dress became more exaggerated as the nobility spent more time and money advertising their affluence. Men's robes became voluminous and were trimmed with fur and jewels. The dress of the young men became more formfitting: short tunics, pulled in with a belt; hose; and long, pointed shoes which showed that the feet in them did not carry the owner to work. Sleeves went crazy: some were monstrous balloons gathered at the wrist; others were so long they trailed on the ground (Figure 4).

Women's clothes, toward the latter part of the Middle Ages, also became more formfitting. Waists were pinched, and skirts grew fuller and heavier until they were quite cumbersome (Figure 4).

Manners and Movements

Every man could ride, hunt, shoot, and fish. For some men it was work, for others sport, but for all life was vigorous and full of action. The bearing should be that of an athlete, striding easily from the hips. In the Tudor period, gentlemen's breeches were padded,

Figure 4.

making their walk a sort of straddle; and the most comfortable standing position would have been with the feet planted wide apart.
Padded breeches make crossing the legs when sitting rather difficult.
Besides, these men were interested in showing off their legs to best
advantage, and crossing them does not display them well. The old
term for bowing, by the way, was "to make a leg." (If the breeches
are not padded too thickly, a good stance is the third position: heel of
the front foot to the hollow of the rear foot, a few inches apart, toes
and knees well turned out. The rear knee is bent, and the rear heel
kept very slightly off the ground; the forward leg is straight, and the
weight is evenly divided between both feet.)

Movements should reflect the fact that men enjoyed wearing
their fine clothes, enjoyed showing off. Once you know this, many
gestures will suggest themselves. If you were sporting a magnificent
ring, for instance, you would hold your collar or a fold of your cloak
with the four fingers tucked inside and the thumb, with its sparkling
rider, poked out in full view. If you had a large, bejeweled belt buckle,
you would hook your thumbs in your belt and thus draw attention to your middle. If your sleeves were full and flowing, you would
keep your hands on your hips to achieve the best effect.

Hats stayed on during this period, especially in England. Men sat at table and danced with their hats on. They uncovered for the king, a lord, a lady, or in church.

When greeting each other, men approached with both arms extended and simultaneously grasped each other above the elbows. In this way, no hands were free to grab a dagger. By the Tudor period, men were grasping hands just above the wrist, but not shaking them. Women kissed each other when meeting.

Gentlemen and ladies held hands, as children do, but when leading a queen or some other high-born lady, the gentleman held his hand forward at shoulder level, palm down, and the lady placed her fingertips on the back of his wrist. This method of leading a lady obtains for future periods as well.

Women should maintain an erect posture; corsets keep the torso straight and stiff. Turn from the waist, not the hips, and avoid letting the full skirt sway from side to side. The effect, when walking, should be that the entire costume is floating smoothly along. Women were not yet in high heels.

Bows

The following bow is correct from the fourteenth century onward to men and from the eleventh century onward to women. The hat is swept off and either held close to the hip (inside of hat next to the body) or extended back. A step backward is taken with one foot as though you were going to kneel. A half-bend is executed with both knees, and then you straighten up. If there is no hat, both arms may be swept back to show the flowing sleeves.

Another type of bow may be used in the Tudor period. The hat is removed and is held either at the side or across the body. The right foot lunges straight forward and both knees are bent. Keep the head erect. Straighten up by bringing the back foot up to the front one as the hat is replaced.

When coming before a lord or a sovereign, kneel on one knee. "Both knees for God, one for fellow man."

Curtsy

For the medieval period the curtsy consists of a bend of both knees, the depth of the dip depending upon the rank of the person being saluted. The skirt is held out and lifted slightly, not because it looks cute but because it gets in the way otherwise. The head may be inclined slightly to one side or slightly forward.

THE ELIZABETHAN PERIOD

The Spirit of the Times

The ancients believed that man was controlled by an inexorable and often irrational Fate, but the Renaissance man was presumed to be an intelligent being, free to choose his own path. God had created everything for man's use; the focus of the age was on the experiences, nature, and culture of the individual man. It was an age in which new worlds were being discovered. Shakespeare's England had grown as a world power. Elizabeth's men were sailing all over the globe; prosperity and political stability gave a feeling of confidence and national pride.

The plays of the period reflect the vitality and high spirits of the times. The Elizabethans were lusty and pleasure loving, and virile with a vengeance. The Renaissance hero was idealized to heroic proportions; he was a courtier, a poet, a soldier. He had sensitivity, passion, and sweep. The Elizabethan stage seemed made to accommodate this hero. The bare, open platform allowed the playwright and the actor free rein and fluid action.

The Dress

Elizabethan dress was at odds with the boisterous, active life of the people inside the dress. Clothes were stiff and sturdy; they "could stand up by themselves," says Lyn Oxenford, a leading authority on historical costume. They were restrictive and made movement difficult. Part of the answer seems to lie in the fact that expanded trade brought new materials and fashions from all over the world, and the Elizabethans tried to outdo each other in putting together the wildest costume concoctions. It was not unusual to see someone wearing an outfit made up of parts from several different countries. Many people tried to dress above their station; clothing became extravagant to the point of caricature, and fashions were the butt of much satire. The fashion parade was led by Queen Elizabeth herself, who can be seen in portraits in her monumental farthingale, ruffs which dwarfed her head, great billowing sleeves, and towering collars.

Men and women dressed for display rather than comfort. Just getting dressed in those days was an intricate affair. A lady's dress consisted of two parts: a bodice and a skirt. The bodice was in two parts: a triangular stomacher was attached to the bodice proper and was stiffened with stays to keep the torso rigid. The neckline was either immodestly low or high with a standing collar or ruff around

Figure 5.   *Figure 6.*

the neck. In addition to the stomacher and tight bodice, women wore boned underbodices. The puffed sleeves were separate and were equipped with rolls on the upper part which very nicely prevented one's arm from being held close to the body (Figure 5).

The skirt was given a bell shape by the farthingale worn underneath. This was a series of hoops which started at the waist and got progressively larger toward the ground. High heels were worn indoors from about 1560 onward. Women's outdoor shoes had thick cork soles like "wedgies."

The man's dress consisted of doublet and hose. The doublet was a tight-fitting jacket into which the torso was squeezed. A padded shirt was worn underneath for warmth, and in the last quarter of the sixteenth century the padding swelled until huge, puffy chests were the fashion. Starch, introduced into England in 1560, made possible high-standing collars and stiff ruffs which reached insane proportions. The hose consisted of breeches, still padded, and stockings. The breeches reached to mid-thigh and the hose were held up by "points," or laces, fastened to the waistline. Men's clothes were fantastically decorated. Men also wore corsets (Figure 6).

Manners and Movements

The Elizabethans were obviously indomitable, for in spite of the shackles of their costume, we are constantly told that the period was a mighty vigorous one. Dances were not stately but unbelievably energetic. Physical prowess was given top priority: movement should be virile and boastful, masculine and swaggering, but with a strong sense of cutting a dashing figure, of showing off one's finery. Men's gloves were perfumed and were slashed at the knuckles to allow the rings to show through. Men wore a lot of jewelry, often a ring in one ear. They fingered lockets and jeweled daggers. Swords or rapiers hung on the left hip, and spurs were often worn. Slung from the belt were a purse and a tobacco pouch — tobacco was chewed. Toothpicks were carried about, gilded and ornamented. And little mirrors were tucked in the hatband; these were consulted after a meal to be sure that no particles of food lurked in the beard or moustache. Waist-high canes were popular, and the dandies carried fans.

After the accession of James I (1603), fashion relaxed a bit. Ruffs shrank and lost some of their stiffness. The doublet acquired a more natural waistline, and the padding departed from the breeches. Movement was a lot easier.

For the women, the great problem was maneuvering the farthingale. Skirts were so wide that women often had to go through doors sideways. The hands could not hang at the sides because of the width of the skirt and also because of the rolls on the sleeves. The hands may either rest lightly on top of the farthingale, elbows curved outward, or be gracefully clasped at the waistline. When holding a fan or other object, the hands move away from the body, outside the circle of the farthingale.

Sitting in a farthingale is a complicated matter. The hands must guide the skirt past the chair, and then the back of the skirt is lifted so that it bunches up slightly in the rear. The lady then sits on that part of the skirt which falls behind the knees. When rising, shift the weight to the forward foot so that the skirt falls clear of the chair. It need hardly be said that ladies never crossed their legs. Wenches did, though, since they were less mindful of manners and, more important, free of corsets.

Ladies carried pomanders attached to the waist. These were round metal containers with scent to shield delicate noses from unpleasant odors. Sometimes a small hand mirror hung from a ribbon at the waist, but a better custom for actresses was that of having a little mirror in the fan. This could be used for surreptitious preening and for seeing behind one's shoulder!

After the Elizabethan period, artificial stiffening went out of fashion and skirts became narrower. Movement became more natural.

Bow

Elizabethan bows and curtsies, thanks to all the starch and padding, are stiff affairs. The man stands with the feet straddled (his usual stance), weight on both feet, one foot in front of the other. The hat is removed as both knees are bent. The knees are straightened, and the hat is replaced.

Curtsy

The arms are outstretched to the sides, the hands resting lightly on the edge of the farthingale. Both knees are bent slightly, and the head is inclined toward the person being greeted. Do not lift the skirt. The curtsy is deeper for the queen; remain down until Her Majesty gives you permission to rise. Curtsy again before leaving the queen.

THE RESTORATION PERIOD

The Spirit of the Times

The Restoration period was gaudy, naughty, and exuberant. It was as though people were making up for the time lost during the Puritan reign when diversions such as theatre-going were prohibited. Ladies and gentlemen indulged themselves with fine clothes, amusements, and love intrigues. Servants did all the work, although a lady might make her own cosmetics with pestle and mortar. Gentlemen in London would occasionally tax themselves by writing a letter or sniffing some snuff.

The Restoration comedies were written for a small, sophisticated set of Londoners, and they, too, burst the Puritanical bonds. The frankness in those plays would shock many modern spectators, but the Restoration audiences found them delightful. Actresses, instead of boys, were now, for the first time, playing the women's parts, and this encouraged playwrights to include many more love and seduction scenes. The plots were intricate love triangles (or octagonals). These plays satirized the manners of the court; and the court was the audience. Manners on stage, then, had to be impeccable. There should be about the Restoration play a neatness and precision which reflect the pride and enjoyment the court took in the faultless execution of their many little points of etiquette.

Figure 7.

The Dress

Lyn Oxenford describes the Restoration man as a "gaudy parrot." He wore a dazzlingly decorated square-cut coat which reached to the knees. The cuffs were wide and stiff, with frilly lace which reached to the knuckles. There was also much lace and ruffles on the shirt front and at the throat. The breeches reached just below the knees, a decorative garter was worn on one leg, and sparkling buckles often topped the high-heeled shoes. Red heels, if you please. On his head was a huge and heavy periwig with curls down to the shoulder, and perched atop the wig was a broad-brimmed, plumed hat. After about 1688 all fashionable gents wore a gigantic fur muff attached to the waist by a belt. Watches hung around the neck or were tucked into waistcoat pockets. Men and women carried long, fancy canes. Both men and women also wore small, black patches on the face; these were stars, crescents, and triangles cut from black silk or velvet. Such patches were also worn during the Elizabethan period. Originally they were used to cover ugly blemishes; in time they became a fashion (Figure 7).

The women wore wide, bell-shaped skirts. The waist was still small but not so stiff as the Elizabethan woman's, and the neck and bosom were often quite exposed. High-heeled shoes were worn. For outdoors, milady wore a long, hooded cloak, reaching to the hem of her skirt. In addition to the indispensable fan, the Restoration lady wore pounds of jewelry, rings on every finger, choker necklaces, earrings, bracelets. She often carried a little parasol, a pomander, and sometimes a small, enameled box for sweets (Figure 7).

Manners and Movement

In spite of the frivolity that lurked below the skin, manners on the surface were formal and polished. Even husbands and wives bowed and curtsied to each other. A gentleman greeted a lady by bowing and kissing her hand. (When kissing a lady's hand, do not clutch it and haul it to you. Offer her the back of your hand, she will place her fingertips on it; and you gently draw her hand to your lips.) And only dolts allowed their noses to touch the lady's hand. Merchants and innkeepers bowed when receiving honored guests and when given orders. Servants bowed and curtsied when entering and leaving a room. Male servants bowed with heels together. The lower classes went arm in arm, but a gentleman offered a lady his outstretched hand and she placed her hand on his sleeve. Because of the wide skirt she could not have gotten much closer even had she wanted to.

The general movement for men should be peacocky, which should not be confused with the delicate, mincing movement of the fops in these plays. There is a peculiar tendency to consider all male characters in Restoration comedies as fops. While most men were proud of their fine dress and loved to show off, they also had a masculine strength and self-confidence. There were lots of challenges to duels in those days. But the Restoration man did not have the same robust, athletic swagger as the Elizabethan, for he was in high heels, which modified his walk; he could not stride or bounce about. Moreover, his costume was very heavy and had to be carried and balanced properly.

The attitude of the Restoration man should be manifested in his stance and posture and in the way he sits rather than in a great deal of dashing about. A good, comfortable stance was with the weight on the back foot, the other foot forward and to the side. This position permitted him to address himself to people scattered over a wide area by simply turning from the waist. The wide cuffs did not permit the hands to hang close to the sides; besides, the cuffs were too beautiful to hide, and the hands were kept high, in a pretty pose, to show off the frills at the wrist. Objects were handled deliberately, in a way which brought the lace-trimmed cuffs into focus.

Snuff-taking, for example, was very common and offered gentlemen a fine opportunity to attract attention to themselves and their clothes. It was not simply a matter of snapping open the lid, snatching a pinch of snuff, and popping the box back into the pocket. Oh, no, it was like a Japanese tea ceremony. The box was carried in the waistcoat pocket and brought out with a flowing, deliberate movement. Before the box was opened, the lid was tapped to make the grains which clung to the top drop back into the box. Very expensive stuff, snuff. A pinch was taken with the thumb and second finger and either applied directly to the nostrils or placed on the back of the left hand, which was then lifted to each nostril in turn. (And do not sneeze afterward or you will betray your poor breeding.) When the box was returned to the pocket, the cuffs and shirt frills were flicked with a handkerchief, for snuff stains were difficult to remove.

When sitting, always maintain an erect posture; never slouch. Make sure the coat falls in a graceful line. In pictures you will notice men sitting on the edges of chairs so that the coat falls in a straight line below the seat of the chair and does not bunch up between the back of the chair and the back of the breeches. And do not cross the legs; keep one foot forward and to the side of the other, both toes well turned out. The hands may rest atop a cane, or one hand may rest on the hip while the other is posed at chest height, showing off some rings.

At this time men started taking off their hats in the house, although they continued to dance in hats until the end of the eighteenth century. Tobacco was smoked only at home.

Gentlemen's movement was all flourishes. Nothing was done casually, or "thrown away," unless the person sought to convey the effect of deliberate casualness. Men did not just stand around, they always posed. The extreme fops carried this to a ludicrous degree, with too much waving of the handkerchief, greater flourishes, mincing walks, and even a quick snap of the head to flick their curls away.

The same feeling for showing off the costume was shared by the ladies. Very much aware of all their charms, they flirted and fluttered and completed every silken movement with a pretty pose. There was much lifting of the skirts, for sitting, curtsying, and getting around corners. The fan was used constantly. There was a whole language of the fan; milady peeked out from behind it, hid behind it, tapped a naughty knuckle with it, gave signals with it. Handkerchiefs had reached a fantastic elegance, especially those made in France. They were of exquisite hand-wrought lace in various shapes, sometimes ornamented with jewels. In the eighteenth century women began to use colored handkerchiefs. These handkerchiefs were, of course, less functional than ornamental. They gave the lady a pretty excuse for waving, and they were superb for accidental dropping near a gentleman.

Bows

Step back with bent knee, hollow of the rear foot in line with the heel of the forward foot as in the stage bow, but this time not quite so far back and with less vigor. After bowing, straighten and bring the forward foot back to the rear foot as though you were taking a step backward. This is just the reverse of the stage bow in which the rear foot is brought up to the forward foot. Several things may be done with the hands while executing this bow: (1) the right hand is brought to the heart; (2) the right hand is placed on the heart before the bow is begun; as you step back and bow, the right hand is brought down before you, palm up, as if to lay your heart at her feet; sweep the hand up with a flourish as you straighten; (3) the right hand takes the hat, which is carried under the left arm, and sweeps it back at arm's length, but low, on the right side; return hat on rising.

A special bow, termed *en passant*, is used when you are out walking and wish to greet someone without actually stopping to talk. Wait until you are level with the person; turn in to him slightly and bow from the waist while sweeping one foot in an arc in front of the other without stopping the walk. A variation is to sweep the foot behind the other; but in either case, the foot swept around is the one nearest the person you are greeting. The other leg is bent slightly to allow for a smooth sweep. The lady makes the same bow, adding a little wave of her fan.

THE VICTORIAN AND EDWARDIAN PERIODS

The Spirit of the Times

Mention of the Victorian era brings melodrama to mind. This form of theatre dominated the stage. The story line was strong and clear, the characters were broad types, and their actions were fairly predictable. There was the helpless heroine, the dauntless hero, the foilable villain; there were railroad tracks, lost mortgages, sudden bequests from unknown uncles. There were thrills, suspense, asides, and soliloquies. Movements were broad and direct. Today we often see Victorian melodramas burlesqued. They shouldn't be.

The stage hero embodied the chivalric code which Victorian

Figure 8.

gentlemen had embraced. Man was the Protector, and woman was there to be protected. The characters in these plays were black or white; and the plays were highly moralistic, another reflection of the life of the times. Girls were sent to finishing schools and were taught to lower their eyes and to blush when any indecent remark was overheard — and almost any remark was considered indecent. The language was filled with euphemisms.

The Dress

Dress during the nineteenth century underwent many changes. Fads in fashion flourished for ten years or so and then vanished. At the start of the century women revealed their shape by wearing no more than two layers of clinging chiffon; as the century progressed, however, they became more and more upholstered. The skirt continued to be cumbersome. (It did not become practical until the first decade of the twentieth century, when many women were working and needed practical clothing.) By 1845 as many as ten petticoats were being worn to hold the skirt out. Soon afterward, the crinoline removed much of the weight but still retained the shape (Figure 8).

Figure 9.

By 1870 the crinoline left and the bustle appeared. The rear thrust of the bustle caused the upper half of the body to be inclined forward to maintain balance. The front of the skirt became tighter and revealed the outline of the leg from the thigh to the knee (Figure 9). This dress is supposed to have driven men wild, for heretofore the bell-shaped skirt hid any hint of a lady's legs. Women considered themselves terribly seductive in this outfit; a sway developed to call attention to the hips, and a good forward stride was used to make sure the legs pushed against the skirt and were clearly outlined. Hats were extreme — either gargantuan or petite. Shoes were slipperlike with blunt toes.

Men's clothing had radically changed by this time. Industry, like a monster vacuum cleaner, had drawn most of the men into its offices. Men relinquished their feathers and ruffs for more practical wear. Even the colors were toned down. The heavy, ornamented coat was now a soft frock coat in which one could move comfortably. Breeches and hose were replaced with trousers (Figure 8). It is interesting to note that the need for more practical clothing did not altogether dispel men's desire for dash and color and for occasional opportunities to display themselves. For during this time when daily dress became rather drab (compared with previous times), there was a significant development in sporting clothes. Special costumes were created for bicycling, tennis, golf, picnics, which gave our man a chance to glitter on weekends. Of course, there were still dandies and gentlemen of leisure, but they displayed not so much a different kind of costume as a finer one—more expensive cloth, diamond stickpin.

Manners and Movements

Manners were still very formal. Bows and curtsies were used until 1870, but by 1840 handshaking was seen. In the 1890's a high, exaggerated handshake was fashionable. Ladies shook hands out of doors but continued to curtsy indoors until the crinoline went out of fashion. (Always curtsy to royalty, whatever the period.) By 1804 it was customary for a lady and gentleman to link arms when walking. Before that time only the lower classes linked arms.

The Victorian man was the "boss" at home and in society. He moved with strong self-assertiveness. He stood solidly, his legs straddled. This does not mean that he moved heavily or awkwardly, for graceful movement was taken to be a sign of good breeding, and it is surely possible to move gracefully and yet with masculinity. When standing, one hand was sometimes held on the heart, or it held the lapel of the coat; the other hand might be held behind the back, bent at the elbow, or it might hang at the side. When sitting, it was as though he were rooted to the earth. The feet were planted on the floor about two feet apart. One hand might be on the knee, elbow out; the other hand might be fingering the watch fob. Men carried canes.

A gentleman was on his finest behavior in the presence of ladies, showing them the utmost courtesy. He opened doors, brought refreshments, stood when ladies entered, and catered in every possible way. Men only lounged or crossed their legs in the company of other men, never when with ladies. Nor did they smoke in front of the ladies until after 1900. Ladies did not smoke in public until about 1912.

Feminine psychology had not changed so much that women were no longer interested in being attractive and in showing off their newest dress. Until the bustle came in, women faced the perennial problem of dealing with wide skirts—guiding them through doors, sitting in them, floating in them about the furniture without knocking things to the floor. The torso was kept erect and a smooth movement was cultivated, helped now by the flat shoes, so that the woman looked as though she were gliding along on skates.

During this time, trains appeared at the bottom of skirts. When turning in a train, it is necessary to pause and raise the train with the foot just enough to move it behind you. The movement should be hardly noticeable, and the ankle should not be seen. Do not kick the train, unless you are angry.

Girls in the Victorian era learned "deportment," how to be "ladylike." They practiced walking with a steel backboard to ensure an absolutely straight back. Stiff corsets aided and abetted. They never crossed their legs when sitting. They learned to exercise self-control, to be polite, and never to show anger or any sort of rudeness. However, it was perfectly proper to scream and faint if some gentlemen in the company were engaged in a violent altercation. Young girls were thought to be forward if they looked anyone straight in the eye, and so they sat with eyes downcast and head lowered. They perfected a knack of raising the eyes to a gentleman while keeping the head drooped.

Pince-nez were used now. Women wore them on a chain attached to the bosom of the dress; men wore them on a black ribbon attached to the buttonhole of the coat.

Servants curtsied and bowed before and after an announcement. The butler bowed from the waist, heels together, hands at the sides with the back of the hands facing front.

Bows

As in previous periods, the bow was used to denote the social standing of the recipient; the bow got deeper as the recipient got more important. Gentlemen bowed to the assembled group when entering a room. During the nineteenth century the bow gradually changed to what we do today. In the early part of the century one foot was placed in front of the other, the front heel slightly raised; the bow was from the waist. Both hands were placed on the heart. A little later, gentlemen bowed while standing in third position (heel of one foot to hollow of the other) with one hand to the heart. During the latter half of the century the heels were put together and eventually the hands were dropped to the sides. Precise information for these changes is difficult to obtain. Actors must be guided by the spirit of the play.

Curtsies

While skirts are still billowing, the stage curtsy may be used. However, when the crinoline is worn, the curtsy develops a bit of a flourish. Instead of a straight sinking down, a little side movement is taken before the dip. Slide the right foot to the side, knee bent, and let it take the weight. Now bring the left foot behind the right (third position), and bend the knees with the weight on the rear foot. Straighten the knees and point the right toe as the body and head lean slightly backwards from the waist and towards the right. The curtsy has four counts: the side movement, the dip, the pointing of the toe, the recovery. A variation of this curtsy emphasizes the pointed toe: the left foot is brought behind the right as before, but instead of a bending of both knees, the left foot takes the weight as the right is stretched out obliquely with the toe pointed.

As skirts become narrower, the curtsy changes. As long as the skirt is full enough to conceal the bent knee, the above curtsy may be used. However, when the skirt is narrow enough to break at the knee, a modification is used to ensure a smooth line. The skirt is lifted slightly at the sides, and a backward step is taken. The weight is shifted to the back foot, the forward leg being kept straight. In this way the skirt will flow in an unbroken line from the waist to the floor. Keep the ankle concealed.

These periods have been selected because they are the ones with which the actor most commonly has to deal. If you find yourself in a play of another period, your research should follow the pattern set forth above. Learn as much as you can about the spirit of the times; find out exactly what kind of clothing was worn and why; and learn the special rules of etiquette that apply to the period. And whether you are using your own research or some of the material offered here, remember that these manners and movements are only a point of departure; they are meant to exemplify, to typify. You must shape them to your character; you must individualize them.

SOURCES

While all the books listed contain useful information, *Manners and Movements in Costume Plays* and *Playing Period Plays* are addressed specifically to the actor, describing the manners and movements of the periods, with particular reference to their execution on stage, the ways of handling costumes, and a wide variety of activities, games, and occupations which were practiced in each period.

Brooke, Iris. *Costume in Greek Classic Drama*. New York: Theatre Arts Books, 1962.
_____. *English Costume from the Fourteenth Through the Nineteenth Century*. New York: The Macmillan Company, 1937.
_____. *Western European Costume and Its Relation to the Theatre*. Vol. 1: Thirteenth to Seventeenth Centuries: Vol. 2: Seventeenth to Mid-

Nineteenth Centuries. London: G. G. Harrap and Company Ltd., 1934.

Chisman, Isobel, and Raven-Hart, H. E. *Manners and Movements in Costume Plays*. London: H. F. W. Deane and Sons, 1934.

Eichler, Lillian. *The Customs of Mankind*. New York: Garden City Publishing Company, 1937.

Flugel, J. C. *The Psychology of Clothes*. London: The Hogarth Press Ltd., 1950.

Hurlock, Elizabeth B. *The Psychology of Dress*. New York: The Ronald Press Company, 1929.

Lester, Katherine M. *Historic Costume*. Peoria: The Manual arts press, rev. 1942.

Oxenford, Lyn. *Playing Period Plays*. London: J. Garnet Miller Ltd., 1958.

Parsons, Frank A. *The Art of Dress*. New York: Doubleday, Doran and Company, Inc., 1928.

eight

The product

It is now time to put everything together, to blend all the individual elements and techniques we have discussed into a smooth, coherent, organic presentation. This involves the choice of scenes for practice, the techniques of rehearsing, and the problems involved in keeping the part fresh and alive during performance.

CHOOSING PRACTICE SCENES

You must start with simple scenes and gradually work your way up to characters and situations which are more complex and finally to scenes which demand verse and difficult styles. Do not leap right into Greek tragedy. Let your first scenes have characters who are not overcomplicated, not torn by ambivalence nor weighted with abnormal psychological problems. Let them be fairly ordinary people, as close to your own age as possible, whose actions and objectives are straightforward and not devious, ambiguous, and difficult to figure out. This does not mean to imply that there will be no characterization, that you will be playing yourself. Every role must be characterized, but we'll save the more distorted and heightened characters for later.

Practice scenes are not included in this book because, given such material, the student will almost invariably do the scene without reading the rest of the play. A bad practice. The scene is part of the whole; what comes before and after has a very direct bearing on the scene. The student must interpret the scene in the light of the entire play. There will be many clues to characterization in other parts of the play which will be lost to the student who attempts to do the scene without studying it in context.

Here are some plays which contain excellent scenes for our first round.

Advise and Consent (Loring Mandel)
Ah, Wilderness! (Eugene O'Neill)
All My Sons (Arthur Miller)
All Summer Long (Robert Anderson)
The Apollo of Bellac (Maurice Valency)
Best Foot Forward (John Cecil Holm)
Born Yesterday (Garson Kanin)
Burning Bright (John Steinbeck)
The Caine Mutiny Court-Martial (Herman Wouk)
Career (James Lee)
Come Back, Little Sheba (William Inge)
A Cook for Mr. General (Steven Gethers)
The Cradle Song (G. Martinez-Sierra)
Darkness at Noon (Sidney Kingsley)
Detective Story (Sidney Kingsley)
The Diary of Anne Frank (Frances Goodrich, Albert Hackett)
Dream Girl (Elmer Rice)
Five Finger Exercise (Peter Shaffer)
For Love or Money (F. Hugh Herbert)
The Fourposter (Jan de Hartog)
The Girl on the Via Flaminia (Alfred Hayes)
Girls in Uniform (Christina Winsole)
Golden Boy (Clifford Odets)
A Hatful of Rain (Michael Gazzo)
Hay Fever (Noel Coward)
Holiday for Lovers (Ronald Alexander)
Home of the Brave (Arthur Laurents)
Janus (Carolyn Green)
John Loves Mary (Norman Krasna)
Journey's End (R. C. Sherriff)
King of Hearts (Jean Kerr, Eleanor Brooke)
Liliom (Ferenc Molnar)
Look Homeward, Angel (Ketti Frings)
The Male Animal (James Thurber, Elliott Nugent)
The Man (Mel Dinelli)
Mary, Mary (Jean Kerr)
The Moon Is Blue (F. Hugh Herbert)
No Time for Sergeants (Ira Levin)

Oh, Men! Oh, Women! (Edward Chodorov)
Our Town (Thornton Wilder)
A Palm Tree in a Rose Garden (Meade Roberts)
Picnic (William Inge)
The Rainmaker (N. Richard Nash)
The Shy and the Lonely (Irwin Shaw)
Three Men on a Horse (John Cecil Holm, George Abbott)
Time Limit (Henry Denker, Ralph Berkey)
The Time of the Cuckoo (Arthur Laurents)
The Time of Your Life (William Saroyan)
Two for the Seesaw (William Gibson)
The Voice of the Turtle (John van Druten)
Waiting for Lefty (Clifford Odets)
Wedding Breakfast (Theodore Reeves)
What Price Glory? (Maxwell Anderson, Laurence Stallings)
The Young and the Fair (N. Richard Nash)

When such scenes as these have been handled successfully, move on to the more disturbed characters, the ones requiring deeper and subtler justifications, the ones with the more severe internal conflicts. Choose scenes from plays by:

Tennessee Williams	Anton Chekhov
Lillian Hellman	Eugene O'Neill
Henrik Ibsen	Friedrich Duerrenmatt
August Strindberg	Jean-Paul Sartre

Next move on to plays which require a polish and finesse, such as those by Oscar Wilde; then see if you can wring all the meaning out of the speeches of George Bernard Shaw. Try next scenes which demand a knowledge of the manners and movements of specific periods, scenes from plays by Nikolai Gogol, Carlo Goldoni, Molière, Federico Garcia Lorca, and the Restoration playwrights. And, finally, attack the verse plays of Maxwell Anderson, Christopher Fry, Shakespeare, and the Greek tragic poets.

Finding Plays

Plays we've read, seen, or heard about have a habit of eluding us when we are rattling our brains trying to think of a good scene to do. I pick up the nearest book on the history of the theatre or on dramatic criticism and turn to the index. There I find a long list of the plays which are mentioned or discussed in the book, and that serves as a wonderful memory refresher.

Treasure troves of plays are available in catalogues from the following:

Applause Books
211 West 71st Street
New York, NY 10023

Dramatists Play Service
440 Park Avenue South
New York, NY 10022

Samuel French
45 West 25th Street
New York, NY 10001

And of course the blessing of our age is the paperback book. Individual plays and anthologies are available for pennies. They appear faster than anyone can list them, and cover the entire spectrum of dramatic literature.

REHEARSALS

You can tell much about an actor by his attitude toward rehearsals. When you find an actor who is bored with rehearsals and cannot wait to reap the glory of performance, you may scratch him from your list of serious actors. The conscientious actor will usually complain that the rehearsal period is nowhere near long enough. And, in truth, he is right. Bowing to assorted commercial and union pressures, American producers and actors have set a four-week limit to rehearsal time on a straight play. Then follows an out-of-town tryout period before paid audiences. This is often a frantic spell during which the actor is getting adjusted to the set and the costumes (which he sees for the first time when he arrives at the first out-of-town theatre) and the playwright is making cuts, additions, and changes in his script. It is not unusual to have daily rehearsals at which the actor is handed pages of new dialogue which he must learn for the evening's performance. The rewriting and reworking of scenes may go on for the entire tryout period, which may be two weeks or two months. All this hectic carrying-on makes it difficult for the actor to continue to deepen his own role. What hasn't been done in the first four weeks of rehearsal may remain undone.

We read of the Moscow Art Theatre rehearsing one play for several months. No opening date is set; the play is shown when the actors and the director feel it is ready. Most American actors are prostrated by the thought of such a long rehearsal period. The customary explanation is that Americans just do not have the "temperament" for protracted rehearsals. Apparently the American temperament favors the crisp, practical, businesslike approach: snap to, get the job done, and move on. Efficiency! Perhaps that's why America has produced more great businessmen than great actors.

When we consider the phenomenal amount of work required to create a role, we realize that we have not a moment of rehearsal time to waste. This is the actor's creative period — far more creative than the actual performance — and it requires all his concentration plus an admirable amount of discipline. He must learn to use rehearsal time to its fullest advantage.

Why do I make an issue of this? Isn't the director responsible for conducting the rehearsals? Why must the actor have his own rehearsal technique? Because he will be working with many different directors and must learn to get the most out of rehearsals regardless of his director's approach. Some directors excel at the visual aspects of production—design, costumes, movement and grouping of actors—but do not know how to help the actor with his characterization. There are other directors who speak to the actor in terms of results or quality desired. "I want this scene to be much faster and brighter," they say; and we already know what happens when an actor tries to be fast and bright. The actor given this sort of direction must go home and try to understand what the director really means. He will not just "become" fast and bright at the next rehearsal, but he will figure out the actions and justifications that will produce the result the director wants. Thus the director is happy and the actor is working organically and creatively. This is why the actor must have a thorough grasp of play and character analysis and must know how to determine his own actions, objectives, and justifications.

Most directors appreciate the actor who brings new ideas to each rehearsal, who is not afraid to try new things. Regard the creation of a role as the sculptor regards the creation of a statue. He starts with a huge block of marble and gradually trims away what he doesn't need. Bring everything you can think of to your role. Fill it to overflowing with character elements and business. You'll never know whether something is going to work until you've tried it in rehearsal with your fellow actors. After a while, you will begin to discard, select, and heighten, until you are left with an artistically edited characterization which is neither cluttered with irrelevancies nor lacking essentials.

When I say to be inventive, to bring everything you can think of to rehearsals, I don't mean all at once. I mean systematically. A monstrous error made by some actors is to strive for performance level early in rehearsal. They try to do everything at once, perhaps because they are afraid they will not have enough time, perhaps because they are insecure and want to "set" their performance as quickly as possible. Some directors push their actors to reach for full emotional intensity at early rehearsals; this is a grievous mistake, for it can only result in the actor's forcing a quality. If your director pushes you, you must push back (gently and tactfully) by explaining that you don't work that way. Rehearsals are not performances; it is the actor's right to use rehearsal time to experiment and to practice. For this reason certain wise directors forbid any visitors to attend rehearsals, for that actor is superhuman who can resist the temptation to start performing when a stranger enters the hall. Who knows who he is? He may be a casting agent.

The first day or days of rehearsal are normally given to round-table readings of the play and discussions. In our American system of casting, the actor has usually auditioned several times — for the director, again for the producer, then for the playwright, once again for all together — which means that he has had the script for a reasonable amount of time and has been able to reread it and study it before the first rehearsal is called. It is therefore impractical to have someone read the play to the assembled company for the "first" time as I have earlier suggested. (In a repertory theatre this technique would be feasible, for the performing company would be the same for each play, obviating the need for the current clumsy casting procedure.)

Having studied the play in advance, then, the actor should come to the first rehearsal prepared to contribute to the discussion. He will listen to the director's concepts and learn how closely they correspond to his own. Minor differences will be compromised during rehearsals, but please remember that, no matter how strongly you may disagree with him, the director is boss. It is his job to coordinate the entire production, and his decision must be final. Major differences had better be discussed immediately, for if you feel that you cannot possibly play the part the way the director wishes, you had better withdraw from the cast. (Otherwise, you'll be fired anyway.) This is asking an incredible sacrifice of the young actor, but if he tries to force himself into the director's image of the part, he will assuredly turn in a wretched performance, and since we Americans are a devoutly practical people, it would be wiser for our aspiring actor to be seen in a part he does well.

Rehearsal Objectives

Before dress rehearsals are reached, each scene should have been rehearsed many times. Don't just run through the scene each time; use each separate period to explore a single facet. If each element of a scene is discovered and made solid, the entire scene with all its complexities will blend effortlessly. You must not rush.

No one can tell you how many rehearsals should be spent on each facet of a scene; that depends on the problems in the scene and the relative ease or difficulty each presents to the actor involved. I suggest you get your actions and objectives down first, since everything you do will spring from these. For the first few times train all your efforts on playing your actions and making your objectives organic for you. You will be deepening your justifications all through the rehearsal period and, if you are a thinking actor, during performance as well.

When you are thoroughly convinced of your actions and objectives, start to probe the other areas. Use at least one whole rehearsal to work on the environment. Don't worry if your actions are not played fully this time; they will return in force when you need them. For now, exhaust the possibilities of the surroundings: what can you use, what can you react to, do you like this place, have you been here before? If the scene poses a special problem, such as jungle heat, go through the entire scene once concentrating just on that.

You may have a physical adjustment in the play—a limp, an aged walk—which will need careful practice so that it becomes second nature. You should also use everything you can to help you get the feel of your character and of the period. We have spoken of the great effect which costumes have on the actor, yet most companies never see their costumes till dress rehearsal. You simply cannot rehearse a Restoration lady in slacks and sneakers. Some producers will provide substitute costumes for rehearsals so that the actors can get used to moving about in long skirts, hoops, or bustles. If these are not offered, do not hesitate to provide your own; you can make a long skirt with an inexpensive piece of muslin. It is vital that you learn to be comfortable and to move gracefully in period clothes. Shoes are important, too, for they affect our manner of walking and our entire carriage. Don't rehearse in flats if you'll be wearing high heels in performance.

Some directors demand props, or at least substitute props, very early in rehearsal. If props are not available, bring your own. The clumsy handling of a prop can spoil an entire scene. It is rank amateurishness not to have these technical elements under absolute control.

Now take a rehearsal or two and forget everything you've worked on. Do next to nothing yourself but concentrate your entire attention on your stage partner. You will be amazed to learn what he has come up with during the time that you were so totally absorbed with your problems! Use these rehearsals to strengthen your relationship. Find out what he is doing, how and why, and react solely to him. You will suddenly find yourself with a wealth of new material.

A Syllogism

All people have days when they don't feel like working.
Actors are people.
Therefore: Actors have days. . . .

This may strike you as a rather obvious bit of logic, but it has important overtones for the actor. While the salesman and the office worker must force themselves through the day with aspirin and black coffee, producing a bumper crop of mistakes, the actor can actually benefit from an off day. Honoring our philosophy of never forcing counterfeit emotions or playing qualities, it will not do for the actor to bludgeon his way through scene after scene. Feeling totally uninspired, he will drag through the rehearsals listlessly and indifferently. He will do little more than repeat mechanically what he did in the previous rehearsal, thereby wasting precious time and offering no help whatever to his fellow actors.

Rather than fight your mood, *use* it. We always feel better when we indulge our ill humors; the attempt to quell a mood binds us, whereas the pampering of it offers us a release and, indeed, a source of energy which we use to vent our mood.

This does not mean that you should march into rehearsal and growl and carry on and display the fact that you are out of sorts. Your creative colleagues will hardly appreciate that. Keep your problems to yourself, but plunge into your scenes. Your mopes will give a slightly different edge to your actions, a little twist to your justification. And the chances are superb that you will accidentally discover a new color for the scene. For you have entered into the rehearsal with a new vigor. Instead of dividing your concentration between the scene and the outside event which brought on your mood, you have directed all your pent-up annoyances and energies into the playing of your role, and the extra dimension which is thus added to that day's rehearsal will supply a considerable note of interest. You see, having analyzed the scene and decided on your actions and objectives, you will very often, in an effort to deepen what you have already set, put up an unconscious barrier against new ideas. You must always be on the lookout for new shadings. For example, in a scene of great merriment you may discover one small moment when a touch of sadness (which had never occurred to you to try before) will add a useful nuance.

If this seems a daring idea, and one that runs counter to most accepted theories, I remind you that acting is a daring task demanding fearless individualism. The only inviolable rule for the actor is that the audience must believe him. For the rest, he's on his own to break or re-make all the other "rules" according to his own needs. Now it may be that by indulging your mood during one rehearsal you will simply vent your spleen and discover absolutely nothing new for your role. At least the rehearsal will not have been any more wasted than if you had dragged through it half-heartedly. It's better to be in the full bloom of your gloom, but at least to be alive and organic, than to walk robotlike through a rehearsal dead from the neck up. In the first instance you can harbor a secret hope that you *may* come up with something you can use; in the second instance you know before you start that you'll be wasting your time.

Improvising the Script

Some directors use an improvisational technique for rehearsing a play. They discourage the actors from learning their lines too quickly and spend time exploring the situations with them. This is a very exciting and creative way to work, though for directors who gain a sense of security by seeing the play neatly blocked and by having the actors know the lines cold at an early stage of rehearsal, the technique is frightening.

The improvisational technique for rehearsing a scene uses the author's characters, situations, actions, but the actor's own words. As we have previously suggested, memorized lines are perhaps the greatest hindrance to the exploration of relationships, environments, actions, and all the other ingredients of a scene. The tendency to "play the words" and not to fill in between them, under them, and all around them is very nearly irresistible.

The written scene is used as an outline. Let it guide you, but do not hesitate to amplify certain elements as you improvise if you feel compelled that way or if you feel you have not exhausted all the possibilities. The scene in which you tease the girl may only be a few lines as written, but by improvising on it and prospecting the many means and ways of teasing, you will eventually be able to select the most suitable, the most exciting, the most interesting means of expression.

Caution: Always remember that your first obligation is to the playwright. That bit of inspiration which strikes you during an improvisation may truly be the funniest bit of business since Don Quixote got caught in the windmill, but if it's wrong for your character, you must discard it.

Etiquette

Readying a play for production is a complex affair, depending as it does upon the contributions of so many different people. If rehearsals are to run efficiently, with each member of the company having the maximum opportunity to prepare his offering, there must be true teamwork. There is no room for prima donnas, temperament, or any other of the colorful but disconcerting displays which are the mainstays of Hollywood representations of theatrical rehearsals. As work progresses, costume designers, prop men, and lighting technicians begin to appear. You may be measured for costumes between your scenes or fitted with a partially made cloak; the prop man may want to know if this cane suits you or if these spectacles fit properly; the director may totally ignore your efforts in a scene while he explains to the lighting designer the effects he would like to have. All these things beg your utmost cooperation and patience.

A cardinal commandment, never to be broken, is this: Do not direct your fellow actors. With the very best intentions, actors have buttonholed a colleague in the wings and said, "You know, in that scene you have with Abigail, you could get a great laugh if you would. . . ." This is not your business. The other actor and the director will attend to his characterization; you worry about your own. Still worse is speaking to an actor with whom you are playing a scene and telling him that you need a certain reaction from him in order for you to make a point or that you would like him to say his line in such-and-such a way so that you may respond in a particular manner. You will incur his everlasting wrath, ire, enmity, indignation, and annoyance. He will feel, rightly, that you are being selfish about the matter and are using him for your own gain. He has a right to create his character in his own way, and your job is to react to what he offers you.

Now it may be that your suggestion is a legitimate one which will enhance the scene as a whole. Take it to the director. Let him arbitrate, choose, sanction, reject. The final decision is going to be his anyway; by going to him at the outset, you will help preserve the harmony of the company.

Between Scenes

If you have a relatively small part, there will be days when you will not be required on stage for hours at a stretch. Don't goldbrick. Use every minute. It is horrifying to note the number of actors who, during dress rehearsal, announce, "I'm going out front to watch Myrtle's scene; I've never seen it." Never seen it! As though the only scenes that mattered were the ones in which they appeared. It is important to watch the rest of the play during rehearsal, for the more you understand of what is being done to the play as a whole, the better will you be able to fit your character into the scheme.

Also, if you have spent your time between scenes swapping funny stories with the other actors, you establish an anti-work mood, and it becomes doubly difficult to buckle down to serious effort when you finally do get on stage. There is no end to the amount of work you can do on your part, and you should be ashamed to claim that you have nothing to do between scenes.

One sure thing to keep you busy during off moments is a duel or a fight scene. There can never possibly be enough formal rehearsal time for these scenes, for they take hours of careful preparation, and the director cannot spare all the time needed. The duel must be carefully choreographed, and then the actors must work by themselves. There are few moments in a production more galling than the ones in which actors pretend to duel, keeping a goodly distance from each other and clacking their swords now this way, now that. A duel should be a high point in the play. What is more exciting, more theatrical than a sword fight in deadly earnest? It is unkind and unprofessional to cheat the audience with a bumbling, amateur display.

If no one in the company knows how to fence, the services of an instructor should be obtained and the fight blocked step by step. It must then be rehearsed in slow motion many, many, many times. Those people who play musical instruments will appreciate the value of practicing slowly. Speed comes of itself along with the absolute certainty of the moves. I sport some beautiful scars as a testimonial to an improperly rehearsed duel scene. There is no margin for error in a staged sword fight or a fist fight, no room for a suddenly inspired tricky move; this is one time when, feel like it or not, you've got to repeat things exactly. Every thrust, every bit of footwork must be counted and measured precisely, and no deviation can be tolerated. With many slow rehearsals you can offer an extremely complicated, realistic, and thrilling bit of seemingly dangerous stage business.

The Big Slump

There comes a time during the preparation of a play—usually just before dress rehearsal—when the actor finds himself in a slump. He suddenly feels dried up and dull, his justifications do not move him any more, his work seems to deteriorate. This is perfectly normal. The first few weeks of rehearsal have been charged with the excitement of discovering his character, finding bits of business that work well, gaining control over the sundry elements and obstacles in his role. He has been working at the peak of his capacity, his energy being constantly recharged by the enjoyment of experimenting and inventing materials for his performance.

However, if the show is to open at the end of the normal four-week period, the end of the third week usually sees the start of run-throughs. The production must begin to cohere, to assume a solid shape, an artistic form; the company cannot experiment until opening night and then let things happen as they will in a free and easy, slipshod manner. The director begins to run through the entire play without stopping in order to ensure a smooth and properly keyed performance. The actor has supposedly discovered nearly everything he will need for his performance, and it is now a question of repeating these things over and over to achieve a fine polish.

And the beginning of this repetitive process is most apt to produce a slump. The work which has been done on the part is not yet at top level, and new ideas must be discouraged or the actor will never polish the old. He feels neither here nor there. As exciting as rehearsals are, creative work is also tiring, and by now he is having some trouble evoking the same old justifications and making them organic. There is a tendency to fall back on playing the words, which makes his scenes dead and mechanical and makes him feel as though he were retrogressing. Another factor is that music, sound, props, and other technical elements are often added at this time, creating distractions and making the actor's concentration more difficult.

It is at this time that some directors give pep talks to the cast: "O.K. kids, let's pick it up today, let's get some pace. Pick up your cues. The show's been dragging. Snap. Energy. Vitality." A foolish piece of advice. Forced energy will make the company twice as tired and produce no worthwhile results. What is needed now are a few tiny sparks that will offer your scenes a new lease on life, something that will jolt you out of that broken-record feeling repeated run-throughs have given you.

One thing to do at this time is to make an objective appraisal of what you are doing in the play—what you are actually doing right now, not what you decided to do two weeks ago. Sometimes, by the third week, we begin to take for granted such things as objectives, justification, and preparation. We substitute for these life-giving, dynamic elements the sureness with which, by now, we are able to spout our lines and move about the stage. We have grown secure on stage and go through our paces with a certain vigor, and we are often not aware that our objectives and justifications are slipping. We have a false sense of security, created by a sound knowledge of the physical aspects of our performance—lines and blocking—and this surface solidity hides the fact that we have lost depth.

Look at yourself honestly: Are you really preparing for each scene? Or has it become easier to stroll on stage without the bother of preparation? Are you still acutely aware of your objectives as you play your actions, spurring them on with all the justifications you have mustered? This is the time to bolster your internal work before the outer façade becomes too thick to penetrate. If some of these internal elements have begun to doze, a reawakening of them will give you the thrust you need to carry you through this flagging period.

All this may not apply to you. You may be conscientiously preparing, sincerely and fully involved with your objectives and justifications. And yet you experience a lag. Well, you know what happens when you gorge yourself with your favorite food: soon you can't stand the sight of it. However stimulating your original prepa-ration for a scene may have been, it can lose its potency after many repetitions. Try another. There is no one-and-only preparation for a scene. The change can be ever so trifling, but it will be enough to give you a fresh start.

You cannot, of course, change your objectives in a scene, but you can slightly manipulate the balance of your justifications. For each objective you normally have several justifications. You are reaching for a certain objective because it will bring you power, wealth, pres-tige, self-satisfaction, and so on. If now one of these justifications becomes slightly more important to you, and then another, you will be able to keep the justification as a whole alive at all times. The tiny shift in balance will be imperceptible to your fellow actors and will not really affect anything you do on stage, but it will be just enough to keep your concentration active and prevent your mind from going to sleep. That really is the crux of what I am trying to say: You must be thinking at all times and must never lapse into acting by rote. When the actor's mind takes a holiday, he ceases to be alive on the stage. These very minor adjustments which I have suggested are enough to give the mind something to latch on to.

Dress Rehearsal

Whatever has happened previously, dress rehearsal brings spirits, energy, and excitement to an all-time high. At last you have an actual staircase to mount, doors to slam, real props to handle; the lights, costumes, and make-up launch the play right out of this world of grubby rehearsal clothes and bleak studios into the wonder-realm of the theatre. There is a renewed and fierce camaraderie among the company, and all this provides a stimulating atmosphere which is most conducive to creative work. Indeed, it is at dress rehearsal that most actors profess to being struck with "inspiration"—a brilliant flash of insight, a sudden sensational piece of business.

Why does inspiration wait till dress rehearsal to strike? Inspira-tion is simply the fruition of all the hard work and thought that has gone into the preparation of your role. At dress rehearsal your con-centration is at its keenest and your energy at its peak. You are operating at full capacity, and all the individual ideas and efforts you brought to different rehearsals are now bundled together for one huge push toward the highest artistic experience you are capable of attaining. This is your most creative moment—nerves may inhibit your freedom on stage on opening night—and it's no wonder if the character you have given birth to springs to life almost independ-dently of your will.

Playwrights and novelists tell us that at times their characters wrest control from them and force the story according to their own wills. What they mean, of course, is that they as authors are incapable of forcing their characters to do things which would contradict the personalities which have been created for them. This idea is more dramatically realized in the case of the actor, whose created character is his very own self. During those occasional instances of highest creativity — and they are too rare — when every single facet clicks into place for a few flashing, beautifully coordinated moments, the actor is truly "possessed." His character becomes so vivid, so vibrantly alive, that it is impossible for him to do anything wrong. Anything he does in that moment will be in character, and the likelihood is excellent that he will do something he has never done before. Later, he will say, "It just came to me"; but it never would have come to him had not the seeds of his characterization been firmly planted during previous rehearsals. And that's inspiration for you.

This has been, necessarily, a rather generalized discussion of rehearsal techniques. Every production will impose different problems which will have to be ironed out during rehearsals. Period plays, modern plays, plays with music for which the actors must learn to dance, directors with varying approaches, and fellow actors with divers methods, all these combine to make the rehearsal period of each play a unique experience. As a member of a team whose success depends in part upon the tightest integration, you must be cooperative and flexible. You may be sure that this will in no way preclude your being as imaginative and as creative as you can.

It is now time to face the audience. (And don't eat too heavy a meal before opening night; it makes one sluggish.)

PERFORMANCE

The very first thing to do is to stop peeping through the hole in the front curtain to see who's in the house. Get back to your dressing room where you belong. Seeing the *New York Times* critic sitting out there and looking as though he had dined on lemons can be distressing. Powder your make-up and concentrate on the world behind the curtain, not the one in front of it.

We all get opening-night fidgets. The biggest stars, with years and years of experience on Broadway, confess to wild palpitations before every opening. So you might just as well accept them and learn to live with them. It means nothing more than that you are alive. As we have seen, if your groundwork for the role has been thorough, and if you involve yourself in your fantasy world, you will have nothing to worry about. The jitters will vanish after one minute on stage. So much for that.

The Real Problem

The great challenge which faces every performer is that of keeping his performance alive and spontaneous each night. Unlike the engraver, he cannot make a die and turn out perfect copies every time. His work is never finished as is the sculptor's, there to stand unchanging for as long as the material lasts. The performer's offering must be fully created every single time, with all the attendant stimuli that went into the original creation. And since his performance is organic, it must grow—either better or worse. It cannot remain the same.

There are actors who like to set their performance exactly, never varying the number of steps they take before turning, always picking up the drink with the same hand and on the same word; and not only do they frown upon the slightest change, but they get confused and upset when another actor changes so much as an inflection. These actors have measured their performance precisely and are able to turn out a carbon copy of their original plan. But it is only a copy. As excellent as the physical technique of these actors may be, their performance must inevitably go downhill. If one is concentrating on the exact repetition of moves and inflections, there cannot be enough concentration left over for the internal, organic elements. The forcing of an entire performance into a rigid mold is a mechanical operation which cannot but grow static. We become aware of the actor's technique, his vocal play, his dexterous movement—and we remain unmoved.

And so we present the actor with another paradox. Heretofore he has faced the problem of being himself and another at the same time; of being beside himself with rage and yet in perfect control. Now he discovers that, unlike other artists, he has no permanently fixed creation but that, within the ordered and artistic framework of his performance, there is a gentle flux which results in myriad creations, each somewhat different from the others.

Let us symbolize a painting by a straight line representing the directness and singleness of purpose which can be achieved only when the conceiver and the executer are one and the same person. A dramatic presentation, then, would be a double line, one line representing the conception of the playwright and the other the experiences and abilities of the actor. Between these two lines lies the actor's performance—his product—and he is vouchsafed a certain leeway. The measure of his greatness as an artist is the ability with which he can steer his way through this artistically structured series of double lines, varying his course slightly but never exceeding the boundaries.

The Recharged Performance

First, foremost, and everlastingly, the actor must understand that there are no short cuts to a good performance. There is no lazy way out. The temptations will be great, especially during a long run, to slacken the reins and glide through some performances with a minimum of effort. Many actors "save" themselves during matinees so that they will have more energy for the evening performance. (Apparently the evening crowd is more worthy of their efforts.) The result is that the matinee audience is treated to a shambles of a show in which the actors do little more than walk through their parts.

If you would maintain a consistently high level of performance, you must reactivate the organic elements of your role every time; it must be reincarnated, literally brought back to life after its death with the final curtain of the previous performance. This means, for one thing, that you must play your actions fully every night—really play them—for, as we have seen, complete involvement with our actions is the only way to evoke organic responses. The action is the handle with which we get a secure grip on the performance. It is possible to feel wishy-washy about our objectives, or unconcerned about some of our justifications, for these are mental and emotional processes and subject to capricious moods. But our actions are physical and are capable of being reproduced completely and accurately. Playing our actions is our greatest source of control. We have only to do them to the hilt, and the genuine emotional response which we elicit will in turn brace a sluggish sense of objective or justification. Our renewed involvement with our objectives and justifications in turn strengthens our actions, and this mutual feeding operation is our lifeline.

Preparation often slides down the drain once performances have gotten under way, for this is one thing the audience never sees and the temptation to dispense with it is especially keen. Fight it. Do your preparation every time; it is indispensable for warming up the motor.

This brings us to the second means of keeping the part fresh, a technique which was introduced when we considered dress rehearsal: the making of very slight adjustments within the context of our double-lined framework. It is obvious that the easiest and least obtrusive adjustments are those which concern the inner, private work of the actor, such as his preparation and personalization. There is no reason at all for sticking to a preparation after it has dried up.

As we have suggested earlier, any one scene can have innumerable preparations. And the only limit to the amount of personalization an actor can bring to his role is the limit of his own experience. You were enjoined to have a specific night club in mind if you had the line, "I went to a night club last night," but there is surely more than one night club you can evoke. As simple a thing as having a new image for the line will give it a freshness, an insurance against the loss of involvement.

Another situation in which it is easy to make adjustments is when you are alone on stage. Take a scene in which you have been ushered into a room to wait for someone. Before he enters, you wander about idly looking at things. What better way to keep yourself alive and interested than by looking at different things each time? You remain true to the playwright's intentions and to your character, and at the same time you prevent yourself from falling into a routine that will soon grow stale.

Somewhat more delicate is the question of making adjustments on stage when other actors are present. You can sing hosannas if your costumed comrades share your philosophy, for then your performances will be vivacious and joyful, crackling with hordes of spontaneous reactions and bits of interplay as you each remain super-alert to the other's new innuendoes and shadings. Indeed, *you* will be more alive if your *partner* is a truly organic actor, for listening carefully and watching closely for his subtlest changes is the liveliest thing you can do; it gives the scene the spontaneous quality which we found so exciting in improvisation.

Let us consider further the types of adjustments and minute changes which may be made. Just how great is the actor's prerogative to deviate from what has been set? There's the rub; it all hinges on what has been set. If by "setting" a performance you mean calculating every intonation and gesture, then there is no latitude whatever. If, on the other hand, you consider it more important to set the living issues of the play, the fundamental actions, objectives, justifications, and character elements without which there is, in fact, no play, then you have a measure of creative freedom. If you are honestly playing your action of pouring out your wrath on someone, then it makes mighty little difference whether you pound the table or the desk. It is not your pounding that brings the scene to life; the pounding is only one of the many possible choices which physically illustrate the real matter of the scene. So tonight pound one, tomorrow the other—a meaningless change, but that small, spontaneous urge that prompts you to pound one rather than the other at a given performance brings life and freshness. Marlon Brando has this to say about keeping the performance fresh:

. . . to keep the heart of the play alive, the actor cannot stay in the same posture all the time. He must move to other areas, shifting and changing to keep his performance from becoming threadbare and fatigued.

Whenever you are unable to depart from the stencil, you quickly exhaust your imagination, and when you are empty, when the performance becomes a habit, working in the theatre can be tedious beyond belief.[1]

There are countless opportunities in a play for impromptu changes. The mere manner in which you sit down with a cocktail affords endless opportunities for variation. One night you hold the drink in your hand as you talk, sipping frequently; another time you place it on a nearby table and ignore it. Once you lean forward during a certain conversation; next time you lean back. Nor do your lines have to be spoken as though they were recorded. A degree more or less of intensity, a subtle change of inflection, a slightly longer or shorter pause — these things will not usually change basic meanings. *If they do, however, they mark the end of the actor's prerogative.* Never forget that your primary responsibility is to the author, and any adjustment which alters his meaning is unwarranted. You must not make changes for the mere sake of making changes.

A test case. Two actors are on stage. One is engrossed in his work, and without stopping or taking his eyes from his work, he asks the other a question. At the next performance, he stops working, turns to his companion, and asks the same question. The variation here might be innocuous, or it might be lethal. Direct confrontation is often indicative of challenge, while the indirect approach suggests a pretended casualness meant to disguise a deep interest. The answer, of course, lies in the action. If the actor knows his action, he will never make the mistake of substituting a challenge for a devious inquiry.

Since actors are quite human, we are all occasionally faced with that moment when our concentration, for whatever reason, suddenly absconds. We find our thoughts floating out to the audience or to our plans for after the show that night. We suddenly hear ourselves speaking lines and wonder whether we said the previous lines. When this happens you must quickly narrow your focus of attention, not to an idea but to a small, material object on stage. If you happen to have anything in your hands, examine it closely, as we did at the very beginning of our work: look for marks, scratches, note the notches, anything at all to rivet your attention on the circumstances

1. Interview with Joanne Stang in *The New York Times*, November 29, 1964. Section 2, p. 11.

of the play or at least on the physical world in which those circumstances are occurring. If you have no prop, focus on something on stage or on your fellow actor. Look at his clothes, count the buttons, see if there are any worn spots. Why should the good doctor have worn spots in his jacket? Perhaps he's not doing as well as he pretends. All this will take only a few seconds, but it will effectively pull you back to the stage and into the play.

The final and most important way to keep your part fresh is this: You must never stop working on it. You must never cease to dig for deeper justifications and involvements. If you are portraying a human being, you know how ridiculous it is to expect to learn all about him in four weeks of rehearsal. We keep learning new things about friends we have known for years. Our four-week rehearsal period is only an introduction to our character. As we go on living with him, our acquaintance grows richer; and as we come to understand him more and more, our justifications become more meaningful. When an actor says he is bored with performances, we know he has stopped growing; but the actor who continues to probe and think will have constant nourishment for his performances whether they run for a month or a year.

Performance Etiquette

Suppose, in this growth process, the actor comes up with an idea that is quite different from what is being done in performance but which would be a fine contribution to the play. We have already said that new ideas should be taken to the director, who will weigh them and decide whether to include them. If the director has vanished after opening night, the stage manager is next in command. You must know and respect the fact that the stage manager is in complete charge of running the show during performance—not only backstage but on stage as well. Under no circumstances should you take it upon yourself to include the new business and surprise the company; that is extremely unfair. If you think there is a chance of even the smallest bit of business startling or confusing another actor, you should approach him before the show, explain it to him, and ask if he is agreeable to your trying it out. The stunts that are pulled in some amateur productions—vinegar in the wine bottle, funny remarks in the telegram instead of the proper message—are childish pranks which have no place in the theatre. The professional attitude should extend not only to those actors who are paid for their work but to every actor who is serious about his business.

While we are on the subject of professional attitude, it is disgraceful to note the number of actors—on Broadway and off—who become lazy and slapdash about their make-up after a few performances. The highlights and shadows they worked on so carefully for opening night have become a chore, and they are content to slap on a little pancake make-up. And how few actors ever bother to do their hands! It is irksome to see an actor raise his hands to his face and to note the ghostly whiteness of the hands next to the pink face. Unfortunately, only rare stage managers exercise their authority to forbid actors to go on stage without the proper make-up.

And while we're talking about make-up: buy your own! Actors have many little idiosyncrasies, especially in the dressing room, and one of them is that they dislike other actors filching their tissues and using their rouge pots. I myself go into a positive frenzy if I see anyone as much as eyeing my cold-cream jar. I do believe the reason for this, if you must have one, is that the make-up kit is magical, it transforms us; and magical things and mystical charms are highly personal and must always be closely identified with their owner. (You may think anything you like of my reasoning, but buy your own make-up.)

What I am trying to say is that until you become a star and have a private dressing room, you will be sharing one with one or several partners in grease paint. Respect their whims, they will respect yours, and the company will stay friendly and happy, an indispensable factor for a good show.

Once the stage manager has called half hour, fifteen minutes, five minutes, and places (and why don't you be that one actor in ten thousand who replies with "Thank you" when the stage manager calls through the door?), you should make it your business not to have to be called again. Be in the wings in good time for your every entrance. (You should be there anyway to do your preparation.) Technically, the stage manager, or his assistant, is responsible for warning every actor of his every entrance, and if an actor misses an entrance, it is considered the stage manager's fault. Take this responsibility yourself; don't burden the stage manager, who has an enormous number of other things to do.

One more warning: the conscientious director will return every now and again to see the play. If he really wants to know what has been happening in his absence, he will sneak into town without notifying a soul and slip into the back of the auditorium wearing dark glasses and a false beard. He will then appear backstage at the end of the play, the stage manager will assemble the mortified actors, and the director will speak a classic sentence, one which has been uttered unchanged by every director worth his blue pencil: "All right, there'll be a rehearsal tomorrow at three to take out the improvements."

The "improvements" of which he speaks are not the small adjustments we have been talking about, or even a new idea that has been added, which may be a good one. One of the actor's special little devils is the one that lurks about waiting for him to find a particularly effective piece of business or a good laugh. He then prods the actor to capitalize on it by building it. If we discover one night that a little shrug of the shoulders at a certain point gets a little laugh, we reason that a bigger shrug will get a bigger laugh. And who can resist getting laughs? So we try a bigger shrug next night, and, bless the comic muse, we get a bigger laugh. Well, why stop there? Next time we raise our eyebrows and toss our palms in the air a bit, and finally we are flinging our arms to the heavens in a wild gesture that all but dislocates our shoulders. And the audience howls. But the chances are a thousand to one that this hilarious gesture is quite out of character. You have improved the laugh but depreciated your performance. Of course, most people in the audience will think you are a hysterically funny fellow and will not care a hoot about your character. They came to be entertained and you have filled the bill. But a few discerning people will know otherwise. And so will you. Your choice will depend upon the kind of actor you want to be.

One thing that all great artists have in common—actors, dancers, acrobats—is the apparent effortlessness with which they perform. When we see a performer straining, overdoing things, we feel that he is working at some sort of disadvantage, that the odds are against him, and that he is probably substituting lots of energy for a polished technique. The lovely ballerina who floats through the air, clunks down on her toes, and wobbles a bit with a desperate look on her face before coming to a dead stop does not earn nearly so much of our admiration as the one who hits the floor with a gentle smile and freezes on the spot. We know how many years of practice have gone into the latter's execution, and it is a joy to see her perform so easily and gracefully. Fine actors always accomplish their ends with a minimum of pyrotechnics. Their performances are neat and uncluttered; they do not belabor points. The *real* actor, when he has gotten a laugh, will try each night to see how much *less* he can do and still keep the laugh. There is a finesse in underplaying which is far more difficult to attain and far more to be admired than the crudeness of overplaying. In a well-written play, the laughs are inherent in the situations, the best laughs coming from the genuineness of the character's response and not from contrived bits.

nine

The audition

I observed a seminar recently led by a well known casting director. There were about 25 actors and actresses in the room. The director opened the session by asking "How many of you like to audition?" Two hands went up. The others twitched and groaned, rolled their eyes to the ceiling and displayed various other signs of fear, displeasure and discomfort. "Good for you two," said the director to the hands in the air. "As for the rest of you, if you want to work in the theatre, you'd better learn to love to audition."

Why such reluctance? Why such fear? Why such stomach churning at the opportunity to put in your bid for a job? (In a profession you profess to love.) I think much of it has to do with not really knowing what the audition process is all about. Wondering if you chose the right material. Not knowing what they're looking for. The crushing feeling that every time you audition you are once again on your knees begging for a job.

Let's get rid of that last one right away. Don't you realize how important it is for the director or casting director to find the most perfect actor for the role? Their reputation is at stake. The greatest director is nothing with a poor cast. They *want* you to be good. They pray for the right person to walk into that room or onto that stage and knock 'em over. You're doing *them* a favor. I know, I know that's a tough one to swallow—that you're actually there to help *them*. But that's the fact of it. And if you can internalize that, you'll walk into auditions with a wholly different attitude. You'll send out vibes that say "I'm confident—I'm sure of myself (but not cocky)—I *belong* on a stage."

Always remember that half your audition (sometimes ALL your audition) is over before you even open your mouth.

Now back to square one. What is the purpose of the audition? To demonstrate your brilliance as an actor? To show off some special skill or accent or the ability to shed real tears? No. The purpose of the audition is to get the job. No more. Getting the role and creating the role are not the same. It's the difference between artistry and marketing. Too many actors are not sure what they are selling—then they wonder why no one's buying.

One of the first things to do is to find out who will be holding the audition. Check with other actors. Different directors look for different things. Some directors want to be assured that you will be able to reach a peak performance when the show opens—and they want to see it all right there at the audition. (This is often due to their own insecurity and their inability to recognize talent that they can work with.) For these directors you have to pull out all the stops and fly. This is especially true for TV and movies where there is hardly any rehearsal before the scene is shot. Now this usually will result in a phony reading, in playing the quality or the result—just the opposite of what I've been preaching—but do you remember what we talked about in Chapter Three? What is your objective? TO GET THE JOB. What is your action? TO DO WHATEVER IS NECESSARY TO REACH YOUR OBJECTIVE. You will go back and do all your proper homework and preparation after you have decorated the dotted line.

Other directors look more deeply. They're looking for truthfulness, for involvement, how you listen to your partner, how you relate, what kind of imagination you have. They want to see beyond the surface to how you work. They don't want to see a performance, but rather those threads of technique and talent that they can work with and weave together into a performance four weeks from now.

There are various kinds of auditions:

Prepared Monologue

If you are asked to bring in a prepared monologue, you will always be told how much time you will be allowed: a three-minute comic monologue, five minutes for two contrasting pieces, etc. Time your piece carefully and NEVER time it to the second. If you run over, most auditioners will be very irritated and many will cut you off. If I'm allowed three minutes, I time my monologue for two-and-a-half.

Your choice of material is crucial. A few rules:

a) Cast yourself ideally. Don't stray from your actual age or physical or emotional type. Choose a role that you would truly be considered for if you were competing with 100 other actors (which you will be).

b) Be wary of those books of monologues for actors, or of scenes from the world's most popular plays. The directors know these scenes and they become crazed after sitting through hours of auditions and seeing the same scene twelve times. Moreover, they have their own notion of how the scene should be played and this could put you at a disadvantage. Much better to do a scene they don't know. This creates interest and obviates comparison. Look at obscure and unpublished plays. There is a wealth of material in short stories and novels. Or write your own scene—some very successful auditions have been written by actors themselves.

c) Make sure that your scene—even of it's only two-and-a-half minutes—"goes somewhere." See that it doesn't end the same way it starts. There needs to be a build, or a decline, or a change of intensity, a growing realization—anything that gives you a chance to show some flexibility and a variety of "colors." I am especially wary of those scenes in which a character is telling a story from the past. The action is often minimal and the actor falls into the trap of telling the tale on one level with few or no changes. After the first 30 seconds, we've seen it all—no need to finish it.

d) If you're asked to do two contrasting scenes, make sure they really contrast. Most people do one comic and one serious scene. If you do a dialect *really well* this might be the time to do it— provided your other scene is straight. Never do a dialect scene if it is the only one you are doing. They want to hear your normal speech. And please don't drag out your stage Irish. There are lots of authentic Irish actors who do it better than you.

e) When your turn is called, step up to the indicated area and go right to it. You will usually be asked "What are you going to do for us?" Give the name of the piece and go right to it. Don't tell the story or describe the action. If what's happening in the scene is not apparent from your performance, you're behind the eight-ball anyway. And don't—DON'T—get up there and go into any "preparation." Some actors turn their backs to the auditioners and go into a 30 second trance, or they bend over and flop their arms about to loosen up. This is amateurish, utterly phony, and it arouses murderous instincts in auditioners.

f) Your piece might be one in which the character addresses the audience. Most auditioners do not like to be focused upon by the actor. It forces them to respond and it makes them uncomfortable. Also, they often make notes while you are performing, and that's difficult to do when you are being stared at. Now some auditioners don't mind being talked to. You never know. So the thing to do, if you feel strongly about talking directly to someone, is to ask the auditioner "Do you mind if I use you?" Then proceed accordingly. If they don't want to be talked to, focus to one side of them so you are facing them three-quarters.

Auditioning for a play in print

Here you will almost always be told what part (or parts) you are being considered for. Get hold of the play and study it carefully. It's usually easy enough to figure out which scenes you'll be asked to read—the meatiest scenes. Prepare a few of them. Either they will tell you what they want to hear or they will ask you which scene you prefer to read. In either case, you'll be well prepared.

Dress suggestively. Not in costume—but you can dress up or down. You wouldn't wear a suit and a tie to read for Stanley Kowalski. But no torn shirts, either. Clean jeans and sport shirt will do. Don't be cute.

Auditioning for a new play

Here, too, you will probably have some idea of the character you're being considered for. Again, you can dress suggestively. Always arrive much earlier than your call so that you can study the scene they will give you. Look for the movement in the scene—Where am I at the start, where do I end up? This will ensure your not playing it on one level. Look for strong attitudes toward the other characters, strong needs within your character. Find humor if you can. Opt for the opposite of the obvious qualities—don't fall into the cliché. Don't get stuck in a chair, but move about; get your body to work as well as your voice. Always find the urgency in the scene, the immediacy. Don't keep your nose glued to the page, but look at your partner as much as possible. He may be another actor or a stage manager slumped in a chair—no matter, make as much contact as you can. This is another reason for getting there early, so that you can familiarize yourself with the script.

When you are called in, one of two things will happen. Either the director will tell you a few things about the character and the scene, in which case you will immediately adjust to his suggestions—or he will tell you nothing. If he tells you nothing, there are two possible reasons: (1) He doesn't really know what he wants and is waiting for an actor to come along and hit the bull's-eye, or (2) he does know what he wants but he wants to see your personal response to the scene. Again, I urge you to make strong choices. Don't play it down the middle—neutrality is dull. Be wrong, but strong. In this way he will see that you have talent and very often will ask you to do it again witha certain adjustment that he will give you. Quite often a director will give you an adjustment even though you are right on target. (Which, of course, you will not know because directors rarely jump out of their chairs and gleefully shout "Right on!") So listen to him carefully and perform his adjustment as fully as you can. He is doing this to see how you take direction. He does not want to work with an actor who is not flexible, who resists his suggestions.

Let me go back for a moment to the director who says nothing. You've gotten past the "How d'you do's" and other pleasantries and he seems to be waiting for you to start. Don't be afraid to ask, "Is there anything you can tell me about this scene?" Again, if he says, "Just let me see what you do with it," you've got to plunge ahead. Of course, as we've said before, if you've done your research on him, you'll know which way to plunge. But if you haven't been able to find anything out about how he works, there's still a chance. He may possibly answer your question. If he does, he will answer it in one of two ways: either he will say, "This guy is furious because his boss didn't give him the promotion and he really wants to knock the boss's head off and tear the whole place apart." Then you know that this director wants a complete performance. Go all out. On the other hand, he might say, "You have been a diligent and conscientious worker for ten years. You truly deserve this promotion, but the boss has given it to someone who does not have near your experience or qualifications." This is a director who is not looking for a result, but for an honest (and not clichéd) response to the situation. Anyone can shout and growl—he wants to see your imagination at work, your involvement, your sense of truth. This will be a very different reading.

A friendly tip: Sometimes you will be given three pages to look over, but will be stopped on page two. Some actors consider this reason enough to contemplate jumping down the elevator shaft. Not at all. There's no way of knowing what an interruption means. It could mean that you're not what they're looking for. It could also mean that they've seen enough to know that they want to call you back. Which brings us to

Callbacks

Wear the same outfit you wore to the first audition. Obviously the chemistry was right. Don't change horses in mid-stream. Besides, they often make notes about what you wore to help them remember you when they are sifting through the candidates afterwards. "Oh, yeah, the guy with the purple pants and the orange sweatshirt."

Auditioning is a special skill, a particular technique. There are many fine actors who do not audition well. Have a repertoire of audition pieces—comedy, serious, classical, contemporary—and keep them polished and always ready to go. Never take an audition with a piece you learned the night before. You must be absolutely solid and comfortable with the piece you do. Learn to like to audition. Unless your uncle is the director, it's the only way you'll get to work.

Parting Thoughts

Well, we've come a long way together—from the examination of a watch on stage to the projection of a living human being for an audience. This book will not do that projection for you, nor will a one- or two-year course. It will take years. Years of hard work. But the deep satisfaction of maturing as an artist-human being, of becoming a secure and articulate craftsman, of developing an artistic integrity which will push you to strive for the finest job you are capable of doing, will be a rich reward.

It would be presumptuous of me to suggest that the techniques offered here constitute the way of working on a role. It is one way; it works for me. There are as many other ways as there are actors. The artist must ultimately find his own method: he borrows this, rejects that, modifies, alters, invents, until he has devised his very own system. To the extent that his method enables him to express fully and effortlessly his profoundest conceptions, he is an artist. If he is a true artist, he will never stop searching and exploring ways to enrich his expression. That is his dedication. It is also his torment, for the artist realizes better than most how inadequate are his simple human resources for expressing his deepest feelings.

Let the techniques here described be but a start, a point of reference. If they work for you, use them; if not, toss them out. With experience you will come to know what your artist-self needs, what stimuli are most effective, what kind of expression is your forte.

And now, before closing, I must acquaint you with one of our inviolable traditions. When, on opening night or any other important theatrical occasion, you want to wish a friend the greatest success and the best of fortune, you must never say g—d l—k to him, for that is sure to bring bad luck. You always say, as I now sincerely say to you,

BREAK A LEG!

Epilogue

Actors' Axioms

- The cat shall not bark, nor the dog meow.
    Develop "actor's language." Don't get dressed; throw yourself together or preen. "Getting dressed" is acting generally. Choose more specific actions.

- He only begins who hath begun.
    Your performance begins in the wings, not when you arrive on stage.

- Let not thy cup runneth over.
    We can expect no more from an actor who has given his all in a scene. He holds our interest who still has a way to go.

- And the camel shall have one hump or two, but never three.
    If it's not part of your character, cut it out. Don't go for cheap laughs at the expense of your character.

- Covet not thy neighbor's garb.
    People at a Halloween party wear costumes. Actors wear clothes. Work as much as possible in your character's clothes. Be as comfortable and natural in Elizabethan dress as you are in your old blue jeans.

- Neither can a man walk on two roads at once.
    CHOOSE. Work with powerful conviction. Be wrong but strong. Neutrality is death.

    - Heed the moving finger which writes and moves on.
        Watch silent movies for the real playing of actions. With the advent of talkies, actions became weaker.

    - Nor shall ye grasp at the first straw.
        Be wary of your first idea; it's usually a cliché.

- As a man thinketh, so he doeth.
  There is no such thing as a wrong thought. If it enters your head, use it. It may give a new and interesting color to the scene.

- He needs not ears who has eyes.
  If I learn more from listening to your words than from watching your actions, your scene is weak. If half the audience were blind and the other half deaf, they should all know what's going on.

- Tell me not thy troubles.
  I do not want to hear how you feel. I want to see what you do when you feel that way. Always remember—if you can do it, don't say it.

- What ye sow, that shall ye reap.
  Words beget words, actions beget actions. Remember that acting is doing. If you *do*, your partner will respond by *doing*.

- In the beginning was the Word, but the Word was dull.
  Start improvs in the middle, otherwise you will use too many words to set up your story.

- Listen to thy heart, but command it not.
  Never determine the emotions of a scene, but the actions. If you try to hit a predetermined emotional level, you are doomed to failure. You will push for the emotion and end up playing a quality.

- If 'twere done when 'twere done, 'twill be seen.
  If the audience can see it, so can the people on stage. Never show the audience anything you don't want your stage partner to see. That makes him look like a moron and you'll be doing some cornball indicating.

- Speak to me only with thine eyes.
  If you can't play your scene without words, you don't really know what it's about.

- Seek the pie beneath the crust.
  Never play the text. Play the sub-text.

- And no two snowflakes shall be alike unto each other.
  Or fingerprints or performances. Don't try to carbon copy your performance. Look for the subtlest change in any part of the scene. A chain reaction will take place that will keep the scene alive and fresh.

- It is more blessed to receive than to give.
  Giving is only half your job. If you focus only what you are giving out, you are losing all that your partner is giving that you should be responding to.

- Always cast the first stone.
  Especially in improvs. Don't wait for your partner to start the "story"—plow right in with a strong action.

- And the meek shall not inherit the earth.
  Take it from me, the meek shall inherit nothing. Because they're dull. One last time: Desperate objectives, powerful actions.

- Do not seek and ye shall not find.
  Don't peek through the hole in the curtain to see who's out there. It might make you too nervous.

- *Crusurem frange.*
  Break a leg.

Appendix

SICILIAN LIMES

by Luigi Pirandello
translated by Isaac Goldberg

CHARACTERS

MICUCCIO BONAVINO, *musician in a country band*
MARTA MARNIS, *mother of*
SINA MARNIS, *singer*
FERDINANDO, *waiter*
DORINA, *maid*
GUESTS
WAITERS

TIME. *The present*
PLACE. *A city in Northern Italy.*

SCENE. *A hallway, furnished simply with a small table and several chairs. The corner to the left of the actors is hidden from view by a curtain. There are doors at the right and the left. At the rear, the main door, of glass, is open and leads to a dark room, across which may be seen a decorated door, likewise of glass, which affords a view of a splendidly illuminated salon. The view includes a table, sumptuously spread.*

NIGHT. *The hallway is in darkness. Some one is snoring behind the curtain.*
Shortly after the rise of the stage curtain FERDINANDO *enters through*

the door at the right with a light in his hand. He is in shirt sleeves, but he has only to put on his dress-coat and he will be ready to serve at the table. He is followed by MICUCCIO BONAVINO, *evidently just from the country, with his overcoat collar raised to his ears, a grimy bag in one hand and in the other an old valise and the case of a musical instrument. He is so cold and so exhausted that he can barely manage his burden. No sooner has the light been brought in than the snoring behind the curtain ceases.*

DORINA *(from within).* Who is it?

FERDINANDO *(placing the light upon the little table).* Hey, Dorina! Get up! Can't you see that we have Signor Bonvicino here?

MICUCCIO *(shaking his head so as to get rid of a drop at the tip of his nose).* My name's Bonavino.

FERDINANDO. Bonavino, Bonavino.

DORINA *(yawning behind the curtain).* And who's he?

FERDINANDO. A relation of madame's. *(To* MICUCCIO*)* And just how may you be related to madame, please? Cousin, maybe?

MICUCCIO *(embarrassed, hesitant).* Well, really, there's no relationship. I am . . . my name's Micuccio Bonavino. You know that.

DORINA *(her curiosity roused, she steps from behind the curtain, still half asleep).* A relative of madame's?

FERDINANDO *(provoked).* Can't you hear? *(To* MICUCCIO*).* Countryman of hers? Then why did you ask me whether *zia* Marta was here? *(To* DORINA*)* Understand? I took him for a relative, a nephew. I can't receive you, my dear fellow.

MICUCCIO. What? Can't receive me? Why, I've come all the way from the country, on purpose!

FERDINANDO. On purpose? What for?

MICUCCIO. To find her!

FERDINANDO. She's not here. I told you she can't be found in at this hour.

MICUCCIO. And if the train just came in, what can I do about it? I've been traveling for two days.

DORINA *(eyeing him from head to toe).* And you look it!

MICUCCIO. I do, eh? Very much? How do I look?

DORINA. Ugly, my dear fellow. No offense.

FERDINANDO. I can't receive you. Call again tomorrow and you'll find her. The madame is at the theatre now.

MICUCCIO. What do you mean, call again? Must I go? Where? I don't know where to go in this town, at night. I'm a stranger. If she isn't here, I'll wait for her. Really now. Can't I wait for her here?

FERDINANDO. I say No! Without her permission.

MICUCCIO. What permission! You don't know me.

FERDINANDO. That's just it. Because I don't know you, I'm not going to get a bawling-out on account of you!

MICUCCIO (*smiling with a confident air and with his finger making a negative sign*). Rest easy.

DORINA (*to* FERDINANDO, *ironically*). Indeed, she'll be just in the proper mood to attend to him this evening. (*To* MICUCCIO) Can't you see? (*She points to the illuminated salon in the rear.*) There's a party on tonight!

MICUCCIO. So? What party?

DORINA. An evening in (*she yawns*) her honor.

FERDINANDO. And we'll get through, God willing, by daybreak!

MICUCCIO. All right, no matter. I'm sure that the moment Teresina sees me . . .

FERDINANDO (*to* DORINA). Understand? He calls her Teresina, he does. Plain Teresina. He asked me whether "Teresina, the singer" was in.

MICUCCIO. Well, what of it? Isn't she a singer? That's what they call it. Are you trying to teach *me?*

DORINA. Then you really know her well?

MICUCCIO. Well? Why, we grew up together!

FERDINANDO (*to* DORINA). What shall we do?

DORINA. Let him wait.

MICUCCIO (*piqued*). Of course I'll wait. What do you mean? I came on purpose to . . .

FERDINANDO. Take a seat there. I wash my hands of it. I must get things ready. (*He leaves in the direction of the salon at the rear.*)

MICUCCIO. This is fine, indeed. As if I were . . . Perhaps because they see me in this condition . . . If I were to tell Teresina when she returns from the theatre. (*He is seized by a doubt and looks about him.*) Whose house is this?

DORINA (*eyeing him and poking fun at him*). Ours—as long as we stay.

MICUCCIO. So, then, things are going well. (*He inspects the place anew, staring into the salon.*) Is it a large house?

DORINA. So so.

MICUCCIO. And that's a salon?

DORINA. A reception hall. Tonight there's a banquet there.

MICUCCIO. Ah! What a spread! What bright lights!

DORINA. Beautiful, isn't it?

MICUCCIO (*rubbing his hands contentedly*). Then it's true!

DORINA. What?

MICUCCIO. Eh, it's easily seen, they're well . . .

DORINA. In good health?

MICUCCIO. No, I mean well off. (*He rubs his thumb against his fore-finger, in a manner to suggest the counting of money.*)

DORINA. Why, do you know who Sina Marnis is?

MICUCCIO. Sina? Ah, yes, yes, now I understand. *Zia* Marta wrote me about it. Teresina. Certainly. Tere-sina: Sina . . .

DORINA. But wait a moment. Now that I think of it. You! *(She calls* FERDINANDO *from the salon.)* Do you know who he is? The fellow that she's always writing to, the mother . . .

MICUCCIO. She can't write, the poor little thing . . .

DORINA. Yes, yes. Bonavino. But . . . Domenico. Your name's Domenico, isn't it?

MICUCCIO. Domenico or Micuccio. It's the same thing. We call it Micuccio where I come from.

DORINA. You're the fellow that was so sick, aren't you? Recently . . .

MICUCCIO. Terribly, yes. At death's door. Dead. Practically dead.

DORINA. And Signora Marta sent you a money order, didn't she? We went to the post-office together.

MICUCCIO. A money order. A money order. And that's what I've come for! I have it here—the money.

DORINA. Are you returning it to her?

MICUCCIO *(disturbed).* Money—nothing! It's not to be mentioned. But first . . . Will they be much longer in coming?

DORINA *(looks at the clock).* Oh, about . . . Sometime tonight, I imagine . . .

FERDINANDO *(passing through the hallway, from the door at the left, carrying kitchen utensils and shouting applause).* Bravo! Bravo! Bis! Bis! Bis!

MICUCCIO *(smiling).* A great voice, eh?

FERDINANDO *(turning back).* I should say so. A voice . . .

MICUCCIO *(rubbing his palms).* I can take the credit for that! It's my work!

DORINA. Her voice?

MICUCCIO. I discovered it!

DORINA. What, you? *(To* FERDINANDO*)* Do you hear? He discovered her voice.

MICUCCIO. I'm a musician, I am.

FERDINANDO. Ah! A musician? Bravo! And what do you play? The trumpet?

MICUCCIO *(at first, in all seriousness, makes a negative sign with his finger; then).* Who said trumpet? The piccolo. I belong to the band, I do. I belong to our communal band up at my place.

DORINA. And what's the name of your place? Wait; I'll recall it.

MICUCCIO. Palma Monetchiaro. What else should it be named?

FERDINANDO. And it was really you who discovered her voice?

DORINA. Come now, my boy. Tell us how you did it, sonny! Wait and listen to this, Ferdinando.

MICUCCIO (*shrugging his shoulders*). How I did it? She used to sing . . .

DORINA. And at once, you being a musician . . . eh?

MICUCCIO. No . . . not at once; on the other hand . . .

FERDINANDO. It took you some time?

MICUCCIO. She always used to be singing . . . sometimes out of pique . . .

DORINA. Really?

MICUCCIO. And then again, to . . . to get certain thoughts out of her mind . . . because . . .

FERDINANDO. Because what?

MICUCCIO. Oh, certain unpleasant things . . . disappointments, poor little girl . . . in those days. Her father had died . . . I,—yes, I helped her out a bit . . . her and her mother, *zia* Marta . . . But my mother was against it . . . and . . . in short . . .

DORINA. You were fond of her, then?

MICUCCIO. I? Of Teresina? You make me laugh! My mother insisted on my giving her up because she didn't have anything, and had lost her father . . . while I, come good or evil, had my position in the band . . .

FERDINANDO. So . . . You're not related at all, then. Lovers, maybe?

MICUCCIO. My parents were against it! And that's why Teresina sang out of spite . . .

DORINA. Ah! Just listen to that . . . And you?

MICUCCIO. It was heaven! I can truly say: an inspiration from heaven! Nobody had ever noticed it—not even I. All of a sudden . . . one morning . . .

FERDINANDO. There's luck for you!

MICUCCIO. I'll never forget it . . . It was a morning in April. She was at the window, singing . . . Up in the garret, beneath the roof!

FERDINANDO. Understand?

DORINA. Hush!

MICUCCIO. What's wrong about that? The humblest of folk can have the greatest of gifts.

DORINA. Of course they can! As you were saying? She was at the window singing . . .

MICUCCIO. I had heard her sing that little air of ours surely a hundred thousand times.

DORINA. Little air?

MICUCCIO. Yes. "All things in this world below." That's the name of it.

FERDINANDO. Eh! All things in this world below . . .

MICUCCIO (*reciting the words*).

> All things in this world below,
> Live their day and then depart;
> But this thorn that pricks my heart,
> Darling mine, will never go.

And what a melody! Divine, impassioned . . . Enough of that. I had never paid any attention to it. But that morning . . . It was as if I were in paradise! An angel, it seemed that an angel was singing! That day, after dinner, ever so quietly, without letting her or her mother know a thing about it, I took up into the garret the leader of our band, who's a friend of mine, uh, a very close friend, for that matter: Saro Malvati, such a kind-hearted chap, the poor fellow . . . He hears her, he's a clever boy, a great leader, so they all say at Palma . . . And he says, "Why, this is a God-given voice!" Imagine our joy! I hired a piano, and before it was got up into that attic . . . Well. Then I bought the music, and right away the leader began to give her lessons . . . Just like that, satisfied with whatever they could give him from time to time. What was I? Same as I am today; a poor, humble fellow . . . The piano cost money, the music cost money, and then Teresina had to eat decent food . . .

FERDINANDO. Eh, of course.

DORINA. So that she's had the strength to sing . . .

MICUCCIO. Meat, every day! I can take the credit for that!

FERDINANDO. The deuce you say!

DORINA. And so?

MICUCCIO. And so she began to learn. You could see it all from the very beginning . . . It was written above, in heaven, you might say . . . And it was heard throughout the whole country, that great voice of hers . . . The people would come from all around, and stand beneath the window in the street, to hear her . . . And what spirit! She burned, she really was afire . . . And when she would finish singing, she'd grasp me by the arm, like this (*he seizes* FERDINANDO) and would shake me . . . Just like a madwoman . . . For she already foresaw. She knew that fame was hers . . . The leader told us so. And she didn't know how to show me her gratefulness. *Zia* Marta, on the other hand, poor woman that she was . . .

DORINA. Was against her career?

MICUCCIO. I wouldn't say that she was against it—she didn't believe it, that was it. The poor old lady had had so many hard knocks in her life that she didn't want Teresina to take it into her head to rise above the position to which she had been so long resigned. She was, in plain words, afraid. And then she knew what it cost me, and that my parents . . . But I broke with them all, with my father, with my mother, when a certain teacher came from outside . . . He used to give concerts . . . A . . . I can't remember his name now—but he had a fine reputation . . . When this master heard Teresina and said that it would be a sin, a real sin not to have her continue her studies in a city, in a great conservatory . . . I broke with them all. I sold the farm that had been left to me by an uncle of mine, a priest, and sent Teresina to Naples.

FERDINANDO. You?

MICUCCIO. Yes, I.—I.

DORINA (*to* FERDINANDO). At his expense, don't you understand?

MICUCCIO. I kept her there for four years, studying. I haven't seen her since then.

DORINA. Never?

MICUCCIO. Never. Because . . . because she began to sing in the theatres, you see, here and there . . . She'd fly from Naples to Rome, from Rome to Milan, then to Spain, then to Russia, then back here again . . .

FERDINANDO. Creating a furor everywhere!

MICUCCIO. Eh, I know all about it! I've got them all here, in the valise, all the papers . . . And in here (*he removes from his inside coat pocket a bundle of letters*) I have all the letters, hers and her mother's . . . Here you are: these are her words when she sent me the money, that time I was on the point of death: "Dear Micuccio, I haven't time to write to you. I confirm everything that mamma has said. Get better at once, become your old self again, and wish me well. Teresina."

FERDINANDO. And did she send you much?

DORINA. A thousand lire—wasn't it?

MICUCCIO. That was it. A thousand.

FERDINANDO. And that farm of yours, if I may ask—that you sold. How much was it worth?

MICUCCIO. How much should it be worth? Not much . . . A mere strip of land . . .

FERDINANDO (*winking to* DORINA). Ah!

MICUCCIO. But I have the money right here, I have. I don't want anything at all. What little I've done, I've done for her sake. We had agreed to wait two, three years, so as to let her make a place for herself . . . *Zia* Marta kept writing that to me all the time in her letters. I speak the plain truth: I wasn't waiting for the money. So many years had passed I could wait a while longer . . . But seeing that Teresina has sent it to me, it's a sign she has enough and to spare; she's made a place for herself . . .

FERDINANDO. I should say! And what a place, my dear sir!

MICUCCIO. Then it's time . . .

DORINA. To marry?

MICUCCIO. I am here.

FERDINANDO. Have you come to marry Sina Marnis?

DORINA. Hush! That's their agreement! Can't you understand anything? Certainly! To marry her!

MICUCCIO. I'm not saying anything. I simply say: I'm here. I've abandoned everything and everybody yonder in the country: family, band, everything. I went to law against my parents on account of those thousand lire, which came unknown to me, at the time I was more dead than alive. I had to tear it out of my mother's hands, for she wanted to keep it. Ah, no sirree—it isn't the money! Micuccio Bonavino, money?—Not at all! Wherever I may happen to be, even at the end of the world, I won't starve. I have my art. I have my piccolo, and . . .

DORINA. You have? Did you bring along your piccolo, too?

MICUCCIO. Sure I did! We're as one person, my piccolo and I . . .

FERDINANDO. She sings and he plays. Understand?

MICUCCIO. Don't you think I can play in the orchestra?

FERDINANDO. Certainly! Why not?

DORINA. And, I'll bet you play well!

MICUCCIO. So so; I've been playing for ten years . . .

FERDINANDO. Would you mind letting us hear something? (About to take the instrument case)

DORINA. Yes! Bravo, bravo! Let's hear something!

MICUCCIO. Oh, no! What would you want, at this hour . . .

DORINA. Anything at all! Please, now!

FERDINANDO. Some little air . . .

MICUCCIO. Oh, no . . . Really! . . .

FERDINANDO. Don't make us coax you! (He opens the case and removes the instrument.) Here you are!

DORINA. Come, now. Let's hear something . . .

MICUCCIO. But, really, it's impossible . . . Like this—alone . . .

DORINA. No matter! Come on. Make a try!

FERDINANDO. If you don't, I'll play the thing!

MICUCCIO. For me, if you wish . . . Shall I play for you the air that Teresina sang that day, up in the garret?

FERDINANDO AND DORINA. Yes, yes! Bravo! Bravo!

FERDINANDO. "All things in this world below"?

MICUCCIO. All things in this world below.

(MICUCCIO sits down and begins to play in all seriousness. FERDINANDO and DORINA do their best to keep from bursting into laughter. The other WAITER, in dress coat, comes in to listen, followed by the COOK and the SCULLION. FERDINANDO and DORINA caution them by signs to listen quietly and earnestly. MICUCCIO's playing is suddenly interrupted by a loud ringing of the bell.)

FERDINANDO. Oh! Here's madame!

DORINA (to the other WAITER). Be off, now. Open the door. (To the

COOK *and the* SCULLION) And you, clear out! She said she wanted to have dinner served as soon as she came back.

(*The other* WAITER, *the* COOK *and the* SCULLION *leave.*)

FERDINANDO. My dress coat . . . Where did I put it?

DORINA. There! (*She points to behind the hangings and leaves in haste.*)

(MICUCCIO *arises, his instrument in his hand, abashed.* FERDINANDO *finds his coat, puts it on hurriedly, then, seeing that* MICUCCIO *is about to follow* DORINA, *stops him rudely.*)

FERDINANDO. You stay here! I must first let madame know.

(FERDINANDO *leaves.* MICUCCIO *is left in dejection, confused, oppressed by an uneasy presentiment.*)

MARTA'S VOICE (*from within*). In there, Dorina! In the drawing room!

(FERDINANDO, DORINA *and the other* WAITER *enter from the door at the right and cross the stage toward the salon in the background, carrying magnificent baskets of flowers, wreaths, and so on.* MICUCCIO *sticks his head forward to get a look into the salon and catches sight of a large number of gentlemen, all in evening dress, conversing confusedly.* DORINA *returns in a great hurry, hastening to the door at the right.*)

MICUCCIO (*touching her arm*). Who are they?

DORINA (*without stopping*). The guests! (*Exit*)

(MICUCCIO *stares again. His vision becomes clouded. His stupefaction and his confusion are so great that he himself does not realize that his eyes are moist with tears. He closes them, pulls himself together, as if to resist the torture inflicted upon him by a shrill outburst of laughter. It is* SINA MARNIS, *in the salon.* DORINA *returns with two more baskets of flowers.*)

DORINA (*without stopping, hastening toward the salon*). What are you crying about?

MICUCCIO. I? . . . No . . . All those people . . .

(*Enter Zia* MARTA *from the door at the right. The poor old lady is oppressed by a hat and a costly, splendid velvet cloak. As soon as she sees* MICUCCIO *she utters a cry that is at once suppressed.*)

MARTA. What! Micuccio, you here?

MICUCCIO (*uncovering his face and staring at her almost in fear*). Zia Marta! Good Lord . . . Like this? You?

MARTA. Why, what's wrong with me?

MICUCCIO. With a hat? You!

MARTA. Ah . . . (*Shakes her head and raises her hand. Then, disturbed*) But how on earth did you come? Without a word of warning! How did it happen?

MICUCCIO. I . . . I came . . .

MARTA. And this evening, of all others! Oh, heavens . . . Wait . . . What shall I do? What shall I do? Do you see how many people we have here, my son? Tonight is the party in honor of Teresina . . .

MICUCCIO. I know.

MARTA. Her special evening, understand? Wait . . . Just wait here a moment . . .

MICUCCIO. If you, if you think that it would be best for me to go . . .

MARTA. No. Wait a moment, I say . . . (She goes off toward the salon.)

MICUCCIO. I wouldn't know where to go . . . In this strange city . . .

(Zia MARTA returns, and signals him with her gloved hand to wait. She enters the salon and suddenly there is a deep silence. There are heard clearly these words of SINA MARNIS: "A moment, my friends!" MICUCCIO again hides his face in his hands. But SINA does not come. Instead, Zia MARTA enters shortly afterward, without her hat, without her gloves, without her cloak, now less burdened.)

MARTA. Here I am . . . Here I am . . .

MICUCCIO. And . . . and Teresina?

MARTA. I've told her . . . I've brought her the news . . . As soon as . . . as soon as she can get a moment, she'll come . . . In the meantime we'll stay here a little while, eh? Are you satisfied?

MICUCCIO. As far as I'm concerned . . .

MARTA. I'll keep you company . . .

MICUCCIO. Oh, no, . . . if . . . if you'd rather . . . that is, if you're needed there . . .

MARTA. Not at all . . . They're having supper now, see? Admirers of hers . . . The impresario . . . Her career, understand? We two will stay here. Dorina will prepare this little table for us right away, and . . . and we'll have supper together, just you and I, here—eh? What do you say? We two, all alone—eh? We'll recall the good old times . . .

(DORINA returns through the door at the left with a tablecloth and other articles of the table service.)

MARTA. Come on, Dorina . . . Lively, now . . . For me and for this dear boy of mine. My dear Micuccio! I can't believe that we're together again.

DORINA. Here. In the meantime, please be seated.

MARTA (sitting down). Yes, yes . . . Here, like this, apart from the others, we two alone . . . In there, you understand, so many people . . . She, poor thing, can't very well leave them . . . Her career . . . What else can she do? Have you seen the papers? Wonderful happenings, my boy! And as for me, I'm all in a whirl . . . It seems impossible that I should be sitting here alone with you tonight . . . (She rubs her hands and smiles, gazing at him through tender eyes.)

MICUCCIO (in a pensive, anguished voice). And, she'll come? She told you she'd come? I mean . . . just to get a look at her, at least . . .

MARTA. Of course she'll come! As soon as she can find a moment to spare. Didn't I tell you so? Why, just imagine what pleasure it would be for her to be here with us, with you, after such a long time . . . How many years is it? So many, so many . . . Ah, my dear boy, it seems an eternity to me . . . How many things I've been through, things that . . . that hardly seem true when I think of them . . . Who could have imagined, when . . . when we were yonder in Palma when you used to come up into our garret, with its swallows' nests in the rafters, remember? They used to fly all over the house, and my beautiful pots of basil on the window-sill . . . And donna Annuzza, donna Annuzza? Our old neighbor?

MICUCCIO. Eh . . . (*Makes the sign of benediction with two fingers, to signify, Dead!*)

MARTA. Dead? Yes, I imagined so . . . She was a pretty old lady even then . . . Older than I . . . Poor donna Annuzza, with her clove of garlic . . . Do you remember? She'd always come with that pretext, a clove of garlic. Just when we were about to send her down a bite, and . . . The poor old lady! And who knows how many more have passed on eh? at Palma . . . Ah! At least they rest yonder, in their last sleep, in our churchyard, with their beloved ones and relatives . . . While I . . . Who knows where I'll leave these bones of mine? Enough of that . . . Away with such thoughts! (DORINA *enters with the first course and stands beside* MICUCCIO, *waiting for him to help himself.*) Ah, here's Dorina . . .

(MICUCCIO *looks at* DORINA, *then at Zia* MARTA, *confused, perplexed; he raises his hand to help himself, sees that they are grimy from the journey and lowers them, more confused than ever.*)

MARTA. Here, over here, Dorina! I'll serve him . . . Leave it to me . . . (*Does so*) There . . . That's fine, isn't it?

MICUCCIO. Oh, yes . . . Thanks.

MARTA (*who has served herself*). Here you are . . .

MICUCCIO (*winking, and with his closed fist against his cheek making a gesture of ecstatic approval*). Uhm . . . Good . . . Good stuff.

MARTA. A special honor-evening . . . Understand? To it, now! Let's eat! But first . . . (*She makes the sign of the cross.*) Here I can do it, in your company.

(MICUCCIO *likewise makes the sign of the cross.*)

MARTA. Bravo, my boy! You, too . . . Bravo, my Micuccio, the same as ever, poor fellow! Believe me . . . When I have to eat in there . . . without being able to cross myself . . . it seems to me that the food can't go down . . . Eat, eat!

MICUCCIO. Eh, I'm good and hungry, I am! I . . . I haven't eaten for two days.

MARTA. What do you mean? On the trip?

MICUCCIO. I took plenty to eat along with me . . . I have it there, in the valise. But . . .

MARTA. But what?

MICUCCIO. I . . . I was ashamed . . . It . . . it seemed so little . . .

MARTA. Oh, how silly! . . . Come, now . . . Eat, my poor Micuccio . . . You certainly must be famished! Two days . . . And drink . . . here, drink . . . *(She pours some liquor for him.)*

MICUCCIO. Thanks . . . Yes, I'll have some . . . *(From time to time, as the two waiters enter the salon in the background or leave it with the courses, opening the door, there comes from inside a wave of confused words and outbursts of laughter.* MICUCCIO *raises his head from his plate, disturbed, and looks into the sorrowful affectionate eyes of Zia* MARTA, *as if to read in them an explanation of it all.)* They're laughing.

MARTA. Yes . . . Drink . . . Drink . . . Ah, that good old wine of ours, Micuccio. If you only knew how I long for it! The wine Michela used to make, Michela, who lived underneath us . . . What's become of Michela, my son?

MICUCCIO. Michela? Oh, she's fine. She's fine.

MARTA. And her daughter Luzza?

MICUCCIO. She's married . . . Has two children already . . .

MARTA. Is that so? Really? She'd always come up to us, remember? Such a happy nature, too! Oh, Luzza. And to think of it . . . Just to think of it . . . Married . . . And whom did she marry?

MICUCCIO. Toto Licasi, the fellow that worked in the customs house. Remember him?

MARTA. Him? Fine . . . And donna Michela is a grandmother! A grandmother already . . . Fortunate woman! Two children, did you say?

MICUCCIO. Two . . . yes . . . *(He is disturbed by another roar of merriment from the salon.)*

MARTA. Aren't you drinking?

MICUCCIO. Yes . . . Right away . . .

MARTA. Don't mind them . . . They're laughing, naturally . . . There's so many of them there . . . My dear boy, that's life. What can a person do? Her career . . . It's the impresario . . .

(DORINA reappears with another course.)

MARTA. Here, Dorina . . . Let me have your plate, Micuccio . . . You'll like this . . . *(Serving)* Tell me how much you want . . .

MICUCCIO. As you please . . .

MARTA *(as above).* Here you are. *(Serves herself.* DORINA *leaves.)*

MICUCCIO. How well you've learned! You make my eyes bulge with astonishment!

MARTA. I had to, my boy.

MICUCCIO. When I saw you come in with that velvet cloak on your back . . . and that hat on your head . . .

MARTA. Necessity, my son!

MICUCCIO. I understand . . . eh! You must keep up appearances! But if they ever saw you dressed like that in Palma, *zia* Marta . . .

MARTA (*hiding her face in her hands*). Oh, good heavens, don't mention it! Believe me . . . whenever I think of it . . . shame . . . shame overwhelms me! . . . I look at myself. I say, "Is this really I, so bedizened?" . . . And it seems that it's all a make-believe . . . as in the carnival season . . . But what's a person to do? Necessity, my son!

MICUCCIO. Of course . . . certainly . . . once you get into that life . . . But, she's really 'way up in the world, hey? . . . You can see that—really 'way up? . . . They . . . they pay her well, eh?

MARTA. Oh, yes . . . Very well . . .

MICUCCIO. How much per performance?

MARTA. It depends. According to the seasons and the theatres, you see . . . But let me tell you, my boy, it costs money. Ah, how much it costs, this life we lead . . . It takes all the money we can get! If you only knew the enormous expenses! It all goes out as fast as it comes in . . . Clothes, jewels, expenses of every sort . . . (*A loud outburst of voices in the salon at the rear cuts her short.*)

VOICES. Where? Where? Where? We want to know! Where?

SINA'S VOICE. A moment! I tell you, only a moment!

MARTA. There! That's she! . . . Here she comes . . .

(SINA *comes hastening in, rustling with silk, sparkling with gems, her shoulders, bosom and arms bare. It seems as if the hallway has suddenly been flooded with light.*)

MICUCCIO (*who had just stretched his hand out toward the wine glass, sits transfixed, his face flaming, his eyes distended, his mouth agape, dazzled and stupefied, as if in the presence of a vision. He stammers*). Teresina . . .

SINA. Micuccio? Where are you? Ah, there he is . . . Oh, how are things? Are you all better now? Fine, fine . . . You were so sick, weren't you? Oh, I'll see you again soon . . . Mamma will stay with you in the meantime . . . Agreed, eh? See you later. (*Dashes out*)

(MICUCCIO *stands amazed, while the reappearance of* SINA *in the salon is greeted with loud shouts.*)

MARTA (*after a long silence, in order to break the stupefaction into which he has fallen*). Aren't you eating?

(MICUCCIO *looks at her stupidly, without understanding.*)

MARTA (*pointing to the plate*). Eat.

MICUCCIO (*inserts two fingers between his neck and his begrimed, wilted collar, tugging at it as if to make room for a deep breath*). Eat?

(His fingers drum against his chin as if in self-confessed refusal, to signify: "I've lost my appetite, I can't." For a while he is silent, overwhelmed, absorbed in the vision that has just left him, then he murmurs) What she's come to! . . . It . . . it doesn't seem true . . . All . . . in that style . . . *(He refers, without scorn, but rather in a stupor, to* SINA's *nudity.)* A dream . . . Her voice . . . Her eyes . . . It's no longer she . . . Teresina . . . *(Realizing that Zia* MARTA *is shaking her head sadly, and that she, too, has stopped eating, as if waiting for him)* Fie! . . . No use thinking about it . . . It's all over . . . Who knows how long since! . . . And I, fool that I was . . . stupid . . . They had told me so back in the country . . . and I . . . broke my bones to get here . . . Thirty-six hours on the train . . . all for the sake of making a laughing-stock of myself . . . for that waiter and that maid there . . . Dorina . . . How they laughed! . . . I and . . . *(Several times he brings his forefingers together, as a symbol of his union with* SINA, *and smiles in melancholy fashion, shaking his head.)* But what else was I to believe? I came because you . . . Teresina, had . . . had promised me . . . But perhaps . . . Yes, that's it . . . How was she herself to imagine that one fine day she'd be where she is now? While I . . . yonder . . . stayed behind . . . with my piccolo . . . in the town square . . . She . . . making such strides . . . Lord! . . . No use thinking of that . . . *(He turns, somewhat brusquely, and faces Zia* MARTA.*)* If I have done anything for her, nobody, *zia* Marta, must suspect that I have come to . . . to stay . . . *(He grows more and more excited, and jumps to his feet.)* Wait! *(He thrusts a hand into his coat pocket and pulls out a pocketbook.)* I came just for this: to give you back the money you sent to me. Do you want to call it a payment? Restitution? What's the difference! I see that Teresina has become a . . . a queen! I see that . . . nothing! Let's drop it! But this money, no! I didn't deserve that from you . . . What's the use! It's all over, so let's forget it . . . But money? No! Money to me? Nothing doing! I'm only sorry that the amount isn't complete . . .

MARTA *(trembling, shattered, tears in her eyes).* What are you saying, my boy? What are you saying?

MICUCCIO *(signals her to be quiet).* It wasn't I who spent it. My parents spent it while I was sick, without my knowledge. But let that make up for the tiny amount I spent for her in the early days . . . Do you remember? It's a small matter . . . Let's forget it. Here's the rest. And I'm going.

MARTA. What do you mean! So suddenly? Wait at least until I can tell Teresina. Didn't you hear her say that she wanted to come back? I'll go right away and tell her . . .

MICUCCIO *(holding her back in her seat).* No. It's useless. Understand? *(From the salon comes the sound of a piano and of voices singing a silly, salacious chorus from a musical comedy, punctuated by outbursts of laughter.)*

Let her stay there . . . She's in her element, where she belongs . . . Poor me . . . I've seen her. That was enough . . . Or rather . . . you better go there . . . Do you hear them laughing? I don't want them to laugh at me . . . I'm going . . .

MARTA *(interpreting* MICUCCIO's *sudden resolution in the worse sense, that is, as an attitude of scorn and an access of jealousy).* But I . . . It's impossible for me to keep watch over her any more, my dear boy . . .

MICUCCIO *(all at once reading in her eyes the suspicion that he has not yet formed, his face darkens and he cries out).* Why?

MARTA *(bewildered, she hides her face in her hands but cannot restrain the rush of tears, as she gasps between sobs).* Yes, yes. Go, my boy, go . . . She's no longer fit for you. You're right . . . If you had only taken my advice . . .

MICUCCIO *(with an outburst, bending over her and tearing one of her hands from her face).* Then . . . Ah, then she . . . she is no longer worthy of me! *(The chorus and the tones of the piano continue.)*

MARTA *(weeping and in anguish, she nods yes, then raises her hands in prayer, in so supplicating, heartbroken a manner that* MICUCCIO's *rage at once subsides).* For mercy's sake, for mercy's sake! For pity of me, Micuccio mine!

MICUCCIO. Enough, enough . . . I'm going just the same . . . I'm all the more determined, now . . . What a fool I was, *zia* Marta, not to have understood. All for this . . . all . . . all naked . . . Don't cry . . . What's to be done about it? It's luck . . . luck . . . *(As he speaks, he takes up his valise and the little bag and starts to leave. It suddenly occurs to him that inside of the little bag there are the beautiful limes that he had brought from Sicily for* TERESINA.) Oh, look, *zia* Marta . . . Look here . . . *(Opens the bag and supporting it on his arm pours out upon the table the fresh, fragrant fruit.)*

MARTA. Limes! Our beautiful limes!

MICUCCIO. I had brought them for her . . . *(He takes one.)* Suppose I were to start throwing them at the heads of all those fine gentlemen in there?

MARTA *(again beseeching him).* For mercy's sake!

MICUCCIO *(with a bitter laugh, thrusting the empty bag into his pocket).* No, nothing. Don't be afraid. I leave them for you alone, *zia* Marta. And tell them I paid the duty on them, too . . . Enough. They're for you only, remember that. As to her, simply say, for me, "The best of luck to you!"

(He leaves. The chorus continues. Zia MARTA *is left weeping alone before the table, her face buried in her hands. A long pause, until* SINA MARNIS

takes it into her head to make another fleeting appearance in the hallway.)

SINA *(surprised, catching sight of her weeping mother).* Has he gone?

(MARTA, without looking at her, nods yes.)

SINA *(stares vacantly ahead of her, engrossed, then with a sigh).* The poor fellow . . .

MARTA. Look . . . He had brought you . . . some limes.

SINA *(her spirits returning).* Oh, how beautiful! Just see . . . how many! What fragrance! How beautiful, beautiful! *(She presses one arm to her waist and in her other hand seizes as many as she can carry, shouting to the guests in the salon, who come running in.)* Didì! Didì! Rosì! Gegè! Cornelli! Tarini! Didì!

MARTA *(rising in vehement protest).* No! Not there! I say no! Not there!

SINA *(shrugging her shoulders and offering the fruit to the guests).* Let me do as I please! Here, Didì! Sicilian limes! Here's some for you, Rosì, Sicilian limes! Sicilian limes!*

CURTAIN

*The new version (1920) has a different ending. Sina, instead of gaily distributing the limes to her guests, stands in tears before her former sweetheart, who, repudiating her remorse, thrusts the money into her bosom and leaves.

LEADING QUESTIONS

DORINA AND FERDINANDO

1. What is their relationship?
2. How old are they? Dorina calls Micuccio "sonny" and "my boy." Are these just phrases she uses, or do they imply an age difference?
3. What can you infer about their physical attributes? Think of whom they work for and the kind of work they are called upon to do. Are they from the city? Wise? Sophisticated?
4. How do they feel about Teresina? Marta?
5. It is Dorina who says, "Let him wait." Why?
6. It is also Dorina who starts to tease him. Why? What makes Ferdinando join in her game?
7. They are both doing basically the same thing—having fun at Micuccio's expense. But what are the differences between these two people?
8. If Dorina and Ferdinando are simply having fun at Micuccio's expense, what are their objectives?
9. After Micuccio's long story, their teasing takes on a different quality. What are their new actions? Why do they change?

MICUCCIO

1. It would seem that Dorina and Ferdinando poke fun at Micuccio because he is a "hayseed." How do they know? How is he dressed? Does he exhibit provincial behavior which is out of place in sophisticated circles?
2. Is Micuccio aware that he is being teased? If not, why not? And if so, why does he "open up" to them and tell the whole story?

3. Be careful of his long speech describing his discovery of Teresina and her training. It may technically be "exposition" as far as playwriting is concerned, but this will not do for actors. What is his action?
4. Don't let Micuccio simply wallow in misery during his dinner with Marta. What is he actually doing? State his actions positively.
5. Beware of playing a quality on his speech after Sina's first exit—his "realization" speech. What is his action?
6. Micuccio has a difficult transition from hang-dog anguish to anger at her not being "worthy" of him; and he finds a new and sudden pride in himself. This needs deep justification. Dig into the attitudes of provincial Italians toward immoral women, etc.

MARTA

1. Describing her entrance, Pirandello says she is "oppressed by a hat and a costly, splendid velvet cloak." Why does he use the word "oppressed"?
2. How has Marta taken to her new luxury? Is she a fish out of water? How can you physicalize the conflicting elements of a provincial woman in expensive, sophisticated surroundings?
3. What other indications do you find in the script to show that Marta is at odds with her environment?

TERESINA

1. Micuccio reads a letter of Teresina's to Dorina and Ferdinando. What do you learn about her character?
2. Sina's treatment of Micuccio is too clear to be misinterpreted. But it lends itself to quality-acting. Define her action when she comes in to speak to him for the first time.
3. A superficial character must not snare the actor into a superficial performance. Sina was not born shallow—she became that way. Why? What is she striving for? Does she like what she has become? Does she approve of herself? Does this affectation come easy to her, or must she work for it?
4. How much of a conscience does she have? What is her action on the one line "The poor fellow . . . ," which she says just after Micuccio has gone? Does she really feel sorry for him? Does she have a moment of guilt, or is she just shrugging him off?

Index

SPEAK WITH DISTINCTION
by Edith Skinner

"Speak With Distinction is the **most comprehensive and accessible speech book available** for teachers and students of speech."

—Joan Washington, RSC, Royal Court
& Royal National Theatre

"Edith Skinner's book is the **best book on speech I have ever encountered**. It was my primer in school and it is my reference book now. To the classical actor, or for that matter any actor who wishes to be understood, this method is a sure guide."

—Kevin Kline

"Speak with Distinction is **the single most important work on the actor's craft** of stage speech. Edith Skinner's work must be an indispensable source book for all who aspire to act."

—Earle Gister, Yale School of Drama

paper•ISBN 1-155783-047-9

MICHAEL CAINE

ACTING IN FILM

An Actor's Take on Movie Making

Academy Award winning actor Michael Caine, internationally acclaimed for his talented performances in movies for over 25 years, reveals secrets for success on screen. *Acting in Film* is also available on video (the BBC Master Class).

"Michael Caine knows the territory...*Acting in Film* is wonderful reading, even for those who would not dream of playing 'Lets Pretend' in front of a camera. Caine's guidance, aimed at novices still dreaming of the big break, can also give hardened critics fresh insights to what it is they're seeing up there on the screen..."
> —Charles Champlin, LOS ANGELES TIMES

"FASCINATING! Wonderfully practical film acting wisdom—all put across in the best Caine style."
> —John Cleese

BOOK/PAPER: $14.95• ISBN: 1-55783-277-3
VIDEO: $29.95 • ISBN: 1-55783-034-7

THE ACTOR AND THE TEXT
by Cicely Berry

As voice director of the Royal Shakespeare Company, Cicely Berry has worked with actors such as Jeremy Irons, Derek Jacobi, Jonathan Pryce, Sinead Cusack and Antony Sher. *The Actor and The Text* brings Ms. Berry's methods of applying vocal production skills within a text to the general public.

While this book focuses primarily on speaking Shakespeare, Ms. Berry also includes the speaking of some modern playwrights, such as Edward Bond.

As Ms. Berry describes her own volume in the introduction:

" … this book is not simply about making the voice sound more interesting. It is about getting inside the words we use …It is about making the language organic, so that the words act as a spur to the sound …"

paper•ISBN 1–155783–138–6

Michael Caine • William Goldman
John Cleese • Eric Bentley
Oliver Stone • John Patrick Shanley
Cicely Berry • John Russell Brown
Paddy Chayefsky • Steve Tesich
Harold Clurman • Sonia Moore
Bruce Joel Rubin • Janet Suzman
Josef Svoboda • Jerry Sterner
Stephen Sondheim • Larry Gelbart

These Applause authors have their work available
in discerning bookshops across the country.

If you're having trouble tracking down an Applause title in your area,
we'll ship it to you direct! Write or call toll-free for our free catalog of
cinema and theatre titles.

When ordering an Applause title, include the price of the
book, $2.95 for the first book and $1.90 thereafter to cover shipping
(New York and Pennsylvania residents:
please include applicable sales tax).
Check/Mastercard/Visa/Amex

Send your orders to: **Applause Direct**
211 West 71st St
New York, NY 10023

Fax: 212-721-2856

Or order toll-free: 1-800-798-7787